Liturgy in a Postmodern World

edited by

Keith F. Pecklers, SJ

continuum
LONDON • NEW YORK

Continuum

The Tower Building   370 Lexington Avenue
11 York Road   New York
London SE1 7NX   NY 10017-6503

www.continuumbooks.com

First published 2003

British Library Cataloguing-in-Publication Data
A catalogue record for this book is available from
the British Library.

ISBN 0–8264–6412–2

Typeset by Ray Davies
Printed and bound in Great Britain
by Creative Print and Design, Wales

Liturgy in a Postmodern World

THE UNIVERSITY OF
WINCHESTER

2 1 APR 2008

16 May '08

Contents

List of Contributors

Francisco F. Claver, SJ, is Apostolic Vicar of the Catholic Mission of Lagawe-Bontoc in the Philippines. He is Bishop Emeritus of the Diocese of Malaybalay in Bukidnon.

Godfried Cardinal Danneels is Archbishop of Mechelen-Brussel in Belgium and a Consultor to the Congregation for Divine Worship and the Discipline of the Sacraments.

Mark R. Francis, CSV, is Superior General of the Clerics of Saint Viator. He has also served as a Consultor to the International Commission on English in the Liturgy (ICEL) and is former Professor of Liturgy at the Catholic Theological Union in Chicago.

Cesare Giraudo, SJ, is Dean of the Pontifical Oriental Institute, Rome, where he also serves as Professor of Liturgy.

Donald Gray, OBE, is Canon Emeritus of Westminster Abbey, London, and former Chaplain to the Speaker of the House of Commons. He is past-President of the International *Societas liturgica* and continues to serve as President of the Alcuin Club.

Jules Kipupu Kafuti, SJ, of the Democratic Republic of Congo is a doctoral student in Philosophy at the Pontifical Gregorian University, Rome.

Léon Ngoy Kalumba, SJ, of the Democratic Republic of Congo is a doctoral student in Christian Spirituality and Theology at the Pontifical Gregorian University, Rome.

Wendelin Köster, SJ, serves as General Counsellor and Regional Assistant for Central Europe at the Curia of the General of the Society of Jesus in Rome. He is also the General's Delegate to the Pontifical German and Hungarian College.

Richard Leonard, SJ, teaches at the United Faculty of Theology, Melbourne. He is Director of the Australian Catholic Film Office and is presently completing a doctorate on Peter Weir at Melbourne University.

Daniel Madigan, SJ, is the founding Director of the Institute for the Study of Religions at the Pontifical Gregorian University, Rome, where he also serves as Professor of Islamic Studies.

Keith F. Pecklers, SJ, is Professor of Liturgy at the Pontifical Gregorian University in Rome and is also Professor of Liturgical History at the Pontifical Liturgical Institute. He was the chief organizer of the International Meeting on Jesuit Liturgy and served as Editor of this volume.

Peter C. Phan is a professor at Georgetown University, where he holds the Chair in Catholic Social Thought. He is past-President of the Catholic Theological Society of America (CTSA) and has served as a Consultor to the Federation of Asian Bishops' Conferences (FABC).

Timothy Radcliffe, OP, is former Master of the Order of Preachers. He currently resides in London and lectures internationally in the area of theology and spirituality. He is the author of the international best-seller *I Call You Friends* (Continuum, London and New York).

Robert F. Taft, SJ, is Professor Emeritus of Oriental Liturgy at the Pontifical Oriental Institute in Rome. He is Editor-in-Chief of *Orientalia Christiana Analecta* and has written extensively on the Christian East. He also serves as Consultor to the Pontifical Congregation for Oriental Churches.

Introduction

The relationship between liturgy and the community's life has been a struggle since the origins of Christianity. Already in the eleventh chapter of I Corinthians we read of tensions and divisions within that community over its eucharistic worship and its treatment of the poorer members. Examples of similar liturgical tensions and even heresies abound in those early centuries. The situation only worsens in the Middle Ages as the divorce between liturgy and life concomitant with a gradual split between clergy and laity, assembly and sanctuary, became ever more acute. Catechized about their unworthiness and no longer able to understand the worship at which they were present, laity became passive spectators and even ceased to make their own communion at Mass, often choosing to adore the host instead.

In the sixteenth century, Martin Luther and other reformers called the Church to a recovery of liturgy's rightful place within the community's life with intelligible vernacular worship, active participation, and 'worldly preaching' (in the words of twentieth-century Lutheran pastor Dietrich Bonhoeffer). But the Council of Trent refuted the reformers, centralized Catholic worship with a new emphasis on rubrics, and liturgy remained the property of the clergy – something done *for* the people rather than *by* the people, until the advent of the Second Vatican Council (1962–5).

Having embarked on a new millennium 40 years after that Council, while we are grateful for the radical liturgical reforms which Vatican II initiated – reforms not so distant from what Luther and his contemporaries begged for in their own day – we find ourselves at a critical juncture, unprecedented in our history. In this postmodern age of extraordinary technological change we are also increasingly secularized – at least in the West. Indeed, the term 'post-Christian' is often

1

linked with 'postmodern' as the role of religion is relegated to something private and personal. Not surprisingly, the recent growth in new religions and in various forms of 'new age spirituality' are often more compatible with the kind of individualistic and at times narcissistic tendencies indicative of postmodernism than what one finds in traditional religions like Judaism or Christianity. What then, is the role of Christianity within such a context? More specifically, what is the role of its worship and the Christian community's relationship to that worship?

In June 2002, over 120 Jesuit scholars and practitioners came together in Rome from 42 different countries for a week of deliberations on the role of liturgy. Most participants were liturgical scholars, although they included bishops, parish priests, artists, and scholars of other disciplines. They were also joined by almost 20 non-Jesuit collaborators, women and men, both Roman Catholic and Anglican, each of whom represented a unique area of specialization. While the particular scope of the meeting was to consider the role which liturgy plays within Jesuit life and mission, it was the desire of the Superior General of the Society of Jesus, Father Peter-Hans Kolvenbach, SJ, that this historic assembly not limit itself to Jesuit life alone, but seriously address the significant liturgical issues brought on by the Second Vatican Council so that the Society of Jesus might find its own place within those reforms and better put its life and membership at the service of the Church.

Now, if you know anything about Jesuits, you will probably be aware that we are hardly known for our liturgical expertise or celebrational style at public worship. The truth be told, as academicians rather than parish priests (with some notable exceptions) most Jesuits are probably more at home in a library than they are in a sanctuary – especially if there are 300 people in front of them. Prior to the Council, the old expression 'Lost as a Jesuit in Holy Week' was not so far off the mark in describing Jesuit presiders fumbling through the Missal at the altar desperately trying to figure out what came next. More current is the description of a good (i.e. successful) Jesuit liturgy which is defined as 'when no one gets hurt'. Jesuits have much to learn from Anglicans in this regard about proper liturgical style. That being said, one can imagine the amusement on the part of some (even in the Vatican!) that Jesuits were having their first international meeting on liturgy in the Society's 450-plus year history. An international meeting on Benedictine liturgy would never have raised any eyebrows, but Jesuits?

Despite our shady reputation in this area, Jesuit liturgists do, in fact, exist. There are, of course, the great Jesuit names like Josef Jungmann, Jean Danilieu, Clifford Howell, C. C. Martindale, Johannes Hoffinger, Herman Schmidt, Edward Kilmartin, Edward Yarnold – all of whom 'have gone before us, marked with the sign of faith'. But there are also the great liturgical scholars of our own day – two of whom, Robert Taft and Cesare Giraudo, presented papers at this meeting. It is also interesting to note that the North American Academy of Liturgy – an interfaith body of over 400 Christian and Jewish liturgical scholars – was founded in 1975 by a Jesuit liturgist, John Gallen. And today in North America, there are more than 25 Jesuits who hold doctorates in the field of liturgics – the largest representation from any order within the Catholic Church in North America. So despite our bad reputation, the idea of a meeting on the topic of Jesuit liturgy may not be so strange after all.

After some discussion on the matter, the meeting's preparatory commission chose to make these texts public, thus the volume, *Liturgy in a Postmodern World*. In the first essay, Godfried Cardinal Danneels, Archbishop of Mechelen-Brussel, evaluates the liturgical reforms of Vatican II and addresses the problem of liturgy's incomprehensibility in a world whose symbolic system has been lost. He calls for a recovery of liturgy's contemplative dimension which is at once sensual and 'inculturated' – expressive of the liturgical assembly which 'has the most important place in the Christian liturgy'. Two short papers offer some added reflection on the important points by Cardinal Danneels from the cultural horizons of Australia and Germany. Australian Jesuit Richard Leonard who specializes in film considers the importance of the media in postmodernity and argues that Christian liturgists will need to 'learn the language' if they are effectively to reach their peers – especially those who are outside the Church. Wendelin Köster writes of his experience as a youth minister and rector of a Jesuit theological school in Germany and asks why liturgy fails to intersect with the lives of the young. Liturgical participation is fundamental to our membership in the Church lest we lose our 'collective memory' and 'forget who we are'.

Robert Taft also considers the topic of Vatican II, but in light of the Society of Jesus and its own history. Taft's piece is instructive as he recounts the liturgical history of an order which gave less emphasis to prayer in common so that the 'liturgy of the world', i.e. apostolic mission with particular care for the needy, might take precedence. Taft argues that such history needs to be viewed in the light of conciliar reforms and calls for regular community prayer in all religious houses – even those of Jesuits – since 'communities that fail to gather together for some form of corporate prayer cannot call themselves Christian'.

From a consideration of postmodernism and an exposition of various interpretations of inculturation, Peter Phan offers a serious critique of how some recent Vatican documents have presented the topic. He makes particular reference to developments within the Asian Church and shows how Asian mission history and Asian theologies can be instructive in better understanding the role of liturgical inculturation within postmodernity. Mark Francis offers a short response supporting Phan's thesis, and comparing recent liturgical documents like *Liturgiam Authenticam* with Curial texts which preceded them. Discussion on the theology of inculturation then shifts to pastoral application as two African Jesuits, Jules Kipupu Kafuti and Léon Ngoy Kalumba, reflect on the Congolese Rite (i.e. 'The Roman Missal for the Dioceses of Zaire') which was approved by the Holy See in 1988, and raise several pointed questions on its relationship to daily life in the Democratic Republic of Congo.

In an important paper on liturgy and social justice, Cesare Giraudo looks at the intimate link between Eucharist and service of others: *Diakonia,* and makes particular application to the Church in Madagascar where he has worked. Significant in Giraudo's exposition is his affirmation that the calling down of the Holy Spirit during the Eucharistic Prayer is not just about the transformation of the bread and

4

wine; the liturgical assembly itself is transformed into Christ's body and blood of Christ, called to be that body for others in daily life.

In a brilliant paper on 'The Sacramentality of the Word' Timothy Radcliffe treats the topic of liturgical preaching and affirms that all preaching begins in silence – in listening – and ends there, as well. Preachers need to be more honest, he tells his readers, especially as they grapple with the problems facing human society today; they need to talk less and listen more if God's word is to be heard afresh.

Basing his text on Karl Rahner's 'Liturgy of the World', Bishop Francisco Claver explores the challenges inherent within Christian worship in its ecumenical and inter-religious context. He writes from his native Philippines where the poor of the Basic Ecclesial Communities have educated the Church's institutional leadership in 'a new way of being Church'. The truth that we have much to learn from one another is a recurrent theme in this paper which has obvious implications when we consider ecumenical and inter-religious worship and the common tasks which lie ahead for liturgical scholars of all faiths. Canon Donald Gray offers a very helpful response to Claver's text from the perspective of the Church of England, and Islamic scholar Daniel Madigan offers his own reflection from the experience of his work with Muslims.

A collection such as this will inevitably be somewhat uneven; certain essays in this volume contain extensive documentation while others contain very little. We deliberately chose to respect the style and wishes of each author in this regard. Moreover, some texts look back to recall our history even as they make bold assertions about the present and offer serious challenges for the future. Other texts offer a certain pastoral analysis on the current crisis in liturgical participation, raising significant questions for our reflection. Several essays in this collection might well evoke very strong reactions – either a robust 'hear, hear,' or equally strong disagreement from others. If such emotions are tapped as you read this book, all the better! It will have served its purpose. For ultimately, as we grapple with the future of liturgy – its credibility and value in the postmodern world – this book is more about questions than answers. It is meant to provoke thought and discussion far beyond the confines of Jesuit communities.

Finally, I wish to express my personal gratitude to Robin Baird-Smith, the Publishing Director at Continuum, for his willingness to publish this work and to Rebecca Mulhearn for her assistance. Thanks go as well to Hiroshi Nakazato and John Hardt of Boston College for their technical assistance.

Keith F. Pecklers, SJ
All Saints Day, 2002

1

Liturgy Forty Years After the Second Vatican Council: High Point or Recession

Godfried Cardinal Danneels

1. A Major Turnabout

For those who have not experienced it for themselves, it must be difficult to imagine just how much liturgical praxis has changed in less than half a century. The evolution which has taken place in the last thirty years is barely perceptible nowadays since the new liturgical model is considered evident practically everywhere. Such a situation is certainly gratifying but does it mean that the profound intentions of *Sacrosanctum Concilium* have thereby been realized? Perhaps now is the appropriate moment for an evaluation.

It is evident that the last half-century has brought about a major change in the relationship between the minister and the people in the liturgy. This change, however, was not without consequence for our understanding of the relationship between the sacred and the profane and even the Church and the world. The situation might be roughly stated as follows: prior to the liturgical reforms the distance between the minister and the people was clearly designated. This was even given material expression in the ordering of church buildings: the distinct choir area reserved to the priest, the altar oriented to the east, priest and people separated by a communion rail. Even more questionable than the features of church architecture was the parallel configuration of the celebration; it was frequently the case that the priest celebrated the official liturgy while at one and the same time the people set about their personal devotions. The use of Latin, of course, had a significant role to play in this parallel configuration. The consequence of all this was the fact that the liturgy came to be considered untouchable, an entity regulated by rubrics to be performed with great obedience and respect. Liturgy was simply a given, and a good liturgist was seen for the most part as an observant performer. The people assisted, of course, but took little or no part in the liturgy itself.

2. Active Participation

From its very beginnings, the aim of the liturgical movement, which originated in Belgium in 1909, was to close the gap between the official liturgy of the priest and that of the people. The term 'active participation' was born out of this movement and has since become part of our common usage. It became a key term in the liturgical constitution of Vatican II. Active participation was first promoted through the circulation of the People's Missals which contained the Sunday liturgy: the faithful were at least able to follow along. Before long, however, a desire for more than just following in the book emerged: people wanted to participate and join in. Vatican II satisfied this desire by introducing the use of the vernacular, by simplifying liturgical symbolism to make it more transparent, by returning to the praxis of the early church and dropping elements which had later come to overshadow the essentials, and by a correct distribution of roles in the service of the liturgy. The result was a far greater involvement of the people, even to the very heart of the liturgy.

3. From Rubricism to Manipulation

The active involvement of the people in the liturgy is, of course, an unparalleled gift from the Council to the People of God. As with every worthy reform, however, there is a shadow side. Active participation in the liturgy, preparing together, concern to get as close as possible to the culture and sensitivity of the faithful can lead imperceptibly to a sort of taking possession of the liturgy. Participation and mutual celebration can lead to a subtle form of manipulation. In such an event the liturgy is not only set free of its untouchable quality – which in itself is not a bad thing – but it becomes in a sense the property of those who celebrate, a terrain given over to their 'creativity'. Those who serve the liturgy – both priests and laity – become its 'owners'. In some cases this can even lead to a sort of liturgical 'coup' in which the sacred is eliminated, the language trivialized and the cult turned into a social event. In a word, the real subject of the liturgy is no longer the Christ who through the Spirit worships the Father and sanctifies the people in a symbolic act. The real subject is the human person or the celebrating community. The exaggerated emphasis from before the 1950s on discipline, obedience, fidelity to the rubrics, the reception and entering of a pre-existent entity is replaced by self-will and by the elimination of every sense of mystery in the liturgy. In this case the liturgy is no longer 'leit-ourgia': the work of the people and for the people with respect to their relationship with God, it becomes a purely human activity. Fortunately, the trend we have outlined is not universal. Nevertheless, any attempt to evaluate liturgical praxis in our time would be wrong to ignore it.

4. The Liturgy is Beyond Us

There is a liturgical ground rule which runs as follows: the liturgy is first 'God's work on us' before being our work on God. Liturgy is datum or prior given in its very essence: it is beyond us and has already existed for a long time, long before we could participate in it. The acting subject of the liturgy is the risen Christ: He is the first and only High Priest, the only one who is competent to bring worship to God and to sanctify the people. This is not only an abstract theological truth: it must become evident and visible in the liturgy. The core of the liturgy is already given in the Lord's acts of institution. This does not mean that the individual and the celebrating community are neither capable nor permitted to make a creative contribution. The community is creative, but it is not an 'instance of creation'. Otherwise the liturgy would no longer be the epiphany of the Christian mysteries through the service of the Church, the continuation of his incarnation, crucifixion and resurrection, the 'incarnation' of a divine project in history and in the world of human persons via sacred symbols. In such a situation the liturgy would become nothing more than the community celebrating itself.

9

The liturgy 'pre-exists': the celebrating community enters into it as into a pre-established, divine and spiritual architecture. To a certain degree this is also determined by the historical location of Christ and his sacred mysteries. The Eucharist as such is not a 'religious meal' but rather the making present of a particular meal: that of Christ with his disciples on the night before he suffered. In this sense the liturgy can never be a self-fashioned concoction of the celebrating community; we are not creators, we are servants and guardians of the mysteries. We do not own them nor did we author them.

5. The Fundamental Attitude of the 'Homo Liturgicus'

This entails that the fundamental attitude of the 'homo liturgicus' – both individually and collectively – is one of receptivity, readiness to listen, self-giving and self-relativizing. It is the attitude of faith and of faithful obedience. It is not because a particular caricature of this attitude of obedience led at one time to slavish and nonsensical dressage and rubricism that the sense of 'entering in to what transcends us' has been so diminished. The 'homo liturgicus' does not manipulate, nor is his or her action restricted to self-expression or auto-realization. It is an attitude of orientation towards God, readiness to listen, obedience, grateful reception, wonder, adoration and praise. It is an attitude of listening and seeing, of what Guardini called 'contemplating', an attitude so alien to the 'homo faber' in many of us. In short, the fundamental attitude of the 'homo liturgicus' is none other than an attitude of prayer, of handing ourselves over to God and letting his will be done in us.

It should not surprise us, then, that in a period of history like our own, with its active intervention in everyday reality and its submission of that reality to our scientific thinking and our technological expertise, it will be particularly difficult to be genuinely liturgically-minded. The 'contemplative' dimension of the human person is no longer evident these days. This being the case, the core of the liturgy is even less evident. Active participation, therefore, has to be situated within this 'contemplative' attitude, in which case it must also bear the particular characteristics of such an attitude.

10

6. The Incomprehensibility of the Liturgy

One of the primary concerns of Vatican II and of the Church is and remains that the liturgy be understood by the celebrating community. Every reform proposed by the Constitution is rooted in that concern. 'Understand what you do' is a basic demand of everything we do, including what we do in the liturgy. The incomprehensibility of the liturgy was blamed, in the first place, on language. Immediately after the introduction of the vernacular, however, it became apparent that it had to do with more than just language usage; the content of the liturgy itself was equally unfamiliar.

The liturgy, of course, is almost entirely structured on the Bible. It is said that the Hebrew Bible or Old Testament is particularly unfamiliar to us. Everything takes place in an agrarian context which barely applies nowadays in many parts of the world. At the same time, the biblical texts are rooted in a rural culture, and a peculiarly Mediterranean one at that. Many images, such as shepherds, flocks or water wells, are no longer part of the day-to-day vista of the modern city-dweller. In other words, the Bible uses a language from a bygone era.

The non-biblical texts in the liturgy are also a little strange, however. The Latin collects with their succinct and metrical structure are simply untranslatable, not so much because the words cannot be transposed into a modern language but because the mentality and culture from which they stem has disappeared. A great many texts, when detached from their musical setting, end up seeming extremely archaic. Think, for example, of the *Salve Regina* and the *Dies Irae* or even the ordinary sung Gregorian Introits and Communion Antiphons leaving aside the archaic image of God which such texts maintain (the God who sleeps, the God of wrath etc.).

Certain symbols – although secondary – no longer seem to function: the drop of water in the chalice, mixing a particle of the host with the wine, the *lavabo*, the washing of the feet. One frequently hears reproaches such as 'old-fashioned', 'passé', 'medieval' and 'monastic'.

11

7. Abbreviate or Eliminate?

People often opt for a short-term solution which barely touches on the real problem. In the case of the liturgy certain terms were replaced with other more understandable terms. There are biblical terms, however, which cannot be replaced. What do we do, for example, with words like 'resurrection', 'Easter', 'Eucharist', *'metanoia'*, 'sin'? They are part of a sort of biblical and liturgical 'mother tongue' which simply cannot be replaced. They have to be learned. It is hard to imagine a Jew using a different term for *'shabbat'* or *'pesach'*.

Certain biblical images are, indeed, barely perceptible in our modern urban culture. The sight of shepherds and flocks is no longer an everyday occurrence. Does this mean, however, that such images are no longer comprehensible in themselves? Is it because no one has ever met a seraph that the metaphorical power of this angelic messenger no longer speaks to us? Half of the poetry ever written makes use of images and terms which are not part of the daily life and environment of the reader. A great many symbols from medieval German culture were taken up in the Roman Pontifical. People sometimes opt for alternative, poetic texts, especially for weddings and baptisms. Leaving aside the fact that there is a profound theological distinction to be made between an aesthetically valuable text and a biblical text, it is also true that many such texts belong to an even more limited culture than the Bible which, it would appear, possesses a much greater universality.

The remedy employed in most cases often does not help. Most of the time it is limited to questions such as: 'What can we drop ?' – 'How can we abbreviate?' – 'What would function better to express what is going on in our lives as individuals and as a community?' Is the latter question justified, however? What precisely do we have to say in the first instance? What is going on in our lives? Or what is God saying to us? In a manner, of course, which we can understand.

There appears to be only one solution: if the liturgy is not simply a structuring of common human religiosity, but rather the epiphany of God in human history (from Abraham to Christ), then we cannot avoid the need for catechesis and initiation. Liturgy demands schooling because it is both proclamation and celebration of mysteries, mysteries which have occurred in the history of Judaism and Christianity.

8. What Is Understanding?

What exactly is understanding? It is evident that if the liturgy is the epiphany of God's dealings with his Church then the deepest core or heart of the liturgy will never be open to our grasp. There is indeed a hard core in the liturgy – the mystery – which is ungraspable. One can only enter into it in faith.

There is more to say about understanding, however. Our contemporaries often conceive understanding as the ability to grasp at first hearing. Something is understandable if we can grasp it immediately. Such an approach is valid for the ordinary objects of our knowledge which can only be grasped at a purely cognitive level, but this is more a question of registering than understanding. Where the depths of human – and divine – reality are concerned this approach does not work. Love, death, joy, solidarity, knowledge of God, can never be grasped at once and on first inspection. In these cases, understanding is more a question of the biblical notion of 'knowing-penetrating'. It is a lengthy and progressive process of becoming familiar with a particular reality. The same is true for the liturgy. It is not an object of knowledge in the commonplace sense of the word. It is not an object of knowledge at all, rather it is a source of knowledge, a source of understanding. This is why analysis is out of place here, only a prolonged listening and familiarization is appropriate. This implies that the liturgy will only be open to understanding from a perspective of 'empathy'. The liturgy lets itself be understood only by those who have faith in and who love it. For this reason it remains inaccessible and incomprehensible outside of the faith.

Moreover, the liturgy is only understandable through its repetitiveness. Profound realities only gradually yield their full significance. This is why we have the phenomenon of 'ritual' in the liturgy; and whoever speaks of 'ritual' speaks of repetition. Many changes in the liturgy in order to make it understandable have been inefficient because they focused on the immediate, cognitive, informative aspect of under-

13

standing. They wanted to explain everything, to provide commentary, to analyse. They never lead to familiarity with the liturgy.

They are surgical and medical interventions (abbreviating, replacing, scrapping, describing) on a dying reality, a sort of palliative care which can never heal the sick individual. The only approach is the 'dialogical' approach: allowing the liturgy time to say what it has to say; listening attentively to its harmonics and allowing its deeper meaning to unfold; not looking for an alternative but letting the liturgy speak for itself and expose its own virtualities.

9. Our Disrupted Relationship with the Liturgy

The incomprehensibility of the liturgy is not so much due to the unintelligibility of its major symbols. Indeed, all of us are well able to grasp the deep fascination which flows forth from symbols such as fire, light, water, bread, wine, laying on of hands, anointing. These major (natural) symbols speak to us all in our archetypal imagination. Secondary symbols can, of course, be more problematic. At the same time, however, they are of lesser importance and Vatican II correctly discarded a number of them.

A more significant contributor to the problem of understanding is the fact that the symbolic universe within which such symbols functioned has been lost. Removed from its proper context, a liturgical symbol is like a fish out of water, and is left bereft of much of its vitality. Proof of this fact can best be found in what one might call 'contrary' situations, where the symbolic universe continues to thrive even today. Why is it so that short Latin phrases and Gregorian refrains continue to function in Taizé but not in the parishes? Because they are in their proper place within the religious community of Taizé and its monastic liturgical life. Why is it that the symbols we have been discussing continue to function in the abbeys, the monastery churches and the charismatic communities? For the same reason! Why does a Gregorian requiem function well at a funeral? Liturgical comprehensibility also depends on a number of non-liturgical surrounding elements. It is our entire relationship with the liturgy – even outside the cultic celebration – that makes so much possible.

14

The incomprehensibility of the liturgy is not only due to the liturgy itself but in part to us. Our own attitude needs to be worked on. We need to examine our global relationship with God, our faith, our lifestyle etc. Does the liturgy give meaning to these dimensions of our life or does it turn them into a *'corpus extraneum'*? We need to be aware of the fact that understanding the liturgy is far more than a cognitive exercise; it is a loving 'entering in'. At the same time our vision or contemplative gaze is weak. Since the Renaissance we have lost our disinterested contemplative ability; it was pushed aside to make way for analytic observation.

10. What Should We Do? What Can We Do?

10.1 Theme and Variations

It is quite clear that 'entering into the already existing' structure of the liturgy does not mean that we must exclude any kind of flexibility in our liturgical style. Far from being ruled out, creativity is actually called for. If the problem does not lie with creativity then where does it lie?

The problem lies with the boundaries of our intervention. One cannot simply transform and rearrange the whole thing. Changes have to be made with intelligence. The liturgy contains certain given themes which, while they cannot be changed, do remain open to possible variation. Some of those clearly delineated and unchangeable liturgical paths were determined by Christ himself. In classical terms they are referred to as the 'substance' of the sacraments, over which even the Church itself has no power. The liturgy remains Christ's liturgy.

There are also more historically derived elements of the liturgy which one cannot change. Certain forms of prayer and certain words and ways of speaking which, like the Bible texts, remain unchangeable. Perhaps even the liturgical order of scripture reading, lyrical response (psalm) and prayer fall into this category. It is more than just a liturgical vagary, it is a deep theological truth: God speaks first and our response follows.

In order to be able to establish the boundaries between theme and variations a thorough liturgical training is indispensable. Liturgy demands knowledge of tradition and history, in short, documentary knowledge. In order to take one's place in the liturgical enterprise one has to know one's craft; liturgy requires instruction and insight together with a good helping of spirituality and pastoral awareness. Perhaps the reason for the evident liturgical poverty in so many places throughout the world can be found here. There is no lack of engagement or dedication or imagination: there is simply a lack of competence. There is no point in setting up liturgical work groups if they are not trained for their job.

10.2 The Duration of the Celebration

It might come across as strange in the ears of many but our liturgical celebrations are for the most part too short. The liturgy needs time to deliver its riches. It has nothing to do with physical time or 'clock' time but with the spiritual time of the soul. Since liturgy does not belong to the world of information but to the domain of the heart, it does not work with 'clock' time but with 'kairos'. Many of our liturgies do not provide enough time or space to enter into the event. In this regard Eastern liturgy provides a worthy example, taking its time and inviting those who participate to 'leave all worldly cares behind' (hymn of the Cherubim). It is not enough that people have heard the liturgy or that it has been spoken. Has it been 'proclaimed to them'? Have they been given the opportunity to integrate it? It is not enough for us to have heard the liturgy, we need to have grasped and appropriated it as well.

A major factor in all of this is silence and the time to interiorize. The liturgy of Vatican II provides time for silence but in practice it is not given much of a chance. Lack of silence turns the liturgy into an unstoppable succession of words which leaves no time for interiorization. Here, too, is a reason for the liturgy's 'incomprehensibility'.

10.3 The Articulation of Word and Gesture

A major handicap of the liturgy as it is practised de facto in the West is its 'verbosity'. In essence, liturgy has become a matter of 'language' and speaking. The word that was once ignored and neglected has made a comeback. How many presiders consider the homily to be the climax of the liturgy and the barometer of the celebration? How many have the feeling that the celebration is more or less over after the liturgy of the Word? Indeed, there is clearly an imbalance in duration between the liturgy of the Word and the liturgy of the Eucharist. At the same time too much attention is given to the 'intellectual' approach to the liturgy. There is not enough room for imagination, affect, emotion and properly understood aesthetics. This leads in turn to the consequence that the liturgy begins to function in an extremely intellectual fashion and fails thereby to reach many of those who participate in it either because they are non-intellectual types or because they do not consider such stuff to be nourishing for their lives.

A liturgy which is almost exclusively oriented to the intellect is also not likely to involve the human body in the celebration to any great extent. It is small wonder that people end up sitting down for almost the entire celebration: sitting being the typical attitude of the listener. (Please note that this is not usually the case in the United States.) There is a serious imbalance in the articulation of word and gesture. Without introducing rhetorical gesticulations and building in theatricality one can still argue, nevertheless, that the tongue and the ear are frequently the only human organs in use during the liturgy. Liturgy then ends up lapsing from celebration into mere instruction and address.

11. The Instrumentalization of the Liturgy

One of the consequences of the verbosity we have been discussing is the danger that the liturgy will be instrumentalized and used for ends which lie outside it. Liturgy, however, is a global, symbolic activity which belongs to the order of the 'playful'. The uniqueness of 'play' is the fact that one 'plays in order to play', one plays for the sake of playing. The death of play is competition and financial interest.

Liturgy will also die if it is subordinated to ends beyond itself. Liturgy is neither the time nor the place for catechesis. Of course, it has excellent catechetical value but it is not there to replace the various catechetical moments in the life of the Christian woman or man. Such moments require their own time. Nor should liturgy be used as a means for disseminating information, no matter how essential that information might be. It should not be forced to serve as an easy way to notify the participants about this, that and the other unless such things are themselves entirely subordinate to the liturgy itself. One does not attend the liturgy on Mission Sunday in order to learn something about this or that mission territory: one comes to the liturgy to reflect on and integrate one's mission from Christ to 'go out to all nations'. The establishment of all sorts of thematic Sundays and thematic celebrations has little or no future, except in the death of the liturgy as such. Liturgy ought certainly not to serve as a sort of 'warm-up' for another activity, even a church activity. It is not a meeting but a celebration. It can indeed follow from the liturgy that one departs from it with a greater sense of engagement, faith and love informing and inspiring one's actions. Liturgy is a free activity: its end is in itself. Although it is the 'source and summit' of all ecclesial activities liturgy does not replace them nor does it coincide with them.

12. The 'Sensorial' Pedagogy of the Liturgy

The uniqueness of the liturgy is that it gives pride of place to 'experience'. Experience comes first, and while reflection, analysis, explanation and systematization might be necessary they must follow after experience. 'Celebrate first, then understand' might seem a strange proposition to some and perhaps even come across as obscuranist and anti-intellectual. Does it imply a call for irrationality or an abandonment of the massive catechetical effort the Church makes in order to prepare people to receive the sacraments? Think, for example, of the creed and confirmation. The Church Fathers adhered to the principle that mystagogical catechesis (in which the deepest core of the sacred mysteries was laid bare) should only come after the sacraments of initiation. Prior to baptism they limited themselves to moral instruction and teaching on the Christian 'way of life'. Immediately after baptism – during Easter week – they spoke about the deep meaning of baptism, chrismation and Eucharist. Their pedagogical approach remained 'sensorial': participate first and experience things at an existential level in the heart of the community and only then explain. Their entire method of instruction was structured around a framework of questions and answers such as: 'Did you notice that...?' – 'Well, what this means is...'.

Perhaps we do not have to adhere to the letter of such a pedagogical approach – the *'disciplina arcani'* also had a hand in things – but it certainly provides a hint in the right direction. One can only understand the liturgy if one enters into it with faith and love. In this sense no catechetical method will succeed if it is unable to depend on good, community celebrations of the liturgy. In the same way catechesis as such will be of little use if it is not accompanied by a liturgical praxis during the period of catechesis. Where the liturgy is concerned, the following rule applies: first experience, first 'live' the liturgy, then reflect and explain it. The eyes of the heart must be open before the eyes of the mind because one can only truly understand the liturgy with the intelligence of the heart.

This has consequences for liturgical work groups; those who desire to work with the liturgy and, as we already noted, 'vary the given theme', will first have to listen attentively to that theme and participate in the celebration of the liturgy as it is. If they do not, then their entire liturgical endeavour will turn out to be nothing more than 'self-expression' and not the shaping of a pre-given entity which has its roots in the liturgical tradition of both the Old and New Testaments and in the living tradition of the Church. What would we think of a composer who refused to listen to his predecessors or a painter who refused to visit a museum? Every musician listens to music and every poet reads poetry. This is simple human wisdom but it applies in full to the liturgy which is primarily God's work with his people. The worthy liturgist listens first, meditates, prays and interiorizes. Only then can he or she 'modulate'.

13. Ritual and Boredom

The very terms 'rite' and 'ritual' summon up the idea of boredom and monotony. 'It's always the same...', we hear day in day out. Ritual is synonymous with rigidity and sclerosis. Is that really so, however? It is true that an exaggerated attachment to particular forms does exist, but that is ritualism, unsound ritual. We have to admit that every good thing has its pathology. Ritual, however, is something other than ritualism. Ritual is priceless and irreplaceable. It has its place in every human activity. Every human being has a morning and evening ritual just as every society has its regular festivities which are celebrated in the same way each year. Ritual is an unavoidably anthropological datum. Every significant human reality is surrounded and protected by ritual: birth, marriage, love, death. Every transition is adorned and embellished with ritual. Every time we encounter something that transcends the human person we 'humanize' it with ritual.

The unique characteristic of every ritual is its repetitiveness and stereotypical nature. In order for us to interiorize profound matters, we need identical stereotypes, the reassuring ceremonial wordings we call ritual. This kind of repetition, however, does not necessarily imply monotony or the stifling of any kind of personal element. Every marriage rite, for example, is stereotypical: everyone marries in the same manner and with the same words and gestures. Yet in so doing those involved are not left depersonalized, a mere number in the line. Every marriage remains unique even though it took place in just the same way as any other. As a matter of fact it is essential for every couple that they are able to take their place in line with every other marriage in and through the fixed marriage rite. In this way the fragility of their personal engagement is socialized and, in their eyes, protected and guaranteed. The same is true for the language of love. It remains endlessly unvarying yet it is experienced as fresh and new each time it is spoken.

Repetitive ritual provides, in addition, the opportunity for in-depth reflection and interiorization. Serious matters (such as the liturgy) cannot be grasped all at once: they need time and time means repetition. Only pure information such as an order or computer language does not require repetition since it can be understood immediately. More profound matters only let their real significance emerge over time.

Ritual, finally, provides a protection against direct, unmediated religious experience. Only the great religious geniuses (such as Moses before the burning bush) are able to negotiate such direct experiences of the numinous; the rest of us need the protective mediation of ritual and the 'decelerating', 'delaying' role of repetition. Indeed, there will always be a certain monotony and perhaps boredom associated with ritual. Perhaps we simply have to be aware of it and reconcile ourselves to it, as long as we continue to bear in mind how necessary this 'tiresome' aspect of ritual can be.

A few further reflections might also be useful. If we constantly emphasize the 'tiresome' aspect of ritual we reveal just how individualistic our experience of the liturgy has become. Ritual, however, is necessary in order to bring a community together and allow it to celebrate. If we turn the liturgy into the most individual expression of the most individual emotion then we wipe out any possibility of communal celebration. If, however, we enter into the eucharistic celebration with its fixed 'ratio agendi' it is because we want to make it possible for many to celebrate in the same rhythm. There can be no community without ritual. We need to bear in mind, furthermore, that we attend the liturgy at God's invitation. The liturgy is not a feast we laid out for ourselves, according to our own personal preferences. It is God's feast. We attend by invitation and not simply to satisfy our own particular needs.

A great deal depends, to be sure, on the person of the presider. He is someone who must lead a community event on God's behalf. He is the living vehicle of something that goes beyond him. He is, therefore, neither robot nor actor; he is a servant.

14. The Cosmic Grounding of the Liturgy

One important fact about the liturgy is its relatedness to the cosmos. Many of its symbols are borrowed from cosmic realities such as fire, light, water, food, bodily gestures. Times and seasons, the position of sun and moon, night and day, summer and winter are also related to the liturgy. In the liturgical event all the major human archetypes have their place. What is important, however, is that the cosmic realities in question are given their chance to appear in their full reality as created things. The liturgy must work with 'real' things. Although everything is to a certain degree transformed by culture it should never be overshadowed by cultural accretions. Fire needs to be real fire, light

21

real light, linen real linen, wood real wood. Time must also be respected, such as the hour for the Easter vigil celebration. Thus liturgy often becomes the true repository of the authenticity of the objects around us. To serve God we use only the best things as he created them. Expediency and comfort need to make way here for authenticity.

We should be aware, however, that all our Jewish and Christian symbols are no longer purely cosmic or natural. They have all been determined and conditioned by the history of God with his people. Although all our Jewish-Christian feasts have an agrarian origin they have all been conditioned by the events of salvation which are historically situated and no longer natural; they are fact-historical. The Passover feast is no longer purely agricultural, it is also the celebration of the exodus from Egypt. *Shebuoth* is no longer a celebration of the first harvest but of the giving of the law on Mount Sinai. With Christian feasts which are entirely determined by the historicity of the Christian mysteries it is even clearer. There are no more purely cosmic, natural feasts. The Christian festal calendar is no longer a purely natural calendar, it consists rather of a series of memorial days which celebrate historical events between God and his people.

15. The Liturgy and the Senses

Liturgy is closely related to the body and the senses. As a matter of fact there is only one fundamental symbolism: that of the human body as an expression of the human soul and thus the primary location of all symbols. All other symbolic gestures can be situated in the extension of the human body.

The eye is the most active of the senses. In the liturgy nowadays, however, it tends to be somewhat undervalued. There is a lot to hear but little to see. At one time the situation was reversed. At a time when the verbal dimension was not understood the visual dimension was pushed to the fore. Certain secondary liturgical gestures, such as the elevation of the bread and wine at the consecration, are a consequence of this fact. Even eucharistic worship outside of Mass has its roots here. We can certainly re-evaluate the visual side of our liturgy but that does not always mean that we have to supply additional visual effects. It is always best to let the great symbols function. How, for example, can baptism symbolize 'reception into the Church' if it takes place in an almost empty church building? (Again this is not always true in the United States.) How can it be understood as a water bath if it turns out to be little more than a sprinkling with water? How can we speak of 'hearing the message' if everyone is sitting with their heads bent reading the texts in their missalettes at the moment when they should be listening? The three great focal points of the celebration: the presidential chair, the ambo and the altar, also have a strong visual significance.

The assembly has the most important place in the Christian liturgy, and rightly so. Liturgy is a celebration of the faith and the 'faith comes from the congregation'. As a matter of fact, if the Christian mysteries being celebrated are all rooted in historical facts and are thus memorial celebrations, then it is equally true that this should be spoken about. History is impossible with the element of 'narrative'. Of great importance is that the different text genres should be respected: a reading is not a prayer, a hymn is not a psalm, a song is not a *monitio* nor is a homily a set of announcements. Each of these genres requires its own *auditive* treatment. Furthermore, it is clear that neither rhetoric nor theatricality nor pathos have a part in the liturgy. Reading is not acting; it is allowing oneself to be the humble instrument of a word that comes from beyond. The exaggerated impact of the personal individuality of the man or woman who reads can kill the liturgy and eliminate its harmonics. Even the place from which the scriptures are read has some significance. It is better not to read from the middle of the community because the word comes to us from elsewhere. It is proclaimed; it does not simply arise out of the community. It is also best to read from the Book of the Gospels and from an ambo surrounded by symbols suggestive of respect (light, incense, altar servers).

The sense of touch finds its most profound expression in the laying on of hands and in anointing. These are among the most physical gestures of the liturgy and they can have an enormous impact on the human person. The significance of praying in the presence of a sick person takes on quite a different character if one places one's hands on that person or anoints them.

23

The sense of smell, to conclude, is almost completely unused in the liturgy. It is not to our advantage that the use of incense has been pushed aside into the domain of superfluity and hindrance. The Eastern Church is much better off than we are in this regard. One rather absurd case is the scentlessness of the chrism which we use to suggest the 'good odour of Christ' to our newly confirmed. Here, too, the Eastern Church is ahead of us (perhaps too generously!) in their use of tens of different scents and spices in the manufacture of their chrism.

16. 'Inculturation'

The problem of 'inculturation' is a recent phenomenon. It was treated in a remarkable document produced by the Sacred Congregation for the Sacraments and Divine Worship in 1994. We cannot discuss every aspect of the problem at this juncture. The principle, however, is clear: if the liturgy is an 'incarnational' fact then it is an inherent requirement that it be inculturated in the various cultures of humanity. Such is evident. Liturgy must be inculturated; or rather, liturgy will inculturate itself if it is lived with faith and love of Christ by people of all cultures.

There are also limits, however. The liturgy is not only a structuring of human religiosity, it gives form to the Christian mysteries. These mysteries took place in history, in a particular place and time and using particular rites and symbols. The Last Supper is not just a common, human religious meal, it is the meal the Lord ate with his disciples the night before he suffered. This implies that all eucharistic celebrations need to be recognizable as such which includes even formal connections and references. No cultural religious meal is equivalent to the Christ meal. In this sense the Eucharist can never be completely 'inculturated'. The liturgy is not only an incarnational datum, it also belongs to the order of salvation. As such it has a salvific impact on the cultures of humankind.

Not every religious practice or popular 'liturgy' can be used as a 'vehicle' for Christian liturgy. There are levels of incompatibility and there are prayers and practices which are not appropriate for use in the Christian liturgy. 'Discernment' here will not always be so simple.

24

Inculturation does not take place so much on the liturgist's desk as in the praxis of liturgy itself. It is not an act of bureaucratic sophistication but rather a faithful loyal discernment which takes place in the celebration itself. Only after long and deep immersion in the real liturgy accompanied by a great desire for Christ and his mysteries, for Church tradition and for the historicizing of the 'natural' liturgy through the coming of Christ will we see the slow but steady emergence of inculturated liturgy. This is how the Jewish liturgy transformed into the Greek and the Greek liturgy into the Roman and the Roman liturgy was supplemented and augmented by the German and Anglo-Saxon liturgy and so forth. Such work of inculturation has always been the fruit of the thoughts and deeds of a few significant Church figures and of the patient sensitivity and faith-filled discernment of the many peoples of the world.

It remains an open question whether we should consider inclusive language to be a question of inculturation. The discussion is still in full swing and would demand a separate and more thorough treatment than is possible here. In fact the question remains if we are being faced with a radical cultural change and if this has religious implications. It appears to me to be more of an anthropological problem which is significant not only for biblical and liturgical texts but for the use of language as such and for the whole dimension of conviviality between men and women.

17. Liturgy and Life

There has been a great deal of discussion in recent years concerning the exotic character of the liturgy and its distance from the everyday life of Christians. It is true indeed that a liturgy which has no impact on or consequences for the way Christians live their lives is off the mark. If, according to Pope Leo the Great, the Christian mysteries have crossed over into the liturgy then it is equally true that liturgy must cross over into the moral and spiritual life of Christians. '*Imitamini quod tractatis*' – 'Do in practice what you do in the liturgy' – resounds the ancient text from the liturgy of ordination.

Some have endeavoured to draw the conclusion from this axiom that the liturgy is not important when compared with our day-to-day lives or that it is a sort of preparation or 'warm-up' for life itself, an option for those who need it but redundant for those who don't. Others have suggested that liturgy and life coincide and that true service to God takes place outside the church in one's daily life. Liturgy does not coincide with life, rather it has a dialectic relationship with life. Sunday is not Monday nor vice versa.

Aside from the liturgy's profound and significant content as an indispensable source of grace and power for life, we must also bear in mind that the Sunday ritual interrupts monotony and differentiates and articulates human time. The liturgy is not life and life is not liturgy. Both are irreducible and both are necessary. They do not coincide. It is sometimes said that the liturgy gives shape to life, that it symbolizes life. This is not entirely incorrect. What we do throughout the week in a varied and diluted way we also do in the liturgy but in a more concentrated and purified fashion: we live for God and for others. Liturgy, however, is not only a symbolization of human life. Liturgy symbolizes and makes present: firstly the mysteries of salvation, the words and deeds of Christ, but also our deeds in so far as they are reflected, purified and redeemed in Christ. His mysteries – made present to us in the liturgy – are our archetypes. This Christological determination of our lives in the liturgy is of the essence.

On the other hand, it is a fact that the liturgy finds its field of application in daily life. It flows over it and nourishes it but never coincides with it nor complies with it. Life and liturgy are in a dialectic relationship: the life of the Christian is built on two things: *cultus* and *caritas*.

2

'Lights! Camera! Worship!' The Cinema and its Challenges to Roman Catholic Worship in Postmodernity

Richard Leonard, SJ

No one who takes postmodernity seriously underestimates how important the media are in relation to every part of people's lives. As Pope John Paul has observed, 'The impact of the media can hardly be exaggerated. For many the experience of living is to a great extent an experience of the media.'[1] Whether we like it or not, even our people's liturgical expectations are now formed by the media. For example in my home country of Australia – and these figures are replicated all around the industrialized world and are emerging in the developing world as well – adults watch an average of three hours and 13 minutes of TV a day. This means that a 70-year-old Australian has spent nine years in front of the TV; 61 per cent of all Australian homes now have two televisions.

The way Catholic liturgy is portrayed on the large or small screen directly shapes people's expectations of it. In an increasingly unchurched society, the most regular exposure to liturgical actions which many people have is what they see on television and in film. When they come to our liturgical rites, they bring images of what the ceremonies will look like from the media. In this regard, their lives mirror those of their favourite characters – many will come to the church for a 'hatching', 'matching' or 'dispatching', with little or no long-term relationship with the worshipping assembly. It can seem as if the church is a set, the ritual is the script and the priest is a supporting actor in a sacramental matinée.

Some other theological disciplines are starting to take the media as seriously as we should. For example, systematic theologian Margaret

Miles, in *Seeing and Believing: religion and values in the movies*, points out that 'the development of popular film coincided historically and geographically with the emancipation of public life from church control and patronage. "Congregations" became "audiences" as film created a new public sphere in which, under the guise of "entertainment", values are formulated, circulated, resisted, and negotiated. The public sphere is an arena in which various overlapping minorities can converse, contest and negotiate, forming temporary coalitions.'[2] In liturgical journals, however, there is a deafening silence on the interplay between media and liturgy. It is as though the two are unrelated.

Where liturgists do speak up, at least in conversation, is in seeing how many mistakes film-makers make in portraying Christian worship. They use liturgical texts unknown to any mainstream Christian Church and incorrect vestments, they know little about liturgical spaces, gestures, seasonal or ritual colours, and they invent or minimize liturgical actions. Films, however, are not meant to be religious catechesis. They show liturgical actions as a way of situating characters as mainstream members of a community, or to open a plot line (a wedding or baptism), or to 'kill off' a character (a funeral).

Society has a bank of images built up over the century in regard to the way liturgy is employed in cinematic narrative. Spencer Tracy was the first talking priest in the cinema and said Mass in *San Francisco* (1938). Later in *Boys' Town* (1938) and *Men of Boys' Town* (1941) the only time the boys could express their fears and hopes was in prayers at Mass. Bing Crosby went to the altar in *Going My Way* (1944) where liturgical music converted young vandals, and in *The Bells of St Mary's* (1946) Ingrid Bergman led the angelic chorus. In different ways *Open City* (1945), *The Keys of the Kingdom* (1945), *The Fugitive* (1947), and *On the Waterfront* (1954) showed how liturgy could sustain a person in the face of persecution and even martyrdom.

Conversely the liturgy brings no comfort to either assembly or presider in *Diary of a Country Priest* (1950) and *Winter Light* (1962), but focuses a loss of faith. Even Jack Lemmon in *Mass Appeal* (1984) confessed to the assembly that his song and dance presiding had been a show for popularity. Hitchcock's *I Confess* (1954) featured the intrigue of penitential divulgences.

28

The liturgy is parodied in *Heaven Help Us* (1971), *Hair* (1979), and *The Meaning of Life* (1983), where the ritual is presented as a means to social control. The *Godfather* trilogy (1972, 1979, 1990) saw the Corleone family abuse nearly every promise they make at every sacrament while displaying financial generosity toward the Church for doing the deeds. On the positive side the liturgy in *Brides of Christ* (1991) mirrors the changes in the Church from 1962–70.

In *Priest* (1994), apart from an invalid confession where a man admits to incest, the Sunday Eucharist is presented as a celebration for the needy, in the person of the minister and the assembly. And in *Four Weddings and a Funeral* (1994) and *Muriel's Wedding* (1994) Christian liturgy is primarily about celebrating the lives of the couple or the memory of the individual.

So what conclusions can we draw from this brief and incomplete survey? The visual media underline in a positive way the need for ritual at important moments in people's lives, but there is often no sense that the characters have any relationship with the presider or that they belong to the worshipping community that usually gathers in the church. Rarely do they demonstrate the Christian commitment they are celebrating in Christ's name.

The cinema faithfully shows the situation of a growing number of unchurched people who only infrequently attend any church. For them, the baby, the couple or the deceased is the focus of the ritual. Hence, many people cannot understand our focus on Christ and the assembly and the way in which these intersect with the liturgical action surrounding the baby, the couple or the deceased.

Another liturgical focus in film is the priest. He is often incompetent, fraudulent, or completely unaware of the family and social context within which the liturgy is being celebrated. Even in recent films, priests do sacraments and congregations watch.

Finally, and most seriously, the portrayal of sacraments on film rarely gives any evidence that the liturgy changes people's lives. Sacraments are reduced to social occasions and rites of passage, Christ is dislocated from the centre of the ritual action, and the individual is worshipped and his or her aspirations glorified.

What can liturgists do about this? Learn the language. When St

29

Francis Xavier, arguably the Church's greatest missionary, left Rome for Portugal and then on to India, St Ignatius Loyola gave him one piece of advice: wherever you go, learn the language. It is hard work to learn a language, especially at an advanced age, but a new understanding and the ease it gives within a culture amply reward the effort involved. The influence of media in creating and reflecting a postmodern, post-Christian culture means there is a new language spoken here and if we want to influence this culture for good we have to learn its tongue.[3] We have to face up to a Western media-saturated culture as it is, not as we would like it to be. We cannot evangelize a culture we do not know or one that we despise.

The Church has commendably been a custodian of high artistic culture, often exemplified in our liturgy and churches. We do not need to abandon that legacy from our past, but marry it with the postmodern popular culture which now forms the people whom we want speak to and influence for good. This task could be understood as the commission to inculturate the Gospel in a media culture. In a direct application of the principle of inculturation to Australia, Pope John Paul II reminded the Aboriginal people in Alice Springs, 'You do not have to be divided in two parts. Jesus calls you to accept his words and his values into your own culture.'[4] If we are serious about liturgy in a Western, postmodern media culture we cannot ask our people to make a similar division when they come to worship.

On a pastoral level we could ask the next couple or family we are preparing for a baptism, marriage or funeral, what images of these liturgies they remember from TV and film. It can become an opportunity to explain how and why we in the Church approach these occasions differently from the media. Another positive initiative we can offer is to help the motion picture industry get liturgical celebrations right. Liturgists could offer their advice to film companies.

Ignatian spirituality holds that God can be found everywhere but in evil. As liturgists, then, we need to enter the modern media market place where, these days, we have unashamedly to compete with other groups for minds, hearts and values.[5] If we take seriously the idea that liturgy intersects with real life and celebrates it, if as liturgists we are aware that public prayer requires a composition of place, then we need to take very seriously the media the assembly watches *before* they walk into the church so as to enhance what they do in the church and what they take away from it.

3

Recovering Collective Memory in the Context of Postmodernism

Wendelin Köster, SJ

My work in Germany both as a youth minister and as the director of a seminary has often confronted me with the question: 'How can I explain what liturgy is to young people?' This question was and is a burning one because fewer and fewer people are going to church. Liturgy and consequently the sacraments, especially the Eucharist, are becoming more and more strange to them – more and more removed from their lived experience.

Looking for an explanation, I remembered an event. When I was a boy of perhaps 16 years, an old lady in the street attracted my attention. She seemed to be helpless. I went up to her and asked her whether I could help. She wanted to go home, she said. 'Where do you live?' I asked. She didn't know. 'What is your name?' But she also didn't know her name. The old lady was totally confused; she had lost her memory.

If the Church is a corporate personality, she also has – analogous to individuals – a memory, an instrument that is collecting all that is necessary to know about who she is, about what makes her an individual. The issue is not that memory is a collection of knowledge and capable of memorizing things. More significant is that deeper memory capable of knowing and understanding who I am, where I come from and where I'm going. Liturgy *is* that collective memory of the Church, I think, and that memory's centre is the Eucharist.

We are sometimes worried about our memory because it is unreliable. We are afraid that, like that old lady, we could become forgetful and even lose our identity. Those same concerns exist for the Church since both she and the communities within her run the same risk of memory defects or even moments of collective amnesia. This happens, I think, when the celebration of the Eucharist is either neglected or taken for granted. Against such amnesia there is only one remedy: constant care and cultivation.

The demand of Jesus, 'Do this in memory of me!', was at once the igniting spark of the memory power of the Church, and also its content. This is not unlike stimulating the powers of concentration. There is a physical aspect of concentration: people react to an invitation and come together in person and in one place, forming an assembly. On the other hand, this concentration is also mental: the assembled people concentrate themselves on a content; namely, on the legacy left to them by the Lord. Observing his last wish, they know who they are, from where they come, and where they are going.

So the eucharistic liturgy has been caused by the word of Jesus Christ: 'Do this in memory of me!' Whoever wants to know what the Church knows, believes, affirms about herself, should look at the liturgy. Whoever wants the Church to be known, should invite the interested people to 'Come and see!', both to experience that corporate worship first-hand, and later to have it explained to them.

What will that visitor see? First of all, he or she will notice that liturgy is a meeting. God and God's people experience a being together of great concentration and intentionality. They have to talk with each other, and they listen to each other. Secondly, there is a table set for a meal. The first happens by reading from the Holy Scripture and by responding to that reading. Those sacred texts show piece by piece the story of the personal relationship which God initiated with God's people. It is a moving love story – a love, threatened by the infidelity of one of the partners and saved by the fidelity of the other, – faithful until death. The second happens within the meal that the faithful One has prepared – and at what cost – for the unfaithful. This meal is a meal of victory and joy.

What might flow from these reflections? Firstly, as members of the Church we are all jointly responsible for strengthening her powers of memory and concentration. This happens first of all when we meet together regularly in the eucharistic assembly and at the common public prayer of the Church, whether in our own local communities or

33

with other Christians. Already the mere fact that we come together for this strengthens the memory of the Church. Despite the common debate about the pros and cons of daily Eucharist, I am convinced that there is nothing wrong with doing this every day, though, in German at any rate, I avoid using the word *feiern,* celebrate. So I don't say, we should *celebrate* the Eucharist daily. Why do I not do so? Because so many people say: 'If it should be a *celebration,* I must confess that often I am not in the right mood; every day cannot be Sunday, and I just don't have the energy to *celebrate* every day.' But the eucharistic concentration is so important for the vitality of the Church universal and the local community that we should not become dependent on the ups und downs of our moods. Our liturgical participation is not determined by how we feel or what our mood happens to be on any given day. Indeed, I find the daily exercise of our collective memory not only possible, but necessary. If we don't take it seriously, we slowly but surely shall arrive at the condition of the confused lady who forgot who she was and where she was going.

Secondly, without a fixed regular integration of the community into the Eucharist and into common prayer it seems to be nearly impossible to lead that community well; Eucharist and other forms of common prayer ground the community in its common life and mission. As individuals and as communities we need the frequent contact with the Lord in the Eucharist. This contact normally cannot be substituted in any other way. To the degree that this contact becomes weak, communities become confused. In the end, we may find that we can no longer say clearly who we are as believers, where we come from and where we are going.

Thirdly, if I can read the signs of the times well, human beings, living in the countries of Western postmodern culture, are suffering a peculiar weakness of concentration. All of us, but especially those of us from the West, are exposed to powerful forces which are able to effectively distract us from what is a maxim of the Spiritual Exercises of St Ignatius: that we are created to praise, reverence and serve God our Lord, and by this means to save our souls. In this postmodern age we are in danger of losing our souls. The one who is losing his or her soul loses the centre in which that unity as a person is rooted, and begins to disintegrate, to come apart and divide into separate parts. I would suggest that we are willing and obedient victims of an effective temptation, which consists in the fact that we are inclined to compartmentalize our lives, taking our self-esteem from different qualities of ourselves rather than from the centre of who we are as a united whole. Certain phases of life, certain parts of the body, certain talents are regarded as overriding values. And those who seek them are easily inclined to break the whole into pieces. Today there are developing ethics which approve of this kind of thinking and acting. But then we can't be sure that human dignity will be respected. Many of our sisters and brothers in the world notice this danger and look for help and guidance. What can we offer to them? We can offer time and room to meet, where they can recollect themselves and be brought back to the centre and to the whole of their personality. That happens especially in the liturgy.

To conclude, I am convinced that Church ministers, who also today want to be good pastors and good companions, should cultivate good liturgy; it is all part of one integrated whole. Because liturgy is concentration on the essential and vital question: Who am I, where do I come from, where am I going?

4

Liturgy in the Life and Mission of the Society of Jesus[1]

Robert F. Taft, SJ

'Man was created to praise, reverence, and serve God,' St Ignatius famously teaches.[2] But Jesuits have long been considered better at the serving than at praising and reverencing, at least in so far as the official public worship of the Church is concerned. If and why that is so can be determined only by an analysis of liturgy in the history of the Society. That is the only way to discover what brought us to where we are now.[3]

1. Liturgy in the Post-Vatican II Catholic Church[4]

The contemporary Catholic view of worship is the outgrowth of the seminal principle of New Testament theology that all salvation history is recapitulated and 'personalized' in Jesus. Everything in sacred history – every event, object, sacred place, theophany, cult – has quite simply been assumed into the person of the Incarnate Christ. He is God's eternal Word,[5] his new creation[6] and the new Adam,[7] the new Pasch and its lamb,[8] the new covenant,[9] the new circumcision,[10] and the heavenly manna;[11] God's temple,[12] the new sacrifice, and its priest;[13] the fulfilment of the Sabbath rest[14] and the Messianic Age that was come.[15] All that went before is fulfilled in him: 'For the law has but a shadow of the good things to come instead of the true form of these realities,' Hebrews 10:1 affirms, and that includes cultic realities. This revelation lays the foundation for any Christian theology of liturgy.[16] Henceforth, true worship pleasing to the Father is none other than the saving life, death, and resurrection of Christ. And Paul tells us that our worship is this same sacrificial existence in us:[17] 'I implore you by God's mercy to offer your very selves to him: a living sacrifice, consecrated and fit for his acceptance; *this is your authentic worship*' (Romans 12:1).[18]

So the liturgy is quite simply the mystery of Christ operative in our midst. Salvation consists in our insertion into the salvific mystery of Christ primarily through the visible continuation of this mystery through the liturgy. As Pope St Leo the Great (440–61) says in his famous aphorism that sums up an entire patristic liturgical theology: 'What was visible in our Redeemer has passed into the liturgical ministry of the Church [*Quod itaque Redemptoris nostri conspicuum fuit in sacramenta transivit*]'[19] – what Christ did visibly during his earthly ministry is the exact same ministry that the Church carries on now in the liturgy. These acts do not merely express the Church; they constitute her.

Liturgy, then, is much more than an individual expression of faith and devotion. It is first and foremost an activity of God in Christ. Christ saves through the ages in the activity of the Body of which he is the head. So liturgy is the common work of Christ and his Church. This grounds the extraordinary claims the Church has made about the nature of Christian worship, as in the striking assertion of the Vatican II *Constitution on the Sacred Liturgy* §2: '...it is through the liturgy that the work of our redemption is accomplished'.[20] Pius XII affirmed the same doctrine in his 1947 encyclical *Mediator Dei*, the 'Magna Carta' of the modern Liturgical Movement: 'It is an unquestionable fact that the work of our redemption is continued and that its fruits are imparted to us during the celebration of the liturgy...' (§29). Hence 'liturgical prayer, being the public supplication of the illustrious Spouse of Christ, is superior to private prayers' (§37), and 'The worship rendered to God in union with her divine Head is the most efficacious means of achieving sanctity' (§26).[21] The implications of this last statement for our spiritual and apostolic lives as Jesuits should be obvious. Liturgy is at the very centre of the redemptive work Christ exercises through the ministry of the Church. Anyone who does not celebrate and live the liturgy of the Church according to the mind of the Church, cannot pretend to be either a Christian or an apostle, true to the Church and therefore to the Society and its ministry.

37

2. Liturgy and Religious Life in the Time of St Ignatius

Nothing could be more different from this Vatican II teaching on the liturgy than how liturgy was understood in the time of St Ignatius (1491–1556).[22] The Catholic Church was then in the throes of the most degenerate period of its liturgical history. The early Middle Ages had already witnessed the end of the ancient system of 'cathedral liturgy',[23] and with it, the 'dissolution of the liturgical community' and the 'triumph of the private Mass'.[24] Previously, Christian communities in the cities and towns of Late Antiquity were organized as one unit under the direction of the bishop. It was the bishop who presided at services in the cathedral, with the numerous lesser clergy[25] assisting him in the celebration of the sacraments and other liturgical services and pastoral duties, which consisted chiefly in celebrating the offices and sacraments – what today we call 'liturgy'.[26] In this system, priests were ordained to minister to a particular community, and not for their own spiritual entertainment, or as stipendiary Mass-machines for votive offerings.[27]

The collapse of this cathedral system rang the death knell to the public celebration of unified community liturgy. Country chapels and lesser suburban churches came to be served by their own clergy.[28] The practice of administering baptism in parish churches every day of the year spelled the end of the old process of Christian Initiation centred in the cathedral baptistry as an integral part of the paschal celebrations.[29] The proliferation of guilds with their own chapels and liturgies[30] exacerbated the fragmentation of liturgical unity and the growing clericalization and privatization of the Eucharist.

Reciting the *Canon Missae* in an inaudible whisper widened the gap between an ever more clericalized liturgy and the people,[31] and fantastic allegorical explanations of the Mass rush in to fill the devotional vacuum this created. 'Seeing the host', with its associated superstitions,[32] replaces communion in the sacred gifts; the Eucharist becomes a sacred spectacle encased in superstitious beliefs, practices and interpretations;[33] exposition of the Blessed Sacrament even begins to displace the Mass itself as the centre of eucharistic worship, adumbrat-

38

ing the subjective and static devotional cult that will later characterize Baroque eucharistic devotion.[34]

As for the Liturgy of the Hours, they had been 'expanded to an unbearable degree, primarily in the monasteries of Cluny' and the clergy 'groaned under the burden'.[35] The encroachment of the full cursus of monastic offices as part of the daily obligation of the non-monastic clergy rendered it impossible to celebrate the Divine Office publicly and get anything else done in the course of the day. The Hours, thus 'swollen beyond all proportions', continued to be celebrated in cathedral, collegial and monastic churches. But the perfunctory manner of their celebration by a debased, ignorant, often semi-literate clergy, marked at times by sheer degradation,[36] showed the choral Hours to have become a spent force.

Trent corrected this mess at the price of 'rigid unification and rubricism'.[37] Much like Baroque art and architecture, a style of extravagance, excess and externalism in which beauty is in the ornamentation, not in the structure itself, liturgy in this period was conceived to be an external shell, the official ceremonial form of the sacraments and worship – and nothing more.[38] Sacraments were 'things' that 'worked' if performed 'validly' for those who 'posed no obstacle'.[39] What counted was the essential 'matter and form'. 'Liturgy' was just the ceremonial frosting, something nice but not essential, useful not in itself, but because it could edify and arouse devotion, lead souls to confession, etc.

This *ex opere operato* minimalism reduced sacramental life to its 'valid' core, and people took refuge in private devotions, missions, retreats, etc., as a surrogate for what the liturgy was no longer accomplishing. Devotional privatization of piety and the ensuing individualism weakened the realization that we are saved as a people, Christ's Body, and that the liturgy constitutes, realizes, and must, because it is sign, express the unity of this people in its salvific relationship to the Father, through Christ, in the Holy Spirit.

No wonder, then, that there develops a more affective, subjective, interior devotional life focused on the person of Jesus and finding expression in meditation and a proliferation of 'devotions', rather than in the more traditional public liturgical offices.[40] The friars had already

begun to foster this shift away from a spiritual life of ritual obser-
vances,[41] and by the Baroque period, when the young Society was
flourishing, this robust new devotionalism had taken over the terrain.[42]
No wonder, then, that St Ignatius felt no qualms about dispensing from
or keeping to a minimum such a formalistic, ritualistic aspect of life
that was thought to have little or nothing to do with prayer.

Nor was Ignatius alone in this. His contemporary Blessed Paul
Giustiniani (1476–1528), reformer of the Camaldolese Hermits of
Monte Corona, also insisted on a liturgy marked by simplicity and
austerity in reaction to the prevalent Renaissance pomp of the day: 'We
do not sing, except very rarely,' he asserted: 'You must not take
pleasure in the pomp of processions.'[43] And St Francis de Sales (1567–
1622), Bishop of Geneva, made the pious resolve to say his beads when
his episcopal duties required him to assist at public Mass, lest valuable
prayer-time be lost![44]

So St Ignatius, like every man born into the world, was a man of his
times. He transcended those limitations in many ways, but in his
thinking on the role of the Church and the sacraments in sanctification,
Ignatius did not break out of the mechanistic, individualistic framework of his milieu. For him, the sacraments were instruments of
personal holiness.[45] Even the Mass was a very personal, private thing,
a time for visions, lights, consolations, tears, and other divine favours,
a means of obtaining grace, of moving heaven.[46] Solemn ceremonies
could be used (not for the Jesuits themselves but for the laity) as a
means of arousing devotion, leading one to confession, etc. (CSJ
§§261, 277, 401–7, 481, 640–44). But Ignatius shows no awareness
that liturgy is not just ceremony. This is perfectly illustrated by his
rejection of liturgical chant (CSJ §587), today considered integral to
the Divine Praises as the very mouth of the Church, and not just its
lipstick.[47] He also shows no awareness of the objective ecclesial and
communitarian character of the Church's prayer, which is not a means
to something else, not even to lead one to devotion or confession, but
which has a value in itself; no awareness of the full significance of
'community' in the Church or the Society, or of common prayer and
worship as indispensable constitutive elements of any Christian community. That final point is, I believe, a fundamental defect in the

Ignatian vision of Christian and Jesuit life. Even the *Constitutions* show little awareness of what a Christian community means. Everything remains almost totally on the level of individualism. Even the frequent exhortations to 'unity' are directed largely at the utilitarian end of preserving apostolic coordination and effectiveness.

3. Towards an Ignatian Theology of Liturgy

What can we salvage from the Ignatian vision that will ground in our Jesuit tradition the clear will of the Church that our prayer and apostolic life become more liturgical? I would like to try a new approach to this question. St Ignatius had no proper appreciation of the liturgy, and there is no use trying to prove he did. But that is not important. *No one* in the sixteenth-century Latin Church understood or appreciated the liturgy as we understand it today. So what Ignatius intuitively rejected was not what *we* call liturgy, but a degenerate medieval view of liturgy, and one cannot understand what liturgy was for Ignatius only by examining what he legislated about liturgy for the Society.[48] We need to penetrate to the more fundamental elements of his Christian vision. Only there will we find a basis for our Jesuit liturgical life. Only in that context can we judge what Ignatius rejected, and what inspired his vision of the nascent Society.

The Ignatian vision is radically supernatural, Christological and ecclesial. Ignatius saw Jesuit life as one of unity in the Spirit through the inner law of charity. The primacy of the divine is on every page of the *Constitutions*: all is subordinate to the glory of God, the praise and service of his Divine Majesty, within the context of service in and to the hierarchical Church. Words like '*reverentia*', '*majus obsequium*', '*servitium*', '*gloria*', '*laus*' are found constantly in the *Exercises* and *Constitutions*. And all this is accomplished by men wearing 'the livery of Christ'. Here is the foundation for our Jesuit liturgical life. For it is in baptism that Christians are 'placed with the Son', there that we 'put on the livery of Christ', according to Galatians 3:27 ('As many of you who were baptized into Christ have put on Christ'). It is in the Eucharist that we glorify the Father in Him, that we create and express our unity in charity, according to I Corinthians 11:17–34. The liturgy

41

and only the liturgy is the primal source of all these quintessentially Ignatian qualities.

The Jesus of the liturgy, like the Jesus of the *Spiritual Exercises,* is not the historical Jesus of the past, but the Heavenly High Priest interceding for us constantly before the throne of the Father,[49] and actively directing the life of his Church.[50] It is this consciousness of Jesus as the Lord not of the past but of contemporary history that is the aim of all Christian spirituality and liturgical anamnesis. It is also the aim of the *Spiritual Exercises.* Both the liturgy and the *Exercises* are a present encounter with God. Salvation is now. The death and resurrection of Jesus are past events only in their historicity. But they are eternally present in God, and have brought the presence of God among us to fulfilment in Jesus.

Nothing could be more Ignatian than this vision. St Ignatius was in many ways very Western-medieval in his use of imagination in contemplation,[51] in his historicizing emphasis on the earthy life of Jesus.[52] But he was also surprisingly Early-Church patristic in many other ways: the markedly trinitarian dimension of his spirituality; his stress on the work of the Risen Christ actively present in the life of the Church now; the resulting robust sense of the ongoing, unfinished process of Salvation History;[53] his total lack of the ritualism that infected the medieval Western piety of his upbringing – and, what is most important for us, his very Pauline view of liturgy.

Ignatius, like the New Testament, may not use the word 'liturgy' in our sense. But as we saw above in Section 1, the New Testament in fact interprets the entire self-giving life of Christ, especially but not exclusively in the Paschal Mystery of his death and glorification in obedience to the Father, in terms of liturgy. And St Paul portrays our life in Christ in the same perspective. That is extremely important for grounding Jesuit liturgy in the Ignatian tradition, because I am convinced that this Pauline vision is what Ignatius taught intuitively. To express the spiritual identity between the self-offering of the Son of God and our worship as the repetition of this same pattern in our own lives, St Paul uses several compound verbs that begin with the preposition *syn* (with): I suffer with Christ, am crucified with Christ, die with Christ, am buried with Christ, am raised and live with Christ, am carried off to heaven and sit at the right hand of the Father with Christ.[54] This is Paul's way of underscoring the necessity of our personal participation in redemption. We must 'put on Christ' (Galatians 3:27), and assimilate him, somehow experience with God's grace the principal events by which Christ has saved us and repeat them in the pattern of our own lives. For by undergoing these saving events, Christ has transformed the basic human experience into a new creation. How do we experience these events? In Christ, by so entering into the mystery of his life that we can affirm with Paul: 'I have been crucified with Christ; it is no longer I who live, but Christ who lives in me' (Galatians 2:20). What could possibly be more Ignatian than this Pauline vision of 'putting on the livery of Christ'? What more could the Vision of La Storta mean by being 'placed with the Son'?

Ignatius grasped intuitively, however, that not everything in Christian life can be reduced to liturgy, and liturgy under the weight of monastic influence has tended in both East and West to swallow up everything else. Ignatian views on prayer are part of the reaction against medieval externalism and ritualistic sacramentalism that the sixteenth-century Catholic reform movement shared with the Protestant reformers.[55]

So Ignatius rejected not liturgy but an overblown medieval ritualism.[56] Besides, in reducing the burden of liturgical prayer Ignatius was doing no more than what most other major religious reformers had done before him, beginning with St Pachomius (†346) at the very origins of cenobitic monasticism.[57] St Benedict (c. 530–60) greatly reduced the amount of liturgy prescribed in the earlier sixth-century Latin *Rule of the Master* from the Italian Campania. The eleventh-century Cistercian reform purged the liturgical indigestion that had overwhelmed Cluny. The thirteenth-century friars, needing more apostolic mobility, adopted the stripped- down office of the papal Curia.[58] In 1568 Pius V pruned the Roman Hours drastically, the Quiñones breviary had done so even more in 1535,[59] and Vatican II performed similar surgery.[60]

In a very real sense, then, Ignatius' view of liturgy, far from being medieval, was very Early-Church and primitive-monastic. *Monastic?* Yes, monastic. Contrary to common mythology, the earliest monks were quite unliturgical,[61] opposed liturgical chant,[62] and adamantly refused to decree set times for common prayer, which they considered contrary to the evangelical command to pray always.[63] No wonder Benedictine Eligius Dekkers' ironically entitled article, 'Were the Early Monks Liturgical?'[64] poured cold water on the romanticism of the nineteenth-century Benedictine revival à la Guéranger and its resumption of the *monachus propter chorum* ideology, which considered the monk a *homo liturgicus par excellence.*

'Finding God in all things' and 'contemplative in action', the formulas that best sum up Ignatius' teaching on prayer,[65] show Ignatian prayer more akin to that of the early Egyptian anchorites, who prayed while they worked and worked while they prayed. What Ignatius did was make the work apostolic instead of basket- weaving.[66] That is why I say Ignatius had a very Pauline and early monastic view of 'liturgy' in its literal sense of 'service'. When he says in *General Examen* §7 that Jesuits vow 'to go anywhere His Holiness will order…for the sake of matters pertaining to the worship of God and the welfare of the Christian religion,' he could not be more Pauline. For both Ignatius and Paul, as well as the earliest monks, the true Christian 'worship of God' is much more than what people do in church.

So Ignatius broke out of the medieval mould and changed the paradigm, and it is only in that hermeneutical framework that we can understand what Ignatius and the early Society was all about with regard to liturgy. English Benedictine 'David Knowles' little classic on the history of religious life, *From Pachomius to Ignatius,'*[67] sees the evolution of religious life as a more or less linear development of the search for perfection, a view premier contemporary historian of the Society, John W. O'Malley, SJ, rightly challenges.[68] What was central for Ignatius was *ministry,* and his stress on the active life of ministry as the core of religious life was really a radical break in the Pachomius-to-Ignatius continuum. Canon 16 of the First Lateran Council in 1123 forbids monks to engage in any ministry whatever: 'They may not celebrate Masses in public anywhere. Moreover, let them completely abstain from public visitations of the sick, from anointings and even from hearing confessions, for these things in no way pertain to their calling.'[69] Bishops and presbyters were supposed to take care of all that; monks were supposed to stay home and pray. *That* is the vision of religious life Ignatius rejected.

The popular adage, 'The family that prays together stays together,' had no meaning in this early Jesuit context, because Ignatius in no way intended Jesuits to be a family that would stay together long enough to pray together. Early Jesuits were meant to be on the road. Ignatius founded not a cenobitic community – in the *Constitutions* he never even uses the word 'community'[70] – but a group of reformed itinerant priests who later decided to organize themselves into a religious order. Far from being 'cenobites', the *Constitutions* §615 decrees that Jesuits were not to stay in any one place for more than three months![71] With the founding of formation houses, colleges, universities, Jesuit life would become much more settled.[72] But the pristine Ignatian vision is peripatetic-apostolic and *ad extra,* not cenobitic and *ad intra.* Ignatius just carried the peripatetic friars' thirteenth-century revolution of religious life to its logical conclusion, rejecting even the trappings of monasticism the friars had retained – convents and cloisters, priors and priories, chapters and choir – to concentrate exclusively on apostolic ministry. Except for our houses of formation, Jesuit liturgy was originally what Jesuits did for others, not for themselves.[73]

So I would like to suggest that if we want to know what 'liturgy' was for St Ignatius we should concentrate on 'ministry', which in the sixteenth and seventeenth centuries characterized both the Catholic Reform and the Protestant Reformation, and on 'mission', a word popularized by the Ignatian tradition.[74] We think of ministry as 'priestly', and of course it is. But in Ignatian sources 'one searches almost in vain for any mention of priesthood or ordination'.[75] It is especially the ministry of God's Word that dominates both Protestant and early Jesuit sources. The Council of Trent took up the refrain, calling the ministry of the Word – preaching – the chief task of bishops.[76] But for Trent and earlier, medieval Catholicism, holy orders and priesthood had more to do with the Church's regimen than with its ministry, a view that reflects a monastic age when the Church knew no ministry but liturgy.[77] Office-orders-ritual was the rule, and none of it had much to do with what Ignatius or anyone today would call ministry or the cure of souls.[78]

45

In sum, then, I would say that the great liturgical genius of Ignatius was to intuit that for the New Testament the real Christian liturgy is not ritual but life and ministry, the 'praise, reverence, and serve God' of the 'Principle and Foundation' lived out in our own lives and preached to others, of which the Church's liturgy is but the source and nourishment. What Ignatius failed to see, because of the state of Catholic liturgy in his day, is that the Church's ritual expression of this lived liturgy is by its very nature irreplaceably public and communitarian: salvation is not an individual but a Body called the Church of Christ.

That does not mean, however, that all is shadows in Jesuit liturgical history. From Ignatius on, Jesuits were in the forefront of the movement for the restoration of frequent communion, the greatest liturgical renewal of all times.[79] Secondly, Jesuits were prime movers in the interiorization of liturgical piety as a necessary antidote to medieval ritualism, formalism and extrinsicism.[80] And in modern times, Jesuits have comprised the largest single body of professionally trained Catholics engaged in the liturgical enterprise both intellectually and pastorally, some of them among the greatest liturgical scholars of the twentieth century.[81]

4. Jesuit Liturgy Today

This, then, is the historical context of our Jesuit liturgical life, a life most of us would agree needs some refurbishing.[82] Anyone who has read the documents of the supreme magisterium from *Mediator Dei* (1947) on can have no doubt that Jesuit liturgical practice is far from ideal. Yet we all wish to remain faithful to the Society's heritage, which in things liturgical is problematic, to say the least. How to navigate these troubled waters?

We must distinguish what is *Ignatius*, what is *Ignatian*, and what is *Jesuit*. It is Ignatian to be a man of the Church. It was Ignatius to be a man of the sixteenth-century Church. So liturgy, to be Jesuit, must be Catholic, Ignatian, apostolic. But it must not be Ignatius, who was devoted to the private Mass and went to confession every day, practices no one competent in liturgy would dream of recommending today. It is Jesuit to be man of today's Church. In the last analysis, then, what counts is not what Ignatius or any other Jesuit, including myself, thinks about the liturgy, but what the Church thinks. It is a truism to say that Ignatius was a man of his times. *Every man* is a man of his times. Far more important for our purposes is to recall that Ignatius was above all a man of the Church. As such, were Ignatius alive today, he would be beyond doubt the first to insist that Jesuits embrace in their lives and in their work everything the contemporary Catholic magisterium teaches on the central importance of the liturgy in the life and ministry of the Church.

The first great irony of liturgical life in today's Society is that for many, it ends with ordination to the priesthood, at which point the public worship of God stops as private Mass takes over. The second great irony is that there is less liturgical life in the Society now than there was before Vatican II. In 'the bad old days' there was daily community Mass in the formation communities, and in some places even the priest-professors were expected to attend.[83] At Jesuit funerals and on All Souls Day, the Office of the Dead was still said in common, as Ignatius himself ordained (CSJ §600-C). And US Jesuit Custom Books of the day prescribed a far richer diet of common prayer than one sees anywhere in today's Society.[84] So we are not only not getting better; we are getting worse.

What to do? Limitations of space force me to restrict my attention here to general issues and their related fallout in Jesuit practice regarding the Eucharist and the Liturgy of the Hours. Problems of liturgy in the Society are problems of heritage and formation. *Heritage,* because we have never adequately come to terms with those basic defects regarding attitudes toward liturgy in our origins, in our foundational documents, and in our way of life.[85] We have been unable to do this, doubtless, because of the hagiographico-mythological view of our historical origins, something inevitable in any religious body. We are the inheritors, via St Ignatius and the early Jesuits, of a medieval view of liturgy and theology of 'priesthood' which can only be deemed defective, one that the Liturgical Movement and its fruit in the Vatican II liturgical teaching and reform has sought to overcome.[86] *Formation,* because we do not receive an adequate liturgical formation in our

47

spiritual training,[87] a formation which teaches young Jesuits that for prayer to be Christian it must also be common, and if our prayer is not that, then we are inadequate as Christians, and especially as *praying* Christians.[88] Apart from Jesuits in formation, Ignatius simply presumed the 'formed' Jesuits would know what to do without special rules or norms. Over 450 years of Jesuit history have shown how delusionally sanguine that idea was!

The solution to these problems must encompass far more than liturgical practice, since they extend beyond liturgy to problems of community, of theology, and of the inevitable individualism that our apostolic way of life tends to foster. Any renewal will imply, necessarily, a renewed theology of liturgy as common prayer, which can only result from a renewed grasp of the liturgical teaching of Vatican II in the context of our community prayer-life and our sacramental ministry *ad extra*. A community that does not pray together regularly cannot claim to be Christian. Ignatius' view of liturgy as apostolic – i.e. as a service Jesuits do for others – does not take adequate account of the internal needs of the Society of Jesus as a group of Christians with its own inner dynamic towards prayer in common. As such, it is one-sided and outdated, superseded by contemporary developments in liturgical understanding, and must be complemented by regular common prayer. Normally, such prayer should be the liturgical prayer of the Church, specifically community Eucharist and the Liturgy of the Hours, and only extraordinarily, other forms of devotion.

Impeding this renewal is the largely privatized eucharistic practice in much of a still largely unrenewed Society. This is the direct result of the theology of the priesthood adumbrated above. It is true that the Church permits what is called 'private Mass',[89] and although that can by no stretch of the imagination be considered an ideal practice in the light of our modern understanding of Eucharist, *the* sign *par excellence* of the gathered Church, I do not intend to waste time telling the Church it should not permit this. What the Church *does not permit*, however, is the solitary Mass still widely practised in today's Society.[90] It is true, as one Provincial argued in a letter to his Province on liturgy, that this reflects the practice of many good and faithful priests, a rule of thumb moral theologians use to justify a custom *contra legem*.[91]

48

How such casuistry squares with the Ignatian *magis*,[92] to say nothing of the Three Degrees of Humility and the Rules for Thinking with the Church, escapes me, to say the least. The issue is not whether solitary Mass is a sin, but whether it is the ideal, an ideal that is crystal-clear in the teaching of the magisterium. When the Vatican II *Decree on the Ministry and Life of Priests* §6, states that 'No Christian community is ever built up unless it has its roots and centre in the eucharistic liturgy, which, therefore, is the indispensible starting point for leading people to a sense of community,'[93] it is referring, obviously, to community, not private, much less solitary Mass! And the Vatican II *Constitution on the Sacred Liturgy* §§26–7 affirms unambiguously that the communal celebration of the Eucharist is to be preferred.[94]

To choose as common practice a less adequate expression of the Church's liturgical worship can never be justified by anyone's private preferences or devotional needs. In the matter of liturgical prayer, which is an expression of the life of the Church, personal preference, taste, and need always give way to the ideal expressed in the tradition and magisterial teaching of the Church. Nothing is more foreign to the Ignatian *magis* than to opt for the lesser good because the Church does not forbid it. This general norm must regulate all liturgical discernment in our personal and community lives. Liturgy must be an adequate ecclesial expression of the nature and life of the Church. Sacraments must show what they signify – i.e., not only be, *but appear to be*, what they mean. Eucharist is the expression of our communion with one another in Christ. To pretend that this is manifested in anything but a common celebration of the Eucharist is sheer nominalism.

Intimately connected with community Eucharist is the question of concelebration. Originally, concelebration was meant to express two realities: 1. communion between local churches, as when a visiting bishop was invited to join the local ordinary at the altar; 2. the communion between the bishop and his presbyterate.[95] Today concelebration has been transformed into a way of providing presbyters with the possibility of 'exercising their priesthood'[96] daily, while avoiding the divisive counter-symbol of the private Mass, which turns the sacrament of our unity into a ritual of our separation. Concelebration, which *Eucharisticum Mysterium* (25 May, 1967) §47 calls the ideal form of community Eucharist in religious communities of presbyters,[97] is encouraged as the solution to this problem. But in religious communities today, some see concelebration as ritualizing the division between presbyters and non-presbyters. This is most strongly felt in celebrations with women religious present, and becomes especially manifest when there are more ministers than those being ministered to. Two guiding norms for all liturgy, including concelebration, are 1. that liturgy be an adequate ecclesial expression of the nature and life of the Church; 2. that liturgy meet the pastoral needs of the entire congregation, not just the celebrating ministers, as well as possible.[98] Presbyters and their devotional needs cede to these overriding norms. On the other hand, concelebration is infinitely superior to the divisive practice of private or solitary Mass, and if concelebration is what we need to get communities together for Mass, so be it.

Another serious problem is our so-called Ignatian attitude to the Church's non-eucharistic liturgical prayer, the Liturgy of the Hours. This is not a problem Jesuits invented but one we inherited. I have no quarrel with the fact that St Ignatius abolished choir for his order. He did not do so, however, from any distaste or disrespect for the Church's public prayer. On the contrary, the evidence for Ignatius' personal devotion to the public Hours and his daily attendance at them during his 'pilgrim years' is beyond challenge.[99] His sole purpose in obstinately refusing to let his men assume the *obligation* of daily, common office in choir was exactly the same as his reason for refusing to accept parishes or the permanent cure of souls: both require fixed residence and the obligation to be in certain places at certain times, and that would have hindered the mobility and freedom Ignatius demanded for the apostolic endeavours he envisaged as the vocation of his men (CSJ §§324, 586, 588–9).[100] In this regulation we discern the essence of the Ignatian spirit. Jesuit work and piety was directed *ad extra*, and Ignatius resolutely refused to legislate *anything* that would interfere with or restrict in any way the Jesuit apostolic obligation to serve where necessary. All else was subordinate to this: prayer, dress, penances – and liturgy. No Jesuit should ever be able to refuse a mission, a service of his neighbour, a ministry, a work of mercy, with the excuse that he had to be at Vespers.[101]

Furthermore, the common belief that Ignatius *forbade* the common recitation of the Divine Office in the Society, or that devotion to the public office is in some way contrary to the Ignatian spirit, is flatly false. The *Constitutions* explicitly state that Jesuits who 'experience devotion in them', according to the pietistic vocabulary of those days, will find plenty of opportunity to assist at the Hours (CSJ §586). *Constitutions* §586 also says the Divine Office can be celebrated in Jesuit houses and churches. What is rejected is the *obligation* to celebrate them *regularly*. Far from being opposed to the Hours, Ignatius prescribed the community recitation of the Office of the Dead at Jesuit funerals (CSJ §600-C), imposed the Little Office of the Blessed Virgin as the daily prayer for scholastics in formation (CSJ §342-3), and, in Jesuit churches, ordered the celebration of Vespers on special days, and Tenebrae during Holy Week (CSJ §587). Even more interesting, according to a little-known text, Ignatius told his secretary Juan de Polanco, 'we remain free to have choir when and where it may seem to contribute to God's greater service. Only the obligation is removed.'[102]

The basic problem for Ignatius, however, was a misunderstanding that is still with us today: a misconception of what the Liturgy of the Hours is. The Divine Office originated in the morning and evening synaxes that were the prayer of the whole Church, obligatory on all, laity and clergy alike. Contrary to what is generally thought, the Liturgy of the Hours is in no way an outgrowth of monastic life. This daily common prayer of the whole Church was later taken over and developed by the monastics, but it became their preserve in the West only after everyone else had abandoned it in desperation at the back-breaking burden monasticization had turned it into, forcing its reduction to a private prayer book for clergy.[103]

Vatican II attempted, with mixed success, to reverse the tide, restoring the Roman Divine Office from a private breviary into the common daily prayer of God's People.[104] Hence its new name, 'The Liturgy of the Hours'. And hence the teaching of the *General Instruction on the Liturgy of the Hours,* promulgated by the Vatican Congregation for Divine Worship on 2 February 1971, which exhorts that 'The Liturgy of the Hours, like the other liturgical services, is not a private function'

($20),[105] and strongly urges that even clergy and religious 'not bound to common celebration [of the Divine Office]...should try to say at least some part of the Liturgy of the Hours in common, particularly Lauds in the morning and Vespers in the evening' ($25; cf. $§21-27).[106]

There is no legitimate basis in history, theology or the present teaching of the Supreme Magisterium for the view that the Ignatian tradition permanently dispenses Jesuits from this traditional Christian obligation of daily prayer in common. In this context the recovery of the pristine vision of the Liturgy of the Hours at Vatican II, as later expressed in this *General Instruction*, with its insistence on the office in common as the ideal for all, applies to the Society of Jesus as to all other members of the Church, as Keith Pecklers affirms in his unpublished 1997 essay 'Liturgy in the Houses of the Society of Jesus':

> From the 'Formula of the Institute' (no. 6) it is said that since Jesuits are priests they should pray the Divine Office 'according to the ordinary rite of the Church' but they normally do so in private. And this was done to avoid the time-consuming commitment of a communal office that normally lasted about seven hours each day. To take that legislation geared as it was to a sixteenth century Church...and to apply it to the contemporary Church is misguided in the extreme – an example of Ignatian fundamentalism.
>
> The Church calls all Christian communities to pray together. Indeed, communities that fail to gather together for some form of corporate prayer cannot call themselves Christian. The Hours are brief enough so that they no longer threaten a hindrance to apostolic involvement. Jesuit communities must find a way in which the Morning Prayer and Evening Prayer of the Church are offered to its members as part of the common life of the community.[107]

So this age-old obligation of morning and evening prayer in common does not conflict with Ignatius' rejection of choir, a medieval concept based in part on the now discredited notion that some Christians can be 'deputed' to pray for others. In monasteries, choir took precedence over all other activities, and precluded apostolic work. In the later, more active mendicant orders, choir impeded total dedication to such apostolic work.

It was this canonical choir obligation, and not the more ancient universally obligatory custom of common prayer at the beginning and end of the day – of which Ignatius, like all his contemporaries, did not have a clue – that the early Society rejected because it precluded apostolic work. Many things in present-day Jesuit life – academic tenure and the limiting demands of professional specialization, for instance – unavoidably place far greater restrictions on apostolic mobility than common prayer would. And Jesuits today see no problem in accepting the cure of souls in parishes, though Ignatius, as we saw above, excluded that for exactly the same reasons that he excluded choir.[108]

To adopt the burden of common prayer except when it would impede apostolic work is not to introduce choir, but to join the contemporary Church in its recovery of the original meaning of the daily common prayer of the Church.[109] The real issue is whether, in the light of what we know of the history of the Hours, any Christian can be considered permanently dispensed from the age-old obligation of praising God in common at the beginning and end of each day.

The solution, then, is to be found neither in the back-breaking Cluniac choir, nor in the liturgical privatism of sixteenth-century pietism, nor in the nineteenth-century romanticism of Solesmes, but in a renewed understanding of what this sort of common prayer is all about in the first place. Myths die hard, however, as references in contemporary books to the Divine Office as originally something for monks continue to show.

5. Conclusion

What to do in the concrete? Ideally – I would like to say even minimally – the norm should be community Eucharist daily in every Jesuit community, plus Morning Praise and Evensong in common as a privileged opportunity for common prayer according to the express will of the Church. To do anything less in our churches, our parishes, and at least in all formation and retirement communities, could hardly be considered faithful to what the Spirit is speaking in today's Church.

But the basic underlying issue is always formation. In large parts of the Society of Jesus, liturgical formation ranges from the seriously wanting to the completely non-existent. There are entire Provinces, indeed, whole Assistancies of the Society without a single Jesuit trained in liturgy. And some of our scholasticates do not provide even a semblance of liturgical training either theological or pastoral. Until this changes, we are wasting our time.

5

Liturgical Inculturation: Unity in Diversity in the Postmodern Age

Peter C. Phan

There is little doubt that one of the thorniest challenges for Catholic theology and in particular for liturgy for some time to come will be inculturation. By this term is meant the double process of inserting the Gospel into a particular culture and inserting this culture into the Gospel so that both the Gospel and the culture are challenged and enriched by each other.[1] The process itself, albeit not the term and the theoretical reflection upon it, has been of course a constant preoccupation of Christianity from its very inception, as it attempted to make its message and way of life, which had been framed within the Jewish matrix, intelligible to the Greco-Roman world, and subsequently, to the peoples of different parts of the globe outside Europe, especially since its massive missionary movement in the sixteenth century.[2]

That inculturation in general and liturgical inculturation in particular are an extremely complex process, is a theological truism. Inculturation, John Paul II himself has warned, is 'a slow journey'.[3] But this journey, arduous as it was in the past, is made even more so by the contemporary cultural context that has been dubbed 'postmodern'. Since inculturation by definition must take into account the cultural context into which the Gospel is to be inserted, it is imperative to inquire how this postmodern sensibility, widely assumed to be the hallmark of contemporary culture, affects the nature and process of inculturation itself.

This essay will focus on liturgical inculturation and will begin with a brief description of postmodernism and the challenges it poses to inculturation. In the second part it will present and evaluate the Fourth Instruction of the Congregation for Divine Worship and the Discipline of the Sacraments on liturgical inculturation in the light of the challenges of postmodernism. The last part will make some proposals for liturgical inculturation from the perspective of mission history in Asia and Asian theologies.

1. Inculturation in the Postmodern Age

My intention is not, nor is it possible within the narrow compass of this essay, to present even a cursory overview of postmodernism.[4] Rather the focus is on the postmodern understanding of culture and how this understanding challenges the process of liturgical inculturation. Conventionally, the overarching term *postmodernism* refers to the cultural and social shift that has emerged since the 1930s and has been making its way from the West to the other parts of the world through the process of globalization.[5] Three or four decades later, during the 1960s, this phenomenon made its influence felt first in architecture and the arts, then invaded literature, philosophy and theology, and by the 1980s became a general characteristic of popular culture.[6] It would be helpful to see briefly how postmodernism has affected some of the cultural expressions of our times.

1.1 The Postmodern World and its Cultural Expressions

In contrast to modern architecture, which in the wake of Frank Lloyd Wright emphasizes organic unity and practical functionality and is typified by the nearly universal pattern of glass-and-steel boxes, postmodern architecture celebrates 'multivalence' by making use of a variety of incompatible historical styles, forms, techniques and materials. By accentuating pluriformity and hybridity postmodern architecture wants to show that behind the principle of organic unity and practical functionality of modern architecture lies the dehumanizing uniformity of standardized mass production, aided and abetted by the power of science, technology and industry.[7]

Similarly, postmodern art rejects the stylistic integrity and 'purity' of modernity and embraces 'multivalence' and heterogeneity. It favours the technique of juxtaposition which assembles cheek by jowl seemingly contradictory styles of diverse origins. In adopting this 'impure' composition it subtly and ironically rejects modernity's claim to universal rationality and the myth of a single artistic author or creator. Two popular techniques of juxtaposition are collage and bricolage, the former bringing together incompatible source materials, and the latter reconfiguring various traditional objects. The result is pastiche, which by means of its eclectic mixture of disjointed and contradictory elements calls into question the modern 'fiction' of objective reality and meaning invested in dominant institutions and canonical traditions.

In theatre too, the same drive towards diversity and pluralism reigns. In theatrical performance, following Antonin Artaud's protest against the idolatry of classical art and his proposal of the 'theatre of cruelty',[8] the postmodern theatre celebrates transience, instead of temporal permanence. Perceiving what it takes to be the repressive power of a script and a director, practitioners of postmodern theatre experiment with immediate performance without a script, thus making each performance unique and unrepeatable, and with improvisation, group authorship and audience participation. They reject modernity's 'aesthetics of presence' and advocate the 'aesthetics of absence' which highlights the lack of any permanent, underlying truth. Life, like the story performed on the stage, is but an eclectic assemblage of intersecting, disconnected and impermanent narratives.

In postmodern fiction as well, juxtaposition is practised so that it is difficult to tell the real character from the fictitious, the author from the fictional work, the author's voice from the fictional story. By means of this technique postmodern fiction blurs the dividing line between reality and unreality, between temporality and atemporality, so that the reader is no longer able to view the world from a privileged and secure vantage point of eternal truths. The two representative genres of postmodern fiction are the spy novel and science fiction. In contrast to the typically modern genre of the detective story in which a seemingly disjointed series of events becomes a unified whole at the end, the spy novel juxtaposes two radically different worlds, the one real in appearance but turning out to be illusory at the end, and the other sinister in appearance but turning out to be more real than the former. In science fiction, reality is by definition eliminated, and an alternative world is depicted as possible.[9]

On the level of 'pop' culture, which postmodernism refuses to distinguish from 'high art', the film world is paradigmatic of the postmodern world – a realm in which truth and fiction merge. The cinematic reality is largely an illusion. Film-making technology allows the viewer to perceive as a unity in time and space what was disjointed in both time and space. The unity of a film does not reflect the real world but is imposed by the editor who assembles into a unified product the footage shot at different times and at various locations. Even the characters may not be the same, as stunt doubles replace them in dangerous scenes. With advanced techniques of computer-generated images and special effects, it is not possible to tell the real from the fantastic, the historical from the fictional.

An extension of the film industry, television (and cable and direct satellite broadcasts with an almost infinite variety of viewing options) brings the postmodern ethos of the film world into the living room and day-to-day life. But television can go beyond film by offering live broadcasting so that viewers can see for themselves events as they are happening anywhere in the world. In this way, the world *as* presented by television, with its interpretation, commentary and editing – often not without bias – becomes the 'real world' for most people, and consequently, what is not presented on television does not appear 'real' to them. Indeed, as the advertising slogan 'as seen on TV' implies, the television world is the guarantee of the reality and truth of the real world! Furthermore, by juxtaposing serious news with commercials, sitcoms and docudramas, television, like other postmodern artistic expressions, blurs the boundaries between truth and fiction, between the important and the trivial.

Add the personal computer to television, with the unlimited possibility of surfing the Web, and reality becomes 'virtual reality' and vice versa. In virtual reality, you have 'been there and done that' and yet need not be there and do that at all!

Perhaps the power of postmodernism to blur reality and fiction is best epitomized by the screen – whether the movie, television or the computer screen. What happens on the screen is neither 'objective' reality out there nor 'subjective' reality within the viewer; rather it is somewhere in between, blurring the distinction between object and subject, the very thing postmodernism advocates.

1.2 The Postmodern Ethos

From this cursory overview several characteristics of postmodernism have emerged. In his description of the postmodern ethos Stanley Grenz mentions pessimism, holism, communitarianism and relativistic pluralism as its main characteristics.[10] Pessimistic, because postmodernism abandons the Enlightenment myth of inevitable progress and highlights the fragility of human existence; holistic, in so far as it rejects the modern privileging of rationality and celebrates emotions and intuition; communitarian because it eschews modernity's individualism and its quest for universal, supracultural and timeless truth, and emphasizes the role of the community in creating the truth; and relativistic and pluralistic, because there being many different human communities, there are necessarily many different truths.

These characteristics do not however constitute a coherent philosophical worldview. Indeed, for postmodernism, there is not a 'world' about which one can construct a unitary true 'view'; there is not a single objective world to which our knowledge must correspond. What we call the 'real world' is, for postmodernism, nothing more than our ever-shifting social creation. Ours is a 'symbolic' world which we create through our common language. Hence, knowledge is replaced by interpretation. As Stanley Grenz has pointed out, postmodern epistemology is built on two basic assumptions: they view 'all explanations of reality as constructions that are useful but not objectively true' and deny that 'we have the ability to step outside our constructions of reality'.[11] With this constructivist rather than objectivist outlook, postmodernism rejects the correspondence theory of truth and adopts a pluralistic view of knowledge.[12]

In terms of culture, postmodernism spells the demise of 'metanarratives', to use Jean-François Lyotard's expression.[13] By metanarrative is meant the system of myths that bind a society together and by which it legitimates itself. Not only do postmoderns no longer cling to the modern metanarrative of progress, which is itself founded on the Christian narrative and is at best a 'useful fiction'. They also reject any appeal to metanarrative as social legitimation. The age of the *grands récits* is over; what is left is *local* narrative which one constructs in one's particular community.

Together with the death of metanarrative, Lyotard points out, came the end of modern science which has been based on the political myth of freedom and the philosophical myth of the progress of knowledge. The loss of credibility of the grand narratives of scientific progress does not however mean the death of science but only of a particular model of science, namely, that of Newtonian mechanistic understanding. Not science as such but only the modern assumption that the universe contains an internally consistent order from which a quantitative analysis will yield universal laws permitting the prediction of other natural occurrences has been questioned. In the post-Newtonian science, other physical theories have been formulated that have fundamentally undermined our previous way of viewing the world, such as quantum theory, the relativity theory, chaos theory and the Uncertainty Principle.

All together, these theories suggest that the universe is not something that can be fully and completely described by science but is ultimately an unfathomable mystery. The ever-changing universe not only *has* a history but *is* a history that cannot be controlled and predicted by scientific methods. Moreover, these theories contend that science is not a culturally neutral fact, as modernity has assumed. Rather, it is a social construction of reality (a 'paradigm', to use Thomas Kuhn's expression) that controls what the scientist sees. Every experiment ultimately rests on a network of interests, theories, opinions, traditions, often buttressed by money and power, and the resulting knowledge is not a collection of objective universal truths but a formulation of research traditions done within a particular cultural community.[14]

1.3 Postmodern Theory of Culture: Culture as
a 'Ground of Contest in Relations'

This leads to the question of how in contrast to modernity, post-modernism understands culture. The modern concept of culture is represented by the anthropological concept of culture that emerged as a theoretical construct after the 1920s, especially on the American scene.[15] This concept was used to account for differences in customs and practices of a particular human society. They are explained in terms of cultures rather than in terms of God's will, racial or generational variations, or environmental factors, or differences in origin. Furthermore, in this understanding of culture, no evaluative judgement is made as to whether a particular culture represents a less noble or less developed stage of human evolution.

This anthropological approach to culture tends to view it as a human universal. This universal is however realized in particular forms by each social group as its distinct way of life. Culture is constituted by the conventions created by the consensus of a group into which its members are socialized. Given this notion of culture as group-differentiating, holistic, non-evaluative, and context-dependent, anthropologists commonly perceive the culture of a social group as a whole, as a single albeit complex unit, and distinguish it from the social behaviours of its members. Culture is seen as the ordering principle and control mechanism of social behaviours without which human beings would be formless. Above all, culture is seen as an integrated and integrating whole whose constituent elements are functionally interrelated to one another. These elements are thought to be integrated into each other because they are perceived as expressing a fundamental, overarching theme, style or purpose. Or they are thought to be consistent with or imply one another. Or they are supposed to operate according to laws or structures, not unlike the grammatical rules in a language. Or, finally, they are supposed to function with a view to maintain and promote the stability of the social order. Thanks to this non-evaluative approach to culture, anthropologists can avoid ethnocentrism, concentrating on an accurate description of a particular culture, rather than judging it according to some presumed norms of truth, goodness and beauty.[16]

The modern anthropological concept of culture has its own advantages. As Robert Schreiter has noted, the concept of culture as an integrated system of beliefs, values and behavioural norms has much to commend it. Among other things, it promotes holism and a sense of coherence and communion in opposition to the fragmentation of mass society, is congenial to the harmonizing, both-and way of thinking prevalent in oral cultures and many Asian cultures, and serves as an antidote to the corrosive effects of modernity and capitalism.[17] Religion as a quest for meaning and wholeness is seen as a boon to these positive aspects of culture.

In recent years, however, this modern concept of culture has been subjected to a searing critique.[18] The view of culture as a self-contained and clearly bounded whole, as an internally consistent and integrated system of beliefs, values and behavioural norms that functions as the ordering principle of a social group and into which its members are socialized, has been shown to be based on unjustified assumptions.[19] Against this conception of culture it has been argued that: 1. it focuses exclusively on culture as a finished product and therefore pays insufficient attention to culture as a historical process; 2. its view of culture as a consistent whole is dictated more by the anthropologist's aesthetic need and the demand for synthesis than by the lived reality of culture itself; 3. its emphasis on consensus as the process of cultural formation obfuscates the reality of culture as a site of struggle and contention; 4. its view of culture as a principle of social order belittles the role of the members of a social group as cultural agents; 5. this view privileges the stable elements of culture and does not take into adequate account its innate tendency to change and innovation; and 6. its insistence on clear boundaries for cultural identity is no longer necessary since it is widely acknowledged today that change, conflict, and contradiction are resident *within* culture itself and are not simply caused by outside disruption and dissension.[20]

Rather than as a sharply demarcated, self-contained, homogeneous and integrated whole, culture today is seen as 'a ground of contest in relations'[21] and as a historically evolving, fragmented, inconsistent, conflicted, constructed, ever-shifting and porous social reality. In this contest of relations the role of power in the shaping of cultural identity is of paramount importance, a factor that the modern concept of culture largely ignores. In the past, anthropologists tended to regard culture as an innocent set of conventions rather than a reality of conflict in which the colonizers, the powerful, the wealthy, the victors, the dominant can obliterate the beliefs and values of the colonized, the weak, the poor, the vanquished, the subjugated, so that there has been, in Serge Gruzinski's expression, 'la colonisation de l'imaginaire'.[22] This role of power is, as Michel Foucault and other masters of suspicion have argued, central in the formation of knowledge in general.[23] In the formation of cultural identity the role of power is even more extensive, since it is constituted by groups of people with conflicting interests, and the winners can dictate their cultural terms to the losers.

This predicament of culture is exacerbated by the process of globalization in which the ideals of modernity and technological reason are extended throughout the world (globalization as *extension*), aided and abetted by a single economic system (i.e. neoliberal capitalism) and new communication technologies.[24] In globalization geographical boundaries, which at one time helped define cultural identity, have now collapsed. Even our sense of time is largely compressed, with the present predominating and the dividing line between past and future becoming ever more blurred (globalization as *compression*). In this process of globalization, a homogenized culture is created, consolidated by a 'hyperculture' based on consumption, especially of goods exported from the USA, such as clothing (e.g. T-shirt, denim jeans, athletic shoes), food (e.g. McDonald's and Coca-Cola), and entertainment (e.g. films, video and music).

Such a globalized culture is not however accepted by local cultures hook, line and sinker. Between the global and the local cultures there takes place a continuous struggle, the former for political and economic dominance, the latter for survival and integrity. Because of the powerful attraction of the global culture, especially for the young, local cultures often feel threatened by it, but they are far from powerless. To counteract its influence, they have devised several strategies of

63

resistance, subversion, compromise, and appropriation. And in this effort religion more often than not has played a key role in alliance with local cultures.[25]

Like the anthropological concept of culture as a unified whole, the globalized concept of culture as a ground of contest in relations has its own strengths and weaknesses. On the positive side, it takes into account features of culture that are left in the shadow by its predecessor. While recognizing that harmony and wholeness remain ideals, it views culture in its lived reality of fragmentation, conflict and ephemerality. Cultural meanings are not simply discovered ready-made but are constructed and produced in the violent cauldron of asymmetrical power relations. It recognizes the important role of power in the formation of cultural identity. Furthermore, it sees culture as a historical process, intrinsically mutable, but without an a priori, clearly defined *telos* and a controllable and predictable synthesis. On the debit side, this postmodern concept of culture runs the risk of fomenting fundamentalistic tendencies, cultural and social ghettoization, and romantic retreat to an idealized past.[26]

1.4 Postmodern Challenges to Liturgical Inculturation

What challenges does postmodernism in all its cultural expressions (from architecture to theatre, fiction, cinema, television and the internet), with its concept of culture as a ground of contest in relations, pose to inculturation, in particular liturgical inculturation? Here I will highlight only a few.

1.4.1. The first challenge regards the concept of inculturation itself. If the Gospel, and more specifically, the liturgy must be regarded as a cultural, symbolic 'world', a social construct with its own interests and idiosyncrasies, then inculturation is not an 'incarnation' of a timeless, unchanging and acultural reality (such as the eternal Logos) into a particular culture, but an *intercultural* encounter or dialogue between at least two cultures. What are the dynamics and rules of intercultural communication that liturgical inculturation must attend to in order to be successful?

64

1.4.2. In this intercultural encounter, according to postmodernism, the issue of power is of paramount importance. It concerns first of all the relation between Roman authorities and the local churches. How does power play out in liturgical inculturation, especially if the process of liturgical inculturation must preserve 'the *substantial unity* of the Roman rite',[27] which is itself a cultural world? Or if it is conceived mainly as translation into the vernaculars of 'the [Latin] typical editions of liturgical books',[28] which themselves embody a particular culture (e.g., Latin/Roman)? Or if these books 'must be translated integrally and in the most exact manner, without omissions or additions in terms of their content, and without paraphrases or glosses'?[29] Why should Latin be used as the official language of the Roman liturgy (incidentally, *which* Latin?) – which itself forms and is formed by a cultural world? Why can't the liturgical texts be composed directly in the vernaculars in the first place? Why should translation of culturally foreign texts be resorted to? Is the unity of the Church maintained and promoted by a common liturgical text? Finally, why should translations, which have been approved by the national episcopal conferences, still need to be given the *recognitio* by the Congregation for Divine Worship and the Discipline of the Sacraments which more often than not has but minimal linguistic skills, if any, in the languages concerned?[30] When the process of inculturation is carried out in this way, is not the Latin/Roman culture imposed on other churches?

1.4.3. The question of power emerges again in the choice of the culture into which the Roman liturgy is to be inculturated. The culture of a particular country or ethnic group is not an integrating and integrated whole, equally and fairly encompassing the beliefs, values and practices of all the people constituting that country or ethnic group. Rather, the economically, politically and religiously dominant elements will exclude or subjugate the weaker ones whose cultures will be as a consequence marginalized. To take an example, which culture will the liturgy dialogue be with in India: the Hindu culture or that of the *dalits*, who make up the larger membership of the Church?

1.4.4. The issue of power looms large again in the question of the place and role of popular religion in liturgical inculturation. Popular religion has often been depicted as the religion of the poor and dispossessed, a form of identity-affirmation and resistance of the 'subaltern class' (Antonio Gramsci) against the ruling class. In liturgical inculturation, the official liturgy will inevitably have to deal with popular religion, not only as it has already been Christianized (e.g. Marian piety) but also as it is practised in non-Christian religions (e.g. the cult of ancestor). How should popular religion with its myriad devotional practices be viewed vis-à-vis the official religion? Is popular religion to be seen as the 'small traditions' as opposed to the 'great traditions'? Should the practices of popular religion be introduced into liturgical worship? How are they to be evaluated theologically?

1.4.5. Christian liturgy re-enacts the great biblical narratives of God's acts in history, especially in Jesus Christ. With the death of meta-narratives in postmodernity, such re-enactment faces difficult challenges, particularly in places where Christianity has to compete with other religious metanarratives. Can liturgical inculturation be carried out without an effective dialogue with these religious metanarratives? What is the connection between liturgical inculturation and inter-religious dialogue? Can liturgy be fully inculturated without making use of religious rituals and sacred texts of other religions?

1.4.6. The scope of liturgical inculturation includes not only sacred texts and rituals but also music, songs, musical instruments, gestures, dance, art and architecture of the local culture. May and should liturgical inculturation embrace the postmodern preference for juxta-position, bricolage and collage, with pastiche as the result, and the 'aesthetics of absence'? How far can and should it go in adopting classical or traditional art forms without falling into archaeologism and nostalgia? On the other hand, how much of postmodern art forms can it adopt without succumbing to ephemeral fads and passing trends? If liturgical celebrations are performances, how far can the community and the presider experiment with improvisation, group authorship and audience participation, and still preserve the unity of faith and worship?

1.4.7. Liturgical inculturation cannot be divorced from theology. How then can it meet the major challenges of postmodernism to such theological themes as God, Christ and Church? How can liturgy justify its pervasive use of anthropomorphic and anthropocentric (and most often sexually exclusive) language for God and God's agency in the world against the postmodern decentring of the human person? How can inculturated Christian worship preserve and proclaim the truth of Jesus Christ as the universal and unique Saviour against the postmodern affirmation of radical religious pluralism that decentres Christ? How can inculturation, through liturgical celebrations, build up a church that is truly local against the globalizing trend of postmodernity that homogenizes everything with its 'hyperculture'?[31]

2. Liturgical Inculturation according to *Varietates Legitimae* in the Postmodern Context

Before exploring how mission history in Asia and Asian theologies can help us meet some of the postmodern challenges to liturgical inculturation, it would be useful to examine how the Fourth Instruction of the Congregation for Divine Worship and the Discipline of the Sacraments *Varietates Legitimae* envisions the scope and process of liturgical inculturation. My intention here is not to offer a comprehensive analysis and critique of the Instruction but only to highlight those points that appear to have a particular relevance for inculturation in the postmodern context.[32]

2.1 Liturgical Adaptation according to *Varietates Legitimae*

Any fair evaluation of *Varietates Legitimae*'s programme of liturgical inculturation must take into account the fact that it is only intended to be an authoritative guide to the 'right application of the Conciliar Constitution on the Liturgy (nn. 37–40)', as the subtitle of the Instruction stipulates, and not a comprehensive manual on inculturation as

67

such. Within this limited scope *Varietates Legitimae* envisages that 'the work of inculturation does not foresee the creation of new families of rites; inculturation responds to the needs of a particular culture and leads to adaptations which still remain part of the Roman rite' (no. 36). Earlier, the Instruction has expressed its preference for the neologism 'inculturation' instead of the traditional term 'adaptation' (*aptatio*) which was used by *Sacrosanctum Concilium*, because the latter suggests 'modifications of a somewhat transitory and external nature' (no. 4), whereas inculturation signifies, according to the Instruction, quoting Pope John Paul II's *Redemptoris Missio*, no. 52, 'an intimate transformation of the authentic cultural values by their integration into Christianity and the implantation of Christianity into different cultures' (no. 4).

The Instruction clearly differentiates between two types of liturgical adaptation, namely, those that are 'provided for in the liturgical books' (as envisaged by nos. 38–9 of *Sacrosanctum Concilium*) and those which are 'more radical' (as contemplated by no. 40 of the same constitution). While detailed procedures are laid down for both kinds of adaptation, the overwhelming focus of the Instruction is on the former which, in contrast to the latter, are presumably less radical and pervasive. After outlining the principles regarding the goal, the limit and the competent authority of liturgical inculturation,[33] the Instruction enunciates norms governing the first kind of liturgical adaptation in language, music and singing, gesture and posture, art, the veneration of sacred images, and popular devotion (nos. 39–45).

The Instruction goes on to show how adaptations of this kind may be carried out with regard to the liturgical books (no. 53), the Eucharist (no. 54), the rites of Christian Initiation (no. 56), the marriage rite (no. 57), funerals (no. 58), the blessings of persons, places or things (no. 59), the Liturgical Year (no. 60), and the Liturgy of the Hour (no. 61). In all these areas, it is presumed that the official liturgical texts are composed by the Congregation for Divine Worship and the Discipline of the Sacraments, known as 'the Latin typical editions', which are then to be translated into the vernaculars, with possible adaptations indicated therein as belonging to the competence of the Episcopal Conferences and to the individual bishops.

As to the 'more radical' adaptations of the liturgy, *Varietates Legitimae* describes them as involving 'more than the sort of adaptations envisaged by the *General Instructions* and the *Praenotanda* of the liturgical books' (no. 63). The Instruction does not give examples of these kind of adaptations, but it says that they should be undertaken only after 'an Episcopal Conference has exhausted all the possibilities of adaptation offered by the liturgical books' (no. 63). These 'more profound' or 'more far-reaching' adaptations can be made in any of the eight areas mentioned above, namely, liturgical texts, the Eucharist, the rites of Christian Initiation, the marriage rite, funerals, the blessings of persons, places or things, the Liturgical Year, and the Liturgy of the Hour, if there are still 'problems about the participation of the faithful' after adaptations of the first kind have been introduced (no. 63). Nevertheless, the Instruction stipulates that 'adaptations of this kind do not envisage a transformation of the Roman rite but are made within the context of the Roman rite' (no. 63).[34]

2.2 *Varietates Legitimae* in the Postmodern Context

At this point it may be asked how well *Varietates Legitimae* meets the seven challenges of postmodernity to inculturation mentioned above. Clearly, undergirding the Instruction is the modern notion of culture as an integrated and integrating whole, which is also that of Vatican II and of most papal documents, including those of John Paul II.[35] Being an instruction on the implementation of *Sacrosanctum Concilium*, *Varietates Legitimae* simply assumes Vatican II's concept of culture and offers no discussion, by way of acceptance or rejection, of the extensive developments in the understanding of culture in the last 30 years. It appears not to have been aware of the momentous cultural shift from modernity to postmodernity, even though, as will be shown shortly, there surface here and there in the document concerns that may be described as postmodern.

Perhaps the most striking deficiency in the Instruction is its lack of understanding of inculturation as an *intercultural* encounter and its failure to attend to the dynamics of intercultural communication (Challenge 1). As has been correctly pointed out by J. Saldanha, in spite of its preference for 'inculturation', the Instruction repeatedly lapses into using 'adaptation', thus perpetuating the older inadequate understanding of the process of inculturating the Christian faith.[36] The document is impervious to the fact that the Roman Rite, however it is understood, *is* itself a cultural form, embodying a particular and local way of seeing the world, performing divine worship, and living the Christian faith, especially through its linguistic medium and the theology enshrined in its texts and rituals. By insisting on the necessity of maintaining 'the *substantial unity* of the Roman rite' in liturgical inculturation, as stipulated by Vatican II, and by holding that 'this unity is currently expressed in the typical editions of liturgical books, published by authority of the Supreme Pontiff, and in the liturgical books approved by the Episcopal Conferences for their areas and confirmed by the Apostolic See' (no. 36), and by requiring the use of translations of the 'typical editions of liturgical books' composed by experts chosen by the Congregation for Divine Worship and the Discipline of the Sacraments, the Instruction in practice imposes the Roman/Latin cultural and religious expressions on the other local churches.

A comparison with the secular strategies dealing with multiculturalism will highlight the strengths and weaknesses of the Instruction's approach to inculturation. John Coleman, an American Jesuit sociologist, speaks of eight ways in which culturally pluralistic societies have historically dealt with ethnic group differences. Four seek to eliminate differences, ranging from the injustice of (a) genocide and (b) forced massive population transfer to the more acceptable strategies of (c) partition or secession and (d) assimilation. The other four seek to manage differences without eliminating them: (e) hegemonic control, (f) territorial quasi-autonomy in a federalist system, (g) territorial autonomy (consocialism), and (h) multicultural integration.[37]

Varietates Legitimae clearly does not intend to eliminate cultural differences, as was often done in the pre-Vatican II era; on the contrary, it seeks to maintain and promote the 'legitimate differences' of the local churches. But its approach to inculturation lies somewhere between assimilation and hegemonic control. The assimilationist strategy proposes an eventual eradication of cultural differences: immigrants are allowed to keep their cultural heritages in the transitional stage but they are expected to 'become like one of us'. Hegemonic control honours cultural differences but insists on some common culture among different ethnic groups, and the culture of the dominant or hegemonic group is imposed on all as such common culture, no matter what lip service is given to the rhetoric of equality and about the right of a people to its own culture and language. In stipulating that the typical Latin editions of liturgical books composed by outside experts be the normative texts of which translations into the vernaculars of the local churches will have to be made, with limited and strictly controlled 'adaptations' and/or new compositions by the Episcopal Conferences allowed, *Varietates Legitimae* is still operating on the assimilationist model at worst and on the hegemonic control model at best. In either case, a genuine inculturation that is modelled on 'multicultural integration' is forfeited. On this model of 'affirmative multiculturalism' culture is acknowledged, as is done in postcolonialism and postmodernism, to be a site of struggle and a ground of contest in relations. In the intercultural encounter which constitutes inculturation, the two cultures – in our case, the local Latin/Roman culture embodied in the Roman Rite and another local culture – ideally should engage with each other as equal partners, challenging, modifying and enriching each other in a two-way exchange.

Unfortunately, as many sociologists and historians have pointed out, most multicultural societies, even those with a strong democratic tradition such as the United States, are at bottom monocultural and assimilationist, exclusive of cultural minorities. Sadly, the encounter among different cultures within the same country has been achieved, as J. Coleman has put it tersely and accurately, 'always imperfectly, never without conflict and almost never with full equality'.[38] This being the case, it is all the more incumbent upon the Church, given its catholicity, to be more committed to genuinely equal partnership in inculturation.

This brings us to another challenge of postmodernity to inculturation, namely, the use of power. This power play, as is indicated above, occurs between the Roman authorities and the other local churches, in the choice of cultures to enter into dialogue with, and in matters of popular religion. I will shortly discuss how *Varietates Legitimae* regards

71

the choice of cultures into which liturgy should be inculturated. Here I will briefly reflect on the Instruction's view of the relationship between the Roman authorities and the other local churches and popular religion.

That liturgical inculturation is not a private affair to be left to the initiatives and fancies of individuals, be they bishop, priest, or lay person, is not disputed. On the other hand, the well-founded need for hierarchical supervision should not be allowed to stifle genuine collaboration and the application of the principle of subsidiarity (Challenge 2). In this respect, *Varietates Legitimae* does at times go overboard in its stipulations of the various procedures to be followed in both the normal and more radical forms of inculturation. For example, at the Special Assembly of the Synod of Bishops for Asia (1998), questions were raised about the necessity of a *recognitio* by the Congregation for Divine Worship and the Discipline of the Sacraments for translations of liturgical books already approved by the local Episcopal Conferences. Likewise, it may be asked why 'concessions granted to one region cannot be extended to other regions without the necessary authorization, even if an Episcopal Conference considers that there are sufficient reasons for adopting such measures in its own area' (no. 37).[39] In either case it appears that the Instruction is motivated by an excessive desire for control and does not respect the relative autonomy of the local churches.

With regard to popular religion (Challenge 4), *Varietates Legitimae* sees it mainly as 'popular devotion' or 'devotional practices' and decrees that their 'introduction into liturgical celebrations under the pretext of inculturation cannot be allowed "because by its nature, [the liturgy] is superior to them"' (no. 45). According to the Instruction, it is the duty of the local bishop to 'organize such devotions, to encourage them as supports for the life and faith of Christians, and to purify them, when necessary, because they need to be constantly permeated by the Gospel' (no. 45). Clearly, from the postmodern perspective of popular religion and the history of the development of popular Catholicism, the Instruction's understanding of 'popular devotion' is too superficial and constricted.[40]

As to the other challenges of postmodernity, *Varietates Legitimae* does not seem to look upon them favourably. For example, with regard to the need to conjoin inter-religious dialogue with inculturation (Challenge 5), the Instruction's position is somewhat ambiguous.[41] On the one hand, it is open to the use of 'expressions from non-Christian religions' in the liturgy (no. 39). On the other hand, its attitude towards them is largely negative and defensive: 'The liturgy is the expression of faith and Christian life, and so it is necessary to ensure that liturgical inculturation is not marked, even in appearance, by religious syncretism. This would be the case if the places of worship, the liturgical objects and vestments, gestures and postures let it appear as if rites had the same significance in Christian celebrations as they did before evangelization. The syncretism will be still worse if biblical readings and chants or the prayers were replaced by texts from other religions, even if these contain an undeniable religious and moral value' (no. 47).[42] Any admission of rites and gestures from the local customs into the Christian liturgy must be 'accompanied by purification and, if necessary, a break with the past …. Obviously the Christian liturgy cannot accept magic rites, superstition, spiritism, vengeance or rites with a sexual connotation' (no. 48).

As to the various expressions of culture in their contemporary, postmodern forms of collage and bricolage, *Varietates Legitimae* has little to say (Challenge 6). Regarding music and singing, gesture and posture, art and architecture, in general it focuses almost exclusively on the local and popular forms,[43] and is in favour of them, provided that they accord with the sacred character of worship (no. 40) and 'are always the expression of the communal prayer of adoration, praise, offering and supplication, and not simply a performance' (no. 42).

Lastly, with regard to the larger issue of the relationship between liturgy and theology, especially in the context of postmodern relativism and pessimism (Challenge 7), *Varietates Legitimae* is aware that in many countries, even those with a Christian tradition, there exists 'a culture marked by indifference or disinterest in religion' (no. 8).[44] To meet the challenges of this type of culture, the Instruction, strangely enough, judges that liturgical inculturation is not the appropriate approach since inculturation 'assumes there are pre-existent religious values and evangelizes them' (no. 8). Rather it suggests the use of

73

'liturgical formation' and 'finding the most suitable means to reach spirits and hearts' (no. 8). In this context it is worth noting that postmodernism is not hostile to religion as such but only to religions with absolute claims to truth and universal validity. As mentioned earlier, postmodernism and even postmodern science have an acute sense of reality as an unfathomable mystery. Only now the mystery is located elsewhere than in religious institutions and official worship. Hence, to dismiss inculturation as an inappropriate means to recover the sense of the sacred in postmodernism because of the alleged lack of 'pre-existent religious values' is a short-sighted policy. Inculturation may turn out to be one of the 'most suitable means to reach spirits and hearts' in postmodernity.

On the positive side, as has been mentioned above, in spite of the fact that *Varietates Legitimae* seems not have been aware of the challenges of the postmodern understanding of culture, it does contain here and there statements that reflect some of the concerns of post-modernism. For example, the Instruction explicitly acknowledges the historical evolution of the Roman Rite which 'has known how to integrate texts, chants, gestures and rites from various sources and to adapt itself in local cultures in mission territories, even if at certain periods a desire for liturgical uniformity obscured this fact' (no. 17). Again, with regard to the choice of cultures into which the liturgy is to be inculturated (Challenge 3), the Instruction notes that 'in a number of countries, there are several cultures which coexist, and sometimes influence each other in such a way as to lead gradually to the formation of a new culture, while at times they seek to affirm their proper identity, or even oppose each other, in order to stress their own existence' (no. 49). In these places, the Instruction warns, the Episcopal Conference 'should respect the riches of each culture and those who defend them, but they should not ignore or neglect a minority culture with which they are not familiar' (no. 49).[45] In these statements one can hear the echo of the postmodern under-standing of culture as a site of struggle and a ground of contest in relations.

3. Liturgical Inculturation: Perspectives from the Asian Churches

Despite its many positive contributions to liturgical inculturation, *Varietates Legitimae* still falls short of offering an adequate strategy for this task, especially in view of the challenges of postmodernism.[46] For a fuller view of inculturation, attention is now turned to the Asian churches whose greatly varied cultural and religious contexts pose the most difficult challenges to inculturation on the one hand, and which, on the other hand, from their experience of colonialism, their missionary history (in particular, the so-called Chinese Rites Controversy) and their own spiritual traditions, seem to offer a rich trove of resources to meet the challenges of inculturation in the postmodern context. I will examine the contribution of the Benedictine Filipino liturgist, Anscar J. Chupungco, whose works deal extensively with liturgical inculturation as well as the theology of the Federation of the Asian Bishops' Conferences.

3.1 Anscar J. Chupungco and Liturgical Inculturation

A former president of the Pontifical Liturgical Institute and Rector Magnificus of the Pontifical Athenaeum of Sant' Anselmo in Rome and founder of Paul VI Institute of Liturgy in the Philippines, Chupungco is internationally known for his works on liturgical inculturation.[47] My intention here is not to present Chupungco's theology as a whole; rather the focus is only on his understanding of liturgical inculturation. One significant strength of Chupungco's reflections on the relationship of the liturgy and its cultural context is their rootedness in the history of the development of the Roman Rite and the teaching of Vatican II.[48] His knowledge of liturgical history impresses upon him the necessity of inculturation and gives him the freedom for liturgical innovation since all liturgies are culture-dependent. As he puts it later, '... Perhaps the root of our woes in inculturation is the failure to recognize the basic fact that all liturgical rites are vested in culture, that no liturgy is celebrated in a cultural vacuum.'[49] On the other hand,

Vatican II's *Sacrosanctum Concilium* provides the terra firma from which he can sally forth into liturgical inculturation.

Undergirding inculturation, according to Chupungco, are three principles which he calls theological, liturgical and cultural. Theologically, it is the mystery of the Incarnation that demands that the Church incarnate itself in every culture. Inculturation is 'an incarnational imperative, rather than a concession of Vatican II'.[50] Liturgically, inculturation is governed by the following principles: (a) the liturgy is worship of God; (b) it is centred on Christ; (c) in it God's written Word obtains primacy; (d) it must be actively participated by the people; and (e) it is composed of unchangeable and changeable elements. Culturally, Chupungco distinguishes three types of liturgical adaptation. The first is *accomodatio* which affects liturgical celebrations *hic et nunc* by the assembly and need not involve cultural adaptation. The second is *acculturation*, which is 'the process whereby cultural elements which are compatible with the Roman liturgy are incorporated into it either as substitutes or illustrations of euchological and ritual elements of the Roman rite'.[51] Acculturation may be achieved in both the formal or the theological elements of the Roman Rite and may be carried out by dynamic translation or by assuming the rituals and traditions of the local cultures as substitutes or illustrations of the ritual elements of the Roman Rite. The third is *inculturation*, which is 'the process whereby a pre-Christian rite is endowed with Christian meaning'.[52]

In his later writings Chupungco seems to prefer 'inculturation' to 'adaptation', as the titles and subtitles of his books indicate and began to elaborate in greater detail what the process of inculturation entails.[53] Following Aylward Shorter, he now explains more clearly that *acculturation* is the encounter between two cultures in which they are juxtaposed side by side on a footing of mutual respect and tolerance but without producing an internal change in either. Put in a formula, acculturation is: A+B=AB. In inculturation, the encounter between the two cultures occurs in three processes, namely, interaction, mutual assimilation and transculturation. Its formula is: A+B=C. Culture A is no longer simply A but becomes C; likewise, culture B is no longer simply B but becomes C. However, culture A does not become culture B, nor does culture B become culture A; each culture retains its essential elements but both cultures are nevertheless internally transformed to constitute a new culture. [54] Liturgical inculturation, for Chupungco, is the process wherereby 'the liturgy is inserted into the culture, history, and tradition of the people among whom the Church dwells. It begins to think, speak, and ritualize according to the local cultural pattern.'[55] Chupungco argues that the Roman Rite is the example *par excellence* of liturgical inculturation understood in this sense.

Describing the process of liturgical inculturation, Chupungco explains that it consists in the meeting of two elements, namely, the typical editions of the liturgical books, presumably composed in Rome, and the patterns of the local culture. In Chupungco's interpretation of culture, the cultural patterns form one of the three components of culture, the other two being values and institutions. The values (e.g. hospitality, community spirit and leadership) are the principles shaping the life and activities of the community. The institutions are the community's rites with which it celebrates the different phases of human life from birth to death. And the cultural patterns are 'the typical ways members of a society think or form concepts, express their thoughts through language, ritualize aspects of their life, and create art forms. The areas covered by cultural patterns are thus: thought, language, rites and symbols, literature, music, architecture, and all other expressions of the fine arts.'[56]

As to the method of liturgical inculturation, Chupungco expands the two ways of dynamic translation and finding cultural equivalents into three: dynamic equivalence, creative assimilation and organic progression. By 'dynamic equivalence', which includes translation, is meant 'replacing an element of the Roman liturgy with something in the local culture that has an equal meaning and value'.[57] By 'creative assimilation', which for Chupungco 'should not be regarded as the ordinary method of liturgical inculturation',[58] is meant 'the integration of pertinent rites, symbols, and linguistic expressions, religious or otherwise, into the liturgy'.[59] 'Organic progression' is not so much a method of inculturation as the necessity of going beyond both dynamic equivalence and creative assimilation (or 'acculturation' and 'inculturation', as Chupungco uses these terms). The reason for this further step is that neither Vatican II nor the post-conciliar typical editions can foresee and provide for all the particular circumstances of the local churches which must create new forms of worship to meet their own needs: 'The work of organic progression should continue on the level of the local churches. The typical editions normally offer a wide range of options and possibilities. But the breadth of inculturation should not be hemmed in by the provisions contained in a document. The typical editions cannot possibly envisage for the local Church all the options and possibilities of inculturation. Thus their provision will prove insufficient and at times also deficient when placed *vis-à-vis* the demand for a truly inculturated liturgy.'[60]

Liturgical 'inculturation' then is only an intermediate step; one must move beyond it to what Chupungco calls 'liturgical creativity'. As confirmation, he cites the statement of the Instruction *Comme le prévoit*, no. 43: 'Texts translated from another language are clearly not sufficient for the celebration of a fully renewed liturgy. The creation of new texts will be necessary.'[61] This does not mean a total disregard for tradition or any pre-existing liturgical material, Chupungco clarifies, but only 'new liturgical forms not based on the Roman typical editions'.[62] He cites as examples the symbolic dance at the offertory procession, the mimetic interpretation of the Gospel reading, and the use of audiovisuals at the general intercessions. Cautiously he calls for *alternative liturgies*, 'whose aim is to give expression to those facets of liturgical tradition or modern life that are not considered by the Roman rite'.[63] In this context he urges the creation of new sacramentals by the local churches,[64] the cross-fertilization between liturgy and popular religiosity,[65] and a liturgical catechesis based not only on the typical editions but also on the rituals created by the local church.[66]

From this brief survey it is clear that Chupungco's theology of and proposals for liturgical inculturation as symbolized by the formula A+B=C goes far beyond *Varietates Legitimae*. He explicitly states that translations of the typical editions (in acculturation) and adoption of local traditions (in inculturation), though necessary and useful steps, are insufficient and calls for 'liturgical creativity' in devising new texts and 'alternative liturgies' by the local churches. Furthermore, though he does not discuss postmodernism as such, Chupungco does address, albeit indirectly, some of its challenges. For example, for him inculturation is necessarily an intercultural encounter, and more specifically, an encounter between the Roman culture with its typical patterns of sobriety, brevity, directness and practicality, and the culture of another local church with its own distinct, and often very different patterns (Challenge 1). Briefly he notes cultural pluralism and warns that power play is at stake in inculturation (Challenges 2 and 3): 'Monoculturalism … is often the arm of conquest and domination'.[67] In addition, he recognizes the irreplaceable and significant role of popular religion in an adequately inculturated liturgy (Challenge 4). Finally, he avers to the existence of contemporary expressions of culture (though not necessarily postmodern) for which the Roman Rite and its typical editions prove largely inadequate (Challenge 6). Indeed, if A+B=C is carried to its logical conclusion, the result of liturgical inculturation can no longer be the Roman Rite as it currently exists.

3.2 The Federation of Asian Bishops' Conferences: A Triple Dialogue as a Way of Being Church

While Chupungco's insights are helpful for a truly inculturated theology, they could be strengthened by the ecclesiology of the Federation of Asian Bishops' Conferences (FABC). If, as Chupungco says, an inculturated catechesis presupposes an inculturated liturgy, *a fortiori* the latter presupposes an inculturated ecclesiology, or better, a new way of being Church. This is what the FABC offers.[68]

By historical accident, Christianity was and continues to be a foreign religion for Asians. Even Pope John Paul II points out the paradoxical fact that 'most Asians tend to regard Jesus – born on Asian soil – as a Western rather than an Asian figure'.[69] Furthermore, the Church in Asia is still burdened by its past connections with colonial powers. Consequently, the FABC emphasizes that the most urgent task for the Asian churches is to become churches not only *in* but also *of* Asia, in other words, to become local churches.

This new way of being Church in Asia demands a different ecclesiology, one that decentres the Church in the sense that it makes the centre of the Christian life and worship not the church but the reign of God. This sort of Copernican revolution in ecclesiology sees the goal and purpose of the mission of the Church to be not the geographical and institutional expansion of the church (the *plantatio ecclesiae*) but rather a transparent sign and effective instrument of the saving presence of the reign of God, the reign of justice, peace and love of which the Church is a seed.

This theme has been repeatedly emphasized by the FABC, especially in its first and fifth plenary assemblies in Taipei, Taiwan, 1974, and Bandung, Indonesia, 1990 respectively.[70] In Taipei, the FABC affirmed categorically: 'To preach the Gospel in Asia today we must make the message and life of Christ truly incarnate in the minds and lives of our peoples. The primary focus of our task of evangelization then, at this time in our history, is the building up of a truly local church.'[71] In Bandung, the FABC spoke of 'alternative ways of being Church in Asia in 1990s' and envisioned four specific ways. The Church in Asia, it said, must be a '*communion of communities*, where laity, Religious and clergy recognize and accept each other as sisters and brothers', 'a *participatory* Church where the gifts that the Holy Spirit gives to all the faithful – lay, Religious, and clerics alike – are recognized and activated', 'a Church that faithfully and lovingly *witnesses* to the Risen Lord Jesus and reaches out to the people of other faiths and persuasions in a dialogue of life towards the integral liberation of all', and a Church that 'serves as a *prophetic sign* daring to point beyond this world to the ineffable Kingdom that is yet fully to come'.[72]

This necessity to be local churches was reiterated by the Seventh Plenary Assembly (Samphran, Thailand, 3–12 January 2000). Speaking of 'an Asian vision of a renewed Church', the Assembly's Final Statement declares that the Church in Asia is moving towards a '"truly local Church", toward a Church "incarnate in a people, a Church indigenous and inculturated" (2 FABC Plenary Assembly, Calcutta, 1978)'.[73] In this way the Church in Asia will become a 'communion of communities', that is, a community of local communities, which, as *Lumen Gentium* 23, teaches, image the universal Church and in which and out of which the one and only Catholic Church exists.[74]

The mode in which this process of becoming the local church occurs is dialogue. It is important to note that dialogue is understood here not as a separate activity, e.g. ecumenical or inter-religious dialogue, but as the *modality* in which everything is to be done by and in the church in Asia, including liberation, inculturation and inter-religious dialogue. It is through this triple dialogue – with the Asian people, especially the poor, their cultures and their religions – that the Church in Asia carries out its evangelizing mission and thus becomes the local church. Hence, dialogue is not a substitution for proclamation or evangelization, as Asian theologians are sometimes accused of doing; rather, it is the way and indeed the most effective way in which proclamation of the Good News is done.

The reason for this modality is the presence in Asia of the many living religions and rich cultures, among whom Christians are but a tiny minority and therefore must, even on the purely human level, enter into dialogue with other believers, in an attitude of respect and friendship, for survival. But, more than the question of number, there is the theological doctrine today, at least in the Roman Catholic Church, that, as John Paul II says, 'the Spirit's presence and activity affect not only individuals but also society and history, peoples, cultures and religions. Indeed, the Spirit is at the origin of the noble ideals and undertakings which benefit humanity on its journey through history'.[75] In light of this divine presence in people's cultures and religions, and not just in individuals, and in view of the socio-historical nature of human existence, it is possible to say, as some Asian theologians have done, that the followers of other religions are saved not in spite of them but in and through them, though it is always God who saves, and Christians will add, in and through Jesus. At least in this restricted sense, then, religions are 'ways of salvation'.[76]

Given this religious pluralism, it is only natural that dialogue is the preferred mode of proclamation, as Michael Amaladoss puts it: 'As soon as one no longer sees the relationship of Christianity to other religions as presence/absence or superior/inferior or full/partial, dialogue becomes the context in which proclamation has to take place. For even when proclaiming the Good News with assurance, one should do it with great respect for the freedom of God who is acting, the freedom of the other who is responding and the Church's own limitations as a witness. It is quite proper then that the Asian Bishops

81

characterized evangelization itself as a dialogue with various Asian realities – cultures, religions and the poor.'[77]

It is important to note also that dialogue as a mode of being Church in Asia does not refer primarily to the intellectual exchange among experts of various religions, as is often done in the West. Rather, it involves a fourfold presence: 'a. The *dialogue of life*, where people strive to live in an open and neighborly spirit, sharing their joys and sorrows, their human problems and preoccupations. b. The *dialogue of action*, in which Christians and others collaborate for the integral development and liberation of people. c. The *dialogue of theological exchange*, where specialists seek to deepen their understanding of their respective religious heritages, and to appreciate each other's spiritual values. d. The *dialogue of religious experience*, where persons, rooted in their own religious traditions, share their spiritual riches, for instance, with regard to prayer and contemplation, faith and ways of searching for God or the Absolute.'[78]

As noted above, the FABC suggests that this dialogue take place in three areas: dialogue with the Asian poor, their cultures and their religions.[79] In other words, the three essential tasks of the Asian churches are liberation, inculturation and inter-religious dialogue.[80] For our discussion on liturgical inculturation, it is vital to note that for the FABC these are not three distinct and separate activities of the Church; rather they are three intertwined dimensions of the Church's one mission of evangelization. As the FABC's Seventh Plenary Assembly puts it concisely: 'These issues are not separate topics to be discussed, but aspects of an integrated approach to our Mission of Love and Service. We need to feel and act "integrally". As we face the needs of the 21st century, we do so with Asian hearts, in solidarity with the poor and the marginalized, in union with all our Christian brothers and sisters and by joining hands with all men and women of Asia of many different faiths. Inculturation, dialogue, justice and option for the poor are aspects of whatever we do.'[81]

3.3 Liturgical Inculturation as Dialogue

It is only in light of the Asian Church's attempt to find a new way of being Church, becoming a fully local church, a church which is a participatory 'communion of communities', integrally engaged in the triple, intrinsically interconnected dialogue with the Asian poor, their cultures and their religions, that, in my judgement, liturgical inculturation can be correctly understood. In this connection, it is very interesting to note that in the 30 years of its existence and its abundant theological production, the FABC has devoted very few pages to the explicit theme of liturgical inculturation.[82] This lacuna, I believe, is not an oversight. Rather it is due to the FABC's overarching and fundamental insight that inculturation, liturgical or otherwise, is not something to be pursued for its own sake, or to make worship palatable to Asian aesthetic and religious tastes. Rather, it must be subordinated to the task of becoming an Asian Church, through the essential mode of dialogue with the Asian poor, their cultures, and their religions.

Of course, it is not the task of the FABC to devise concrete forms or programmes of liturgical inculturation. These fall within the competence of each bishop and each conference of bishops. The FABC recognizes that the Church in Asia still 'remains foreign in its lifestyle, in its institutional structure, in its worship' and that 'Christian rituals often remain formal, neither spontaneous nor particularly Asian'.[83] Hence, it urges, in general terms, a renewal of all aspects of the Church's prayer-life, including 'its liturgical worship, its popular forms of piety, prayer in the home, in parishes, in prayer groups'.[84] One step of this renewal is the use of 'venerable books and writings' of other religions for prayer and spirituality.[85]

With regard to Asian popular religion in particular, the FABC recognizes that its worldview is heavily influenced by Confucian and Taoist thought which emphasizes that 'the human person is a spiritual being living in a spirit-filled, mutually interacting and interdependent world' and that 'the underlying aim of customs, ritual, worship, etc. is the maintenance of harmony between humankind and the natural world'.[86]

In spite of these rather general indications, the FABC does provide two very useful guidelines for an authentic liturgical inculturation. First, liturgical inculturation must be undertaken always in conjunction with and as an intrinsic component of inter-religious dialogue and the work for human liberation. Without inter-religious dialogue, liturgical inculturation would operate in the void, at least in Asia, since it would lack the context into which it can insert Christian worship on the one hand, and would have nothing to bring into Christian worship on the other, as the twofold movement of inculturation implies. This inculturation of Christian liturgy must be carried out in two areas, namely, the metacosmic religions or soteriologies (e.g. Hinduism, Buddhism, Taoism, Confucianism, Islam, Shintoism, etc.) with their official forms of worship and prayer and the cosmic religion which is often embodied in popular devotions commonly practised at home and in the family. Even in the United States, where the prevalent context is not yet religious pluralism, albeit a rapidly growing phenomenon, liturgical inculturation must still take into account the American culture and its civil religion, not to mention the Black and Hispanic/Latino cultures and their religious traditions. At any rate, the separation of religion from culture, which is often made in the West and which permits an inculturation of liturgy into culture without facing the religious issues, makes no sense in Asia where culture and religion form an indivisible whole.

Furthermore, as a form of inter-religious dialogue, liturgical inculturation will not be undertaken simplistically as the 'incarnation' of a culture-free Gospel or culture-free liturgy into another culture, which at times the model of incarnation for inculturation seems to suggest. As Michael Amaladoss and Aylward Shorter have reminded us, inculturation is always *interculturation*. It is an encounter among at least three cultures – of the Bible, of the Christian Tradition, and of the people to whom the Gospel is proclaimed.[87] I will broach the dynamics of power play in this intercultural encounter in the last part of my essay; here suffice it to note that liturgical inculturation without an adequate sensitivity to its intercultural dimension runs the risk of imposing a particular culture, e.g., that which is implicit in the Roman Rite, on to others.

Without the struggle for human liberation, liturgical inculturation runs the risk of being an elitist enterprise, perhaps with a purely aesthetic and archeological interest.[88] Worse, it may be a disguised form of cultural chauvinism, especially when the culture into which the liturgy is inculturated is that of the dominant class.[89] For instance,

Dalit and Tribal theologians in India have consistently argued that Brahminic Hinduism is not the only culture and religion of India, and therefore liturgical inculturation cannot assume it as the only partner with which it must dialogue.[90] Similarly, *minjung* theologians of Korea have chosen the 'people' – that is, the mass that is politically oppressed, economically exploited, socially alienated, religiously marginalized, and culturally kept uneducated by the dominant group of the society – as the embodiment of the Messiah.[91] Among Asian theologians no one has argued more forcefully for the unity between inculturation and liberation than the Sri Lankan Jesuit Aloysius Pieris who insists that the Church *in* Asia, in order to be *of* Asia, must undergo a double baptism in the river of the 'religiousness of the Asian poor' and the 'poverty of religious Asians'.[92]

If this coupling of liturgical inculturation with liberation and inter-religious dialogue is objected to on the grounds that it is made into an exceedingly complicated affair, then my point has been understood. Indeed, we should disabuse ourselves of the notion that liturgical inculturation consists mainly in the adaptation of local language, music and singing, gesture and posture, and art while maintaining the '*substantial unity* of the Roman rite', as *Varietates Legitimae* insists. In fact, in such a strategy, there is a serious danger of what Aloysius Pieris calls 'theological vandalism', that is, picking and choosing elements of non-Christian religions, and 'baptizing' them for Christian use, with no reverence for the wholeness of non-Christians' religious experience.[93]

The second important insight of FABC on liturgical inculturation concerns popular religion. By focusing on dialogue with the Asian poor, the FABC see popular religion primarily as the religion of the poor people. This popular religion or cosmic religiosity in Asia is characterized, according to Pieris, by seven features: it has a this-worldly spirituality, it is animated by a sense of total dependence on the divine, it longs for justice, it is cosmic, it accords women a key role, it is ecological, and it communicates through story.[94] By engaging with and retrieving this popular religion, liturgical inculturation will tap into its potential for human liberation. In popular religion believers seek for immediate satisfaction of physical and material needs, they feel God as a close liberating presence, they appeal to the spirits for protection and deliverance, they accord equal roles to women and men in their rituals, and their religious symbols can function as rallying points for the mass. An example of this liberative power of popular religion, from the Christian perspective, is the People Power in the Philippines which has demonstrated the power of popular devotions to unite the people in their effort to overthrow dictatorship, and recently, to remove a corrupted presidency.

In conclusion, in the postmodern age with its manifold challenges to the Christian faith, a truly inculturated liturgy capable of meeting these challenges can no longer, it seems to me, be conceived mainly as a transposition of the Roman Rite with its inherited rituals and centrally composed typical editions, even in the 'accommodated' and 'inculturated' forms, by way of both 'dynamic equivalence' and 'creative assimilation'. This method of inculturation will be regarded, and rightly so in an age deeply suspicious of power play, as an unjustified imposition of a particular culture with its patterns and institutions on to another culture and will inevitably fail to respond fully to the needs of the local churches. The starting point of a genuine inculturation must be a vibrant new way of being Church, characterized by the triple dialogue as advocated by the FABC, out of which a new ritual family, with its own texts, rites, sacramentals, forms of popular religiosity, and various expressions of worship will eventually be constituted. Only in this way is the unity of faith preserved and promoted amidst cultural pluralism. This is no revolutionary approach; after all, that is what the Roman Rite did, in its own way.

6

A Response to Peter Phan

Mark R. Francis, CSV

I would like to thank Professor Phan for his lucid exposition of many of the complex issues surrounding liturgical inculturation in our globalized, postmodern world. As I have come to expect from Peter, he presents his ideas clearly and offers springboards for further reflection on the present dilemma in which the Church finds itself. That dilemma can be stated quite simply: official Curial pronouncements centralizing all major decisions regarding liturgy are severely restricting the possibility of a genuine inculturation of the Roman Rite. I would like to comment on Fr Phan's treatment of these documents and offer some further considerations.

It is no secret that Fr Phan does not think very highly of the scholarship underlying recent documents issued by the Congregation for Worship over the past several years. He advances some very trenchant arguments why a document of the CDWDS such as *Varietates Legitimae* is bound to be unpersuasive since it presupposes a deficient understanding of culture. The same is true of the recent document on translation, *Liturgiam Authenticam*. It, too, comes under fire in his paper for its lack of attention to interdisciplinary scholarship and its call for Curial micro-management of the approval of vernacular versions of the liturgical books at the expense of local bishops' conferences. I very much suspect that he would cast an equally critical gaze on the newly released *Direttorio su pietà popolare e liturgia* as well as the *editio typica tertia* of the *Missale Romanum*, especially the new last chapter of the *General Instruction* that deals with liturgy and culture.

At heart, Fr Phan's critique of recent Roman documents on the liturgy is not just a quibble over the details of implementing rubrics or a debate about nuanced points of translation theory. Rather it is in

87

reaction to a dramatic change in the ecclesiological assumptions of those who now staff the Congregation for Divine Worship. While invoking the documents of the Second Vatican Council, both *Varietates Legitimae* and especially *Liturgiam Authenticam* make some basic assumptions about the role of the Roman Rite in the life of the Church that are clearly not the same that first undergirded liturgical reform since the Council. To be clear: the first stage of liturgical reform (1963–70), being more faithful to the spirit of the Council, allowed greater leeway to local initiative in interpreting liturgical tradition.

One only need compare two official documents on translations, *Comme le prévoit* (1969) and *Liturgiam Authenticam* (2001), to see that the Dicastery for Worship has unilaterally repudiated many of the bedrock assumptions that guided the first translations of liturgical books. One of those assumptions was that a liturgical text is a medium of communication. As such, it is now the 'voice of the church' (CLP 5, 6) and not only needs to take into consideration the message contained in the text but must also be sensitive to whom the text is addressed. As *Comme le prévoit* elucidates:

The prayer of the Church is always a prayer of some actual community assembled here and now. It is not sufficient that a formula handed down from some other time or region should be translated verbatim, even if accurately, for liturgical use. The formula translated must become the genuine prayer of the congregation and in it each of its members should be able to express himself or herself (20 c).

Liturgiam Authenticam, on the other hand, emphasizes that the words of Sacred Scripture and other utterances spoken in liturgical celebrations 'express truths that transcend the limits of time and space' (LA 19). For that reason, 'the original text, insofar as possible, must be translated integrally and in the most exact manner, without omissions or additions in terms of their content, and without paraphrases or glosses' (LA 20). The instruction promotes a literal translation that is much more concerned about rendering the text – both vocabulary and syntactical style – than in the understanding or participation by the congregation in the liturgical celebration. If original texts are to be proposed, LA stipulated that they 'are to contain nothing that is inconsistent with the function, meaning, structure, style, theological content, traditional vocabulary or other important qualities of the tests found in the *editiones typicae*' (LA 107). In others words, the original texts – to be orthodox – have to sound like translations. This is obviously a very different understanding from that of *Comme le prévoit* which encouraged original vernacular compositions in order to promote a fully renewed liturgy (43).

As Fr Phan has pointed out, the questions of meaningful translation and adequate inculturation of the rites go beyond the translation of texts to a real dialogue of the Roman Rite with the whole panoply of signs and symbols of a local culture. This dialogue necessarily touches on questions surrounding authority and power in the Church. Who, indeed, should have the preponderant word in deciding if the language of worship and the interpretation of the received rites used in celebration by a local church is faithful to the Catholic tradition – the local bishops who understand the evolving language usage and customs of their country or 'experts' in the Roman Congregation for Divine Worship who often know the language and culture imperfectly or not at all? It is not surprising that the call to restore the right of Bishops' Conferences to judge the suitability of translations has been a constant theme in the responses to the *lineamenta* of the various continental Synods celebrated here in Rome: Africa, Asia, Oceania. Tragically, the cries of the bishops of local churches for more say in the way their churches celebrate have not been heard. Inculturation, even its most modest forms, will not be a possibility until the Church comes to grips with its new identity as a multicultural, globalized entity, the majority of whose members are no longer of Western European background.

A Question of Method

I think it is useful to point out that one of the key differences between recent Roman documents dealing with culture and liturgy and those, like Fr Phan, who are uncomfortable with them is the question of the starting point. Recent Curial pronouncements tend to present the issues 'from the top down', arguing from previous liturgical legislation and precedents drawn from a rather focused history of the liturgy and liturgical books of the Roman Rite. The overarching concern of the CDWDS is obviously one of preserving the 'substantial unity of the Roman Rite' as it is proposed by the *editiones typicae* in order to insure that the liturgy is able to transmit the teachings of the Church in a faithful and complete manner. Article 398 of the new GIRM describes well the attitude of the current CDW regarding inculturation: 'inculturation requires a necessary amount of time, lest in a hasty and incautious manner the authentic liturgical tradition suffer contamination.' The choice of adjective is important here since it betrays an attitude of caution. The liturgical tradition is authentic or 'pure' and risks being 'contaminated' by inculturation. As stated earlier in the same document, 'the Roman Rite constitutes a notable and estimable part of the liturgical treasure and patrimony of the Catholic Church, and its riches are of benefit to the universal Church, so that were these riches lost, this would be gravely damaging to her' (397). Thus, the Congregation's starting point is the 'pure' Roman Rite that needs to be protected as an absolute good – as an end in itself.

Fr Phan's starting point is quite different. While not ignoring the liturgical tradition, he begins with the challenge of proclaiming the Gospel in a way that is understandable in the context of the postmodern, globalized world. This world is characterized by diversity and pluralism. It is multivalent and heterogeneous, constructed by means of collage and bricolage into a collection of juxtaposed cultural elements that eschew the kind of 'purity' so valued by the Roman documents. It is also a context that challenges the exclusivist interpretation of the Christian 'metanarrative'. In short, his approach begins with the ecumenical and inter-religious human experience of our time and looks at the liturgical tradition from that vantage point. From this point of view, one can see this new-found dicasterial concern for 'Roman liturgical purity' as a fundamentalistic reaction to the challenges posed by postmodernity.

It is rightly said that whenever we Catholics gather for liturgy we move back and forth between at least three hybrid cultural expressions of the faith: the cultures of the Bible, themselves diverse (Hebrew,

Hellenized Greek); the Roman Rite (the culture of the late Roman Empire, medieval Franco-Germanic elements, post-Tridentine and Baroque formulae); and the culture of the local church at prayer (which also may be quite diverse – especially in a multicultural community). It is to the extent that we are conscious of the cultural richness of our tradition – to its *lack* of 'purity' – and sensitive to the people gathered in the name of Christ to celebrate the liturgy, that the Roman Rite – in all 'legitimate varieties' – will be an effective vehicle for proclaiming what we all know to be much more important than the formal elements of the rite itself: the Good News of Jesus Christ.

7

The Zairean Rite: The Roman Missal for the Dioceses of Zaire (Congo)

Léon Ngoy Kalumba, SJ

I would like to discuss what is commonly known as the Zairean Rite of Mass but which was approved by the Holy See under the title the Roman Missal for the Dioceses of Zaire – meaning it is an adaptation of the Roman Rite to the cultural realities of the Democratic Republic of Congo.[1]

One cannot understand 'the Zairean Rite' without locating it in the context of the evangelization of the African continent (and, in this case, of the Democratic Republic of Congo), the pastoral concern and the Christian duty to see the evangelic message be incarnate in the hearts of those who receive it and in the cultures that welcome it. For this reason, I will first address the process of inculturation in Africa (which is the equivalent of talking about the path of theology in Africa) and second, the Zairean Rite itself.

1. The Inculturation or Incarnation of the Gospel

We can divide the history of evangelization of the African continent into three main stages. The first stage took place during the early centuries, during which the northern part (Egypt) received the baby Jesus, accompanied by his parents, who were seeking refuge, and sheltered an intense Christian and theological activity, particularly the School of Alexandria. The second stage (around the sixteenth century) was the one during which the Capuchin missionaries started their work of evangelization in the sub-Saharan part of Africa, Black Africa, and especially in the Kingdom of Congo; this evangelical activity was interrupted by a lack of continuity on the part of the missionaries and a lack of autonomous local support, not to mention the implication of certain missionaries in the slave trade, which certainly did not make them sympathetic figures in the eyes of Black Africans. The third wave of the evangelization of Africa is the one that started at the end of the nineteenth century and continues today. We therefore understand that in the Democratic Republic of Congo, we talk about the second evangelization, the centennial of which we celebrated about fifteen years ago. If I take this course, it is, among other things, to underline the presence of several rites in Africa, of which certain are almost as old as Christianity (for instance the Coptic and Ethiopian rites).

Notably, the announcement of the Gospel in the course of this second wave of evangelization necessitated an effort to translate the missionary's language into the vernacular of the local populations. Homage is due to the catechists who served as translators and followed these missionaries on their itinerary, but also to the numerous missionaries who mastered the native languages of the people and tried to understand the local cultures, with the goal of converting these people to Christianity. We must also acknowledge the first generation of African Christians who consented to be evangelists to their brothers and sisters, employing some of the cultural elements of their ancestors.

Inculturation in this stage of evangelization consisted of a 'transplantation', a 'translation or adaptation': the transplantation of ecclesiastical structures and the Christian way of life from the native countries of the missionaries to the African environments; the translation and adaptation of these same elements to African environments.

But inculturation means going beyond simple adaptation. It is a question of incarnation, that is to say, 'the need of integral implanting of the Gospel in Negro African socio-cultural environments, including all the aspects of life, without excluding any'; following the example of Jesus 'who had settled body and soul in the Hebraic socio-cultural universe, adopting all the Semitic being, except the sin (Hebrews 4:15; John 8:46; II Corinthians 5:21; I John 3:5); this concretely included all languages, ways of thinking and speech, mentalities, religious traditions and inherited wisdom, etc.'[2].

It is this progress towards deep inculturation that theology in Africa is currently bringing to fruition – a theology that would like to unify 'deep Africanity' and 'Catholicity'. The diverse denominations[3] that have accompanied its birth illustrate well the concern of African theologians to see the Gospel become incarnate in the local environments, a double concern that expresses a double fidelity to Christ, to Christian traditions, and to that ancestral inheritance compatible with the Christian faith.

Theology in Africa is essentially a theology of inculturation or of incarnation, in response to the repeated recommendations of recent popes. During his visit to Uganda in 1969, Paul VI declared: 'Yes, you have human values and characteristic forms of culture that can elevate themselves to proper perfection, able to find in Christianity, and through it, a superior and original plenitude, and therefore able to have its own richness of expression, truly African.'[4] John Paul II said that 'Africa was in need of a space of liberty and creativity' (during his second visit to Africa in 1982); and, speaking to bishops of Kenya, said: 'Not only Christianity, but Christ himself, through his members in Africa, is African.' 'It is all of Christian life that needs to be inculturated,' declared the African Synod held in Rome in 1994. The bishops emphasized liturgy: 'a special attention must be brought to liturgical and sacramental inculturation, because it directly concerns all the people who bring their participation to it.'[5] It is in this large frame that the Zairean Rite of Mass must be located.

2. The Zairean Rite of Mass

Following the recommendations of the Encyclical *Mediator Dei* of 20 November 1947, which recommended among other things the 'active participation' of the faithful in the liturgy, there arose in Africa during the decade 1950–60 several African musical versions of the Mass; for instance: the Mass of the Savannahs in Burkina Faso, the Fang Mass in Gabon, the *Misa Luba* and the *Misa Katanga* in the Democratic Republic of Congo, the Creole Mass in Senegal, the Mass of the Boatmen in Congo-Brazzaville, and so on.

Encouraged by the words of Vatican II (*Sacrosanctum Concilium*), different dioceses engaged in pastoral efforts at active and participative liturgical celebrations. In effect, the *Sacrosanctum Concilium* stipulates

94

that 'the faithful do not witness this mystery of faith as foreign and mute spectators, but participate actively in the sacred action (n. 48); in order to promote active participation, we will favour acclamations of people, responses, canticles and also actions or gestures and corporal attitudes' (nn. 30 et 38).

It was in 1972 that the Episcopal Conference of the Democratic Republic of Congo (then Zaire) asked the evangelization commission to undertake a methodic study of the appropriate modes of expression for the celebration of the Eucharist in Zaire. Taking as a base the Roman Rite and gaining inspiration on the one hand from the Ambrosian, Ethiopian and Oriental Rites, and on the other hand from the socio-cultural context of local traditional congregations (which insist on welcoming, listening, debating with dialogue and feast-festivities), the commission created the Zairean Rite. Approved by the Holy See on 30 April 1988 under the title Roman Missal for the Dioceses of Zaire,[6] this rite is performed in the following stages: Opening Rite – Liturgy of the Word – Liturgy of the Eucharist – Concluding Rite.

2.1 Description

Opening Rite

- Introduction by the host: presents the celebrants and then the visitors.
- Entry of the priests and ministers, accompanied by dancing.
- Veneration of the altar: salutation, with the forehead touching the altar on all four sides.
- Greeting of the congregation.
- Invitation to the congregation to put themselves in the presence of God and to unite with all who preceded us in the faith.
- Invocation of the saints, including our ancestors (the Holy Virgin Mary – patriarchs and prophets – apostles and evangelists – all the saints of heavens – ancestors who were right at heart, etc.).
- *Gloria* and homage to God.
- Opening prayer (preceded by the invitation to the people to pray and to lift their hands).

Liturgy of the Word

- Blessing of the readers, proclamation of the Word, acclamation of the people – Gospel – homily – profession of faith – penitential act – greeting of peace.

Liturgy of the Eucharist

- Presentation of the gifts by the faithful (accompanied by dancing), then by the priest to God, the prayer of the offerings, the eucharistic prayer (preface prayed alternatively), communion, *Agnus Dei*.

Concluding Rite

- Final prayer and blessing.

We realize that the Zairean Rite presents new elements and a change of order in relation to the Roman Rite: the invocation of the ancestors, the litany of the saints that precedes the *Gloria*, the *Kyrie* that comes after the *Gloria* and the exchange of peace that precedes the presentation of the gifts.

2.2 Originality and Characteristics

Originality

'The originality of this liturgy is due to its dynamic vision of global inculturation. It strives to harmonize, in a sacred action, unified and realistic, the salvific mystery of faith and the local socio-cultural universe; it aims to progressively eliminate the alienating parallelism or dichotomy between both.'[7] This originality is based on the spiritual vision of life in Africa: the communion of the visible and the invisible worlds.[8] Conscious of this reality, the African 'seizes as finitude in the presence of a reality that has the quality of the infinite, to know the Sacred, God in person'; he celebrates it in those forms of worship in which he seeks to render present in the visible world the invisible world, and holds fast to the 'invisible or sacred world, which we seek

96

proximity to in order to participate in its power and be beatified by it'.[9]

Characteristics

The change of order of certain elements of the rite, compared to their order in the Roman Rite, can be explained as follows:

(a) The invocation of the saints, including ancestors. The presence of God materializes itself through the invocation of the saints, which means entering into communion with the celestial family of God, where our own ancestors preceded us, the saints of our terrestrial families, men with good hearts, allied of God, mediators of his kindness. Ancestors are, for Africans, those from whom came life, wisdom and the kindness of which only God is the source and the plenitude; those whose good example guides our communal march towards the Father. The invocation of the saints and ancestors concludes with the joyous singing of the *Gloria* to the Triune God.[10]

(b) The *Kyrie* comes after the proclamation and the explication of the Word of God and the utterance of fidelity to God (*Credo*). It is immediately followed by the exchange of peace: in the African palaver, speech implies listening, total frankness, the integral freedom of the participants, dialogue and communion, and it can be completed with a sacrifice (the resolution of a conflict through language). Listening to the Word of Christ involves all of these same elements. God calls his people together, gathers, questions. The Word of God is efficient and liberating. The exchange of peace that follows means 'reconciliation, harmony'. The sharing of the peace implies both a vertical reconciliation with God in the communion of the saints, and a horizontal reconciliation of ourselves with our neighbours. Then, with a lightened heart and a transparent conscience, we are admitted to present prayers and offerings, in accordance with the teachings of Jesus himself (Matthew 5:23–24). God loves the one who gives with joy (II Corinthians 8:7).[11]

(c) Corporal expression. Liberated from artificial inhibitions and constraints, the believer expresses faith through bodily movement and moves to a sacred dance, like David dancing in front of the Ark of the

97

Covenant (II Samuel 6:20; Matthew 11:17); these bodily expressions of faith translate into attitudes, gestures, acclamations and light sways of the body. It is the whole man who prays, body and soul. The rhythmic movements express the participation of the whole self in prayer.[12]

3. Conclusion

The fruit of a long process of research and dialogue with the Holy See,[13] this rite establishes a communion between the people and the divine mystery. It is faith expressing itself in a given cultural context. A Catalonian liturgist who worked for many years in Bolivia observed this rite and said it 'contains a certain number of elements that can offer valid suggestions for research in other countries ... the celebration of the Zairean Rite of Mass gives me, sometimes, the impression of drawing closer to the majesty of the Oriental Rite than to the stripped severity of the Roman Rite.'[14] A rite is not celebrated from the outside; it invites you to live it from the inside, not only to better understand its values, but also to pray as one of the people.

As for that which concerns the Company of Jesus in Africa, while we find colleagues who celebrate this rite with success and eloquence in the parishes and locations where their obedience sent them, we also note that this rite is surprisingly absent inside the Company; this is probably due to the lack of liturgism that characterizes us, but perhaps also because of the inadequate measure of conviction that inculturation is given among our priorities.

8

Questions on the Liturgy: The Case of the Congolese (Zairean) Rite

Jules Kipupu Kafuti, SJ

From the liturgical reforms of Vatican II, we have recovered a sense of the fundamental importance of the liturgy in our Christian and religious life. This development is good news for the Church throughout the world. But my concern is at another level, and has to do with the implementation of this liturgy in the particular contexts where we live. The difficulty could be this: how can we fully live the liturgy of a local church when this liturgy is only perceived as the Roman Rite in disguise?

I come from a country, the Congo, where the Church has worked hard on inculturation in the field of liturgy. The Congolese Rite of Mass is the fruit of a long theological, pastoral and liturgical work, extending itself over many years, having as its purpose the adaptation of the Christian religion to the religious and cultural genius of the Congolese people. Coming out of the work of the inculturation of Christianity on Congolese soil, the rite is based on triple fidelity: fidelity to faith and to the apostolic tradition; fidelity to the intimate nature of the Catholic liturgy; and fidelity to the religious genius of the African and Congolese cultural heritage. The question of Congolese liturgy necessarily requires the implementation of the principles of inculturation.

But this inculturation is not unproblematic: it is here that we perceive the difficulty of maintaining the correct balance between unity and diversity in Christian liturgy. If our liturgy is that of the Church, must we not know of which Church? And we cannot avoid this tension between the unity of the Christian liturgy and the diversity of forms that liturgy can take inside the same universal Catholic

Church. In the understanding of the Congolese Episcopal Conference, the Congolese Rite of Mass is the authentic expression of the encounter between the people of God and their Creator, in joy, festivities and dance; it proposes a liturgical celebration in which the human person – spirit, heart and body – participates actively. All the joy and the genius of our culture we have wanted to put at the service of our faith and celebration. It has never been a question of simply adding a little local colour to the Roman Rite. This is true even if the Congregation for the Doctrine of the Faith indicated to the Congolese bishops that the definite title kept for 'the project of the liturgy of mass in Congo, was the Roman Missal for the Dioceses of Congo'.[1] But Congolese Christians continue to believe that inculturation must be both creative and faithful, that inculturation is not worth anything if it remains just a simple disguise and pure folklore, despite what many think of this Congolese Rite. To reduce our liturgical celebrations to songs and dances is to truly misunderstand everything that lies at the base of this project of the Congolese Rite, and, as a result, to refuse to perceive all the richness that the Church of Congo, like every particular church, can offer to the universal Church.

Would the universal Church continue to hold as external to the essence of the Christian liturgy the theological and cultural contributions that have issued from other people and other civilizations? Then inculturation would be merely a pretty word that did not mean anything after all. How then can we live this tension between the local church and the universal Church? What can we do for our liturgy to be fully that of the Church in which we work? In this context, how can we work to render the liturgy a living part of our communities and how can we train liturgical leaders to celebrate the praises of God according to the liturgy of a particular church?

I believe we always enter into a local church that lives a determinate liturgy: we must take this into account in liturgical training. This supposes, of course, an adequate knowledge of the culture and the deep and religious meaning of the people of God who form this church. Two examples could clarify what I want to say here. First, the Congolese Rite of Mass is based on the style and the structure of the African dialogue. All the penitential celebration of this rite is based on

100

this structure. But how is one to appreciate this structure when it is perceived as long and useless chatting? We have talked a lot about the South African Commission 'Truth and Reconciliation': this commission, as we know, has done its work relying on the structure of the African dialogue. But could this constitute, in its structure, an enrichment for the universal Church? Secondly, we observe here in Europe, at least in certain Catholic churches, that the litany of the saints is lengthened with names of persons who are not always Christian Catholics or canonized (Martin Luther King, Gandhi). The Congolese Rite of the Mass brings something new to the universal Church when it integrates faithful, right-hearted ancestors into the invocation of the saints.

Yes, we must strive to rediscover the fully ecclesiastical and communitarian liturgical life. Yes, it is necessary to integrate liturgy in our catechetical life. But, how can we do this in a context in which the specificity of a culture imposes a fundamental liturgical reform which is not simply a pure remake in local colours of the Roman Rite? How can we live our faith in the universal Church without betraying our duty to a local church that strives to live its faith in a liturgy which is specific to it, but badly perceived?

9

The Eucharist as *Diakonia*: From the Service of Cult to the Service of Charity

Cesare Giraudo, SJ

1. The Eucharist amidst Feelings, Devotion and Little Else

If one were to investigate what expressions recur most often in the spontaneous introductions of the Sunday eucharistic celebration, many would report the one presiding to say things like: 'Brothers and sisters, we are gathered here today to celebrate/to celebrate together/to celebrate around the one table.' On important occasions, such language would be choreographed together with joyful singing, colourfully costumed dancers, enthusiastic applause and blinding camera flashes. The presider has announced a party, has invited active participation in it, and the assembly responds enthusiastically. Far be it from me to disparage the efforts of those who try to translate difficult concepts into accessible terms. Being together and joyful are precious experiences, ever more needed by our culture that is increasingly exposed to the dangers of loneliness, alienation and discomfort. Nevertheless, such an interpretation of the Eucharist leaves me deeply unsatisfied, and leads me to ask, 'Is the Eucharist only about joy – the joyful sharing in a meal – or are there other elements within our corporate worship which reflect the hungers within human society which cry out for our attention?'

I realize that in this festive encounter it is not easy to bring up the doctrine of the sacrificial nature of the Mass, which the Council of Trent insisted on so strongly. In the Roman Catholic context, the presider himself would be the first to recognize that the Mass is a sacrifice. But, finding the explanation of this truth arduous, he would leap over it to land smoothly, systematically and with legitimate pastoral satisfaction on the far easier path of the festal-convivial explanation, which I have just described. And what is to be said of sacramental communion? Naturally that we communicate with the real and ongoing presence; in other words, that in the Eucharist we receive the actual body and blood of the Lord who enters into us and remains as long as the eucharistic species do. When we recall the fishermen surprised by the sudden storm on the Sea of Galilee who tried to shake Jesus awake, or Nicodemus who sought Jesus out by night to relish his words in secret, or the woman who touched the hem of his cloak, or the many others who, even though stifled by the crowds, threw themselves upon him certain of obtaining a miracle, do we not say to ourselves, 'Oh, lucky them! Aren't they lucky to have seen Jesus, to have talked to him, to know his voice, his gestures, his attention! It has not been our lot to receive all this grace from God. No, with the gift of the real and ongoing presence, we walk in faith with him, talk with him in his sacramental presence, we "visit" him in church; we keep company with the Divine Prisoner of the Tabernacle! Even if Thomas could consider himself fortunate to have placed his hand in Jesus' side, the beatitude was not pronounced for him but for those who believe even though they have not seen (John 20:29); and we are they.' These reflections, and so many others that alternate by turns in the secret of our hearts, while dogmatically unobjectionable, nevertheless pose a serious limitation. They are accompanied by an exclusively static understanding of the real and ongoing presence, as if the mystery of the Eucharist did not include anything else.

In short, given the notions most often inculcated by presiders and catechists, the mystery of the Eucharist is forced by an exclusively convivial presentation and by a static understanding. In the former the limitation is expressed by the adverb 'exclusively' and in the latter it is expressed by the adjective 'static'.

As people were leaving church from this Eucharist, what if a voice would challenge them to respond to the question, 'Returning to ordinary life, what resolutions do you carry with you?' I bet that many would find the question odd – too invasive or demanding, perhaps, saying, 'What? Was this confession? Weren't we taught that good resolutions come out of a good confession? What does this have to do with Mass?'

Given such a static, devotional and detached understanding of the Eucharist associated with so many of our celebrations, we have to ask ourselves, for example, 'Is this all there is to the theology of the Eucharist? Does such a static-devotional understanding of the Eucharist truly respond to the purpose for which the Lord Jesus, on the eve of his Passion, wanted to institute the sacrament of his body and blood? For example, couldn't participation in the Eucharist be expressed in a renewed commitment to justice?'

To respond to these questions, we must let ourselves be formed and shaped by the *lex orandi* – by the very liturgy we celebrate – exactly as the Church did in the first millennium, during the time of the Fathers. Then, especially with regard to the theology of the Eucharist, mystagogues and neophytes prayed first and then believed; they prayed in order to believe, they prayed to know how and what to believe. That was the rule of prayer then – of the eucharistic prayer – and it is the rule of prayer now – to be transformed by that Eucharist which we celebrate.

By framing my reflection in terms of the prayer by which the Church has always celebrated the Eucharist, I am guided by two fundamental themes: Eucharist and *diakonia*. These are two very rich themes that interact and illuminate each other.

2. Eucharist: The Semantic Breadth of an Ancient Word

The term 'Eucharist', which took shape in the Greek language, has two millennia of active Christian use. An early witness to its antiquity is Justin, who already used it to refer to the memorial of the Lord. We know that this illustrious Church Father, born in Samaria to Greek colonists, who converted from paganism and who was put to death for his Christian faith in Rome around the year 165, was neither bishop nor presbyter nor deacon, but – as we would say today – a committed lay person. In his famous Apology, directed to the pagans of Rome to defend Christians from defamatory accusations, he left us the oldest description of the Mass.

2.1 The Pair 'Eucharistèin / Eucharistia' in Justin's Account

After describing the first part of the Sunday celebration, that is the liturgy of the Word, Justin proceeds like so:

> Then bread, wine and water are brought, and the one who is presiding stands up and supplicates and eucharistizes [i.e. presides] as he is able, and the people express their approval by acclaiming Amen. Then the eucharistized elements are distributed, and received by each person; by means of the deacons some is sent to those who were not present.[1]

This account highlights two structural elements of the eucharistic prayer: thanksgiving and supplication. We should not be surprised that Justin seems to reverse the order. It is his style to say first what should logically come second, and vice versa. All the Old Testament and Jewish prayers praise God first, then make supplication. It is important to pay attention to Jewish and Christian prayers together, for Christianity grew up out of the Old Testament by means of Judaism, and people often forget that the first generations of Christians for a long time continued to pray to God the Father with formulas used by Jesus the Jew.

Apart from calling the first part of the eucharistic prayer the Eucharist, Justin also speaks of the eucharistized elements. This expression certainly suggested itself to him by the convivial nature of the Jewish liturgy, which was the context of the Last Supper. The Jerusalem Talmud, faithful interpreter of Jewish tradition, allows the father of a family to entreat each and all of the guests by means of the following expression of courtesy: 'Take the bread, it is blessed.'[2] This is a contracted expression, which should be understood to mean 'Take the bread upon which a blessing has been pronounced.' In Jewish teleology, what is blessed is never the elements of the meal but always

105

and only God who is blessed 'on the bread', that is, because of the bread, the wine, and all the other gifts by which God feeds and sustains us.

Obviously, from a faith point of view there is a gap between the convivial Jewish context and the Christian Eucharist. In the Jewish context, the bread and wine remain simple bread and wine, even though the blessing pronounced upon them gives them a sacred character. In the Christian context, because of the eucharistic prayer pronounced upon them, they are substantially transformed such that – as Justin solemnly declares – they are no longer 'common bread nor common drink' but 'the flesh and blood of Jesus who became incarnate'.[3] Once we recognize the radical difference between the convivial elements in the two contexts, we can legitimately conclude that it was precisely the rapid designation of the sacramental body and blood as eucharistized elements – that is as elements on which the entire thanksgiving has been pronounced – that named the memorial of the death and resurrection of the Lord with the specific denomination of 'Eucharist'.

2.2 The Semitic Ground of the Pair
'Eucharistèin/Eucharistia'

We continue our word investigation. Justin's insight that defines the first part of the prayer as Eucharist is confirmed in the Greek formulas. In these, the controlling verb of the preface, and therefore of the entire prayer, is undoubtedly 'eucharistèin', which the ancient Latin version of the anaphora in the Apostolic Tradition recorded in the Verona palimpsest expresses as 'gratias referre', which is a version of 'gratias agere'.

When translating the semantic group 'eucharistèin' and 'gratias agere' into, for example, Italian, some readily choose 'to thanks', for 'to give thanks' is not really ordinary usage. Nevertheless, it is legitimate to ask, What is the proper meaning of 'gratias agere' in the framework of the eucharistic prayer? Is it synonymous with 'benedicere' [to bless] with which it forms a dyad with the institution narrative?

106

In order to appreciate the theological breadth of the verb '*gratias agere*', we must be ready to undertake an extensive retrospective into the past. We skip over its immediate etymological meaning from ordinary Latin to go back to the Greek verb '*eucharistèin*' which it is supposed to translate. In turn, the New Testament and liturgical verb '*eucharistèin*' itself cannot be understood in terms of its immediate etymological meaning in ordinary Greek, for the Christian use of '*eucharistèin*' pertains in effect to the religious and sacral language of biblical Greek. Consequently, it must be read in terms of its originating Hebrew matrix, which the term is supposed to translate.

In our journey back into the past, Syriac must also guide us. Syriac has the honour of being a Christian language, thoroughly rooted in New Testament Greek, while at the same time it is also a Semitic language – called pure Eastern Aramaic – since it is a variant of the language spoken by Jesus and the apostolic generation. The whole of Syriac literature, liturgical as well as patristic, demonstrates that the origin of the semantic pair '*eucharistèin/eucharistia*' is the pair '*yadà/tawdita*', which is identical to the Hebrew pair '*yadàh/todà*' (to confess/confession), typical of Old Testament eucology. To understand their exact meaning, one need only read the account that frames the long penitential prayer of Nehemiah 6:37. There the text says that the Sons of Israel 'maintained a religious attitude and confessed their sins and those of their fathers, and they confessed [the Lord] and adored the Lord.' (Nehemiah 9:2-3).

The religious usage of the Old Testament root '*yadàh*' eminently expresses the attitude of a vassal – and thus of a supplicant – who is about to be reintegrated into the relationship. In fact the Hebrew '*yadàh*', when referring to a term that expresses culpability, means that the supplicating vassal confesses his own sin; when referring instead to God, it means that the human partner is confessing his Lord. However this does not mean two different confessions, for the two connotations imply each other. Understood in a cultic context, the attitude of the human partner who 'confesses' and who 'confesses himself' is neither pure contemplation of divine transcendence nor a self-flagellating contemplation of one's own sinful condition. When the human partner resolves to confess his own sins, he adverts that the ultimate term or goal of the confession is not 'his' sin, but the Lord who alone is able to re-establish him in a covenant relation which is ever new.

Although the verb to confess (to give thanks), in its proper praise dimension, combines readily with all the verbs of celebration – and thus becomes synonymous with 'to bless', 'to praise', 'to celebrate', etc. – nevertheless the semantic group '*yadàh/eucharistèin/gratias agere*' does not lose its other originating connotation of confession of sin. This is why the first section of the eucharistic prayer is the ritual anamnesis of a double story of relationship, that is, a historical confession of God's faithfulness and our unfaithfulness, a historical confession of grace and a historical confession of sin.

Despite the practical equivalence of the above semantic group to the related verbs, its full breadth cannot in any way be reduced to our poor modern way of thanking or of saying 'thank you'. We know that when the biblical supplicant turns to God – and so the Church celebrating the Eucharist – it is wholly stretched or extended towards the One from whom come the 'mighty works' of the shared story of relationship, without dwelling pettily on each single gift received. The fact that the Old Testament '*yadàh*' became the New Testament Greek '*eucharistèin*' and then in the old Latin versions '*gratias agere*', must be understood in the context of the translations of inevitable semantic slippage: once it is combined with the verb 'to bless' the verb 'to confess' becomes understood in a way that limits it to the connotation of praise and gratitude. Thus we must be careful not to understand the term to be translated in terms of what it expresses in ordinary 'profane' language, but rather in terms of its semantic antecedents, understood as expressions of religious language.

With complete respect for the choices made by the ancient translators, however, I believe that to continue down the track that '*gratias agere*' leads to thanking would only make it more difficult to access the theological richness that the original pair '*yadàh/todà*' (to confess/confession) has effectively transmitted to us and still transmits today to the Aramaic and Syriac-speaking Churches. With regard to our situation, to maintain wisely a certain formal level of language can give pastors points for fruitful catecheses, while a rushed adoption of ordinary language would make this impossible.

The configuration of the group '*yadàh/eucharistèin/gratias agere*', as the controlling verb of the anaphoric formula, should not be confused with the configuration of the verbs '*eucharistèin*' and '*eulogèin*' in the institution narrative. To understand the latter, one must turn to the standardization of the Jewish liturgy, which favoured the group '*baràk/eulogèin*' (to bless), imposing it as the absolute beginning of every horizontal expression. New Testament literature, perhaps distancing itself from the Jewish standard in order to begin a new Christian standard, reverted to the ancient verb '*yadàh*' (to confess), rendering it in Greek not as '*exomologèisthai*' or '*exagoreùein*' – both with the double Old Testament meaning of 'confession' – but as '*eucharistèin*'. With this substitution, the scriptural institution narratives attest a moment of instability, allowing sometimes one, sometimes the other verb to prevail. Instead the institution narratives in the anaphoras, because of the notable tendency of their horizontal texts to pile up synonyms, usually combine the two verbs in pairs. Then their recurrence, which takes on an immediate celebratory note, assumes the meaning of the two brief institutive 'blessings' that Jesus pronounced on the bread and the chalice. Finally it must be noted that the foundational double connotation of '*eucharistèin*' as principal directive guiding verb in the anaphoric expressions subsists, even with the material absence not only of the verb itself but also of any other verb that is habitually associated with it for a celebratory meaning. In effect the anaphoric expression, as with any other Old Testament, Jewish or non-anaphoric Christian prayer, is not linked to the material recurrence of this or that verb, but stands in virtue of the structure that makes it a literary form.

2.3 The Historic Depth of the Anaphoric 'Confession'

Let us now consider the teleology of the first part of the anaphora, the part that Justin designates as Eucharist and which in the fairly linear structure of the Antiochene anaphoras goes from the preface to the anamnesis properly so called. We shall be guided by the *lex orandi*, which we will interpret on the basis of the ancient anaphora of the Apostolic Constitutions, found in the eighth book of an anthology of liturgical texts called 'Apostolic Constitutions'.[4] It is the longest known eucharistic prayer, so long that many scholars believe that it was never used, that a prolix interpreter simply interpolated a very brief anaphora from the Apostolic Tradition as an exercise. Textual analysis, however, belies this interpretation. In fact the anaphora of the Apostolic Constitutions comes from an ancient tradition that goes directly back to the Jewish synagogue prayer. The key comes from a Judeo-Greek formulary in the seventh book of the same Apostolic Constitutions.

I presuppose that the celebratory dimension, that is, the confessional and praise dimension, of this first section is expressed by the single opening verb 'to extol' ('*anamnèin*'), which is echoed by a repeated 'thanksgiving' ('*eucharistèin*') in the anamnesis that frames the institution narrative. The verb 'to extol', understood as a laudative variation of '*eucharistèin*,' leads a particularly broad and detailed development of confession. Here are a few brief passages from the Apostolic Constitutions.

It is truly right and just first of all to extol you, you who are truly God, who exist before all generated things, from whom every paternity in heaven and on earth takes its name, the only ungenerated, without beginning, without king and sovereign, without need, dispenser of every good, superior to every cause and origin, always and in everything identical to yourself, from whom, as from a storehouse, every thing comes into existence. You brought all things into existence out of nothing by means of your only-begotten Son. Indeed by means of him, eternal God, you made all things, and by his means you deemed everything worthy of suitable providence; by means of him you give existence and by his means you also grant a comfortable existence.

In this introduction to praise (or preface), God is celebrated for God's sake, then for the sake of creation in which his Son participated equally. Here the text swells to an impassioned proclamation that exalts the greatness of creation, to arrive at the creation of humankind recalling with praise what is narrated in Genesis 2:

You indeed, almighty God, by means of Christ planted a garden in Eden, in the east, adorning it with every kind of edible plant, and there, as in a sumptuous dwelling, you inserted humankind; in creating it, you gave it the innate law, so that it would have within itself the seeds of divine knowledge. And by placing it in this garden of delights, you granted humankind power over all things for sustenance; but of only one thing did you forbid the tasting in the hopes of better goods.

At this point the idyll is interrupted. The memory of the other event in the primordial relationship is inserted here:

And when, because of the serpent's deceit and the woman's advice, he violated the commandment and ate of the forbidden fruit, he was justly expelled from the garden.

Adam did not reciprocate the plan that his Creator and Father had conceived for him. But God does not behave like a human parent who has been deprived, who had counted on the daughter or son and, disappointed, is disheartened. God always has the remedy handy. So the text proceeds thus:

Nevertheless in your goodness you did not despise forever that which was dying – who indeed was your work – but you who had submitted all creation to him gave him the means to procure food and by his sweat and labour, while you make everything sprout and grow and ripen. Then after putting him to sleep for a short while, with an oath you called him to regeneration and, having dissolved the limits of death, you announced life to him through the resurrection.

The text of the anaphora, rereading Genesis 3, speaks of the transgression of the commandment 'because of the serpent's deceit' and of Adam's just expulsion from the garden. This rereading of the punishment is exceedingly serene, far more serene and indulgent than the biblical text itself. It affirms that, even though the logic of the Covenant required the removal from the relational space of the one who had already excluded himself, nevertheless God did not disdain (*hyperoràn* [literally: look down from above]) him definitively, refraining from pronouncing a definitive sentence of death. The condemnation to eat 'by sweat and toil' is met by the attentive commitment of God who makes everything sprout, grow and ripen.

The same is said of physical death, which is here compared to a dream, indeed a short dream. Because Adam has violated the commandment, for punishment he is put to sleep 'for a brief time', rather like a disobedient child (cf. Romans 5:19). But in the very same instant that God, with motherly pedagogy, places him on the bed – in other words, in the tomb – with an oath God guarantees him a swift reawakening. Even though common sense and scientific observation tell us that the world is young, and that Adam's and our sojourn in the sepulchre will last centuries and millennia, such long stretches of time are nothing compared to the solemnity of the oath by which God announced to the progenitor Adam the resurrection and life. Indeed, in the very moment when death seems to take definitive control of the human condition, the limit (*'horòs'*) of its possession is definitively dissolved and its power made vain, because the day of Christ's resurrection is already shining on Adam.

From recalling Adam's story, the prayer moves on to that of his descendants. These are considered through a review of Old Testament personages that begins with Abel and concludes significantly with Joshua, which in Greek (*Iesoús*) corresponds exactly to the name of Jesus. Clearly the Greek homonym plays an evocative role between the figure of the guide who brought people into the Promised Land, and the figure of the Messiah.

After the preface comes the angelic hymn, and then the post-sanctus, which is a celebratory memorial of Christology in history:

Holy also is your Son the Only-begotten, our Lord and God Jesus Christ who, serving you in all things, his God and Father, in the great variety of creation and in appropriate providence he did not disdain dying humankind. After the natural law, after the exhortation of the Law, after the appeals of the prophets and the interventions of the angels, he himself took delight in your decision that the creator of the universe should become human, that the legislator be submitted to the law, that the high priest become victim and the shepherd become sheep; you, his God and Father, he made well disposed and reconciled you with the world, and freed all from the wrath that was threatening.

Christ did not 'disdain' the human race. The Greek verb is *'perioran'* which means 'to look around, here and there'. Christ did not regard us in a distracted fashion but with compassion, and he suffered with the human race 'that was dying'. If the eucharistic prayer really could be reduced to a simple 'thanksgiving', then what would be the sense of mentioning our disobedience alongside the divine faithfulness? Would it not be excessive to thank God for that? The text continues:

He lived as an honest citizen and taught according to the laws. He expelled every sickness and wasting; he worked signs and wonders among the people, and he who feeds all who need nourishment and fills every living creature with good things himself ate, drank and slept. He made your name manifest to those who did not know it, he chased away ignorance, he reawakened pity, fulfilled your will, completed the work you gave him to do. And, when he had fulfilled all these things, he fell into the hands of the impious and being submitted to every dishonour with your permission, he was handed over to the governor Pilate, the judge was judged, the saviour was condemned, the impassible one was nailed to the cross, the one who was immortal by nature died, who gives life was buried. To free from suffering and to snatch away from death those from whom it had come, and to break the chains of the devil and to free people from his deceptions. He rose from the dead on the third day and, after having lingered for forty days with his disciples, he was assumed into the heavens, was seated in the heavens and sat at your right hand, his God and Father.

At this point the commemoration of Christology in history converges on and is summed up in the institution narrative. The proclamation of Christology in history and of the institution narrative are in all the eucharistic prayers, precisely to remind God that Christ, having made himself equal to us in all things but sin (cf. Ephesians 4:15), charged himself with our sin. On the other hand, when he instituted the Eucharist, the Lord himself repeatedly asked to eat his body and drink his blood which were about to be handed over and scattered 'for the remission of sins'. The Church dwells on the Lord's insistence precisely by means of the proclamation of the institution narrative and the subsequent anamnesis.

An attentive reading of the eucharistic prayer in light of the tradition leaves us to understand that the first part is confession of God's faithfulness and our sin, confession of his grace and of our continuing expectation of redemption. Only on the juridical basis of this humble yet exalting double confession will the voice of the praying Church be able to go beyond this to ask God, in the next intercession, to transform us into the one ecclesial body through our communion with the sacramental body.

So far our study has concentrated only on the Eucharist. Read in the light of the Semitic ground represented by the semantic pair '*yadàh/todà*' (to confess/confession) this notion basically expresses the vertical relation that binds the vassal to its Lord, and thus the individual and God. But in the context of the liturgical celebration, the notion of Eucharist-confession expresses the whole relationship of the entire celebrating community to its divine partner, more than the individual's relationship to God. The fact that all the principal verbs of the anaphora constantly appear in the plural confirms that the community is the subject of action, the community who says 'we confess you' ('*eucharistoumèn soi*'). In so far as the community gathered under the presidency of the bishop or presbyter proclaims the eucharistic confession, it already implies the 'communitarian' dimension, transversal relationship among individuals. Such a sacral relation, both vertical and horizontal, is confirmed and further specified by the other term – '*diakonia*' – a guiding theme of the present reflection.

3. *Diakonia*: A 'Bridge' Between Liturgy and Life

Scholars investigating the Old Testament basis of any New Testament word form know from experience how fruitful it is to pay attention to the Septuagint, given the importance of this ancient translation for New Testament, liturgical and patristic literature. However, the same scholars also know from experience that their hopes are not always rewarded, which is the case with our semantic pairs, *'eucharistèin/eucharistia'* and *'diakonèin/diakonia'*. In the former case, the Septuagint's parsimonious use of *'eucharistèin/eucharistia'* offers a glimmer of hope for research, while it remains inexorably silent in the case of *'diakonèin/diakonia'*. Of course, this inexplicable silence does not mean that the notion expressed by *'diakonèin/diakonia'* is absent from either Septuagint Greek or biblical Hebrew. Let us say rather that the notion of service, linked with precise New Testament terminology, is expressed by a complex of related terms in biblical Hebrew and in Septuagint Greek. Nevertheless, given that it is impossible to proceed on the basis of strict lexical correspondence, we must look for further Semitic substrata for the notion of service.

3.1 Adam as Liturgist: the Liturgical Connotation of the Service of Relationship

In this study I will restrict my attention to one particularly significant biblical verse, which I will consider in the light of some interpretations and reinterpretations of the faith of ancient Israel. It is Genesis 2:15, which in the Masoretic text reads like this:

> And the Lord God took Adam
> and placed him in the garden of Eden,
> so that he would serve it and care for it.

Let us examine the third verse. The verb that I translate as *'serve'* is the Hebrew *''abàd'*, a term which, like so many others, has two meanings: 'to work' and 'to serve'. While at the level of the narrative's immediate

115

sense the expression means 'so that he would work it and care for it', on the theological level it expresses the service that the vassal Adam must render to his Lord, attentively caring for the new relationship described by means of the image of the garden and of the relational barrier.

From the verb *"abàd"*, a privileged term in the covenant typology, the specifically theological connotation is carried by the noun *"abodà"*. In the book of Exodus the positive form of this noun expresses the service of a relationship, that is, the new relationship between Israel-vassal and her Lord, and the negative form expresses the previous 'slavery' to Pharaoh. In the *Targums*, as often happens, Genesis 2:15 becomes more robust. Indeed these ancient translations intended for cultic use are concerned to stretch the density of the scriptural text for theological, homiletic and pastoral reasons. Let us look at the verse in the three *Targum* versions of the Pentateuch.

The *Onqelos Targum* reads:

> And Adonai Elohim led Adam
> to dwell in the garden of Eden,
> so he would cultivate [*palàh'*] it and care for it.

The *Neofiti I Targum* reads:

> And Adonai Elohim took Adam
> to dwell in the garden of Eden
> so that he might render cult [*palàh*] according to the Law and
> care for the commandments.

Finally, the *Pseudo-Gionata Targum* says:

> And Adonai Elohim led Adam from the mountain of cult
> [*palàh*], where God had created him,
> to dwell in the garden of Eden,
> so that he might render cult [*palàh*] according to the Law and
> care for his commandments.

In the *Targum* redactions, the Hebrew verb *"abàd'* (to work/to serve) is always translated with the Aramaic verb *'palàh'*, which connotes the idea of 'to cleave'. Biblical Hebrew will use it to say, for example, 'to cleave the earth with the plough' (cf. Psalms 141:7). Targumic Aramaic and Syriac literature will often use it to mean either 'to cultivate the earth' (cf. Genesis 2:5) or, as in our case, 'to offer cult to God'. These are related connotations, analogous to the Latin expressions *'colere argum'* and *'colere Deum'*. Even the terms 'cultivation', 'culture' and 'cult' are related. Just as the cultivation of the field is 'cultivation' and the cultivation of the mind is 'culture', so the cultivation of one's feelings toward the divine becomes 'cult'. One should not be surprised then that the *Neofiti I Targum* and the *Pseudo-Gionata Targum*, which belong to the same tradition,[5] deliberately underline Adam's cultic vocation. The *Midrash Beresìt Rabbà*, commenting on Genesis 2:5, clarifies: 'the expression "to serve it and to care for it" refers to the sacrifices.'

These cultic interpretations are not surprising, especially when we remember that in a Jewish context the term *"abodà'* (service) means cultic service, understood as service *par excellence*.

For the sake of completeness, it should be pointed out that alongside the verb *"abàd'* the Hebrew Bible often places the verb *'seret'*, from the root *'saràt'*, as an analogous meaning and with direct liturgical connotations. Nevertheless, the fact that Hebrew does not have a noun derived from the root *'saràt'* – indeed *'serutà'* is used only in Aramaic – means that it must use the noun *"abodà'* to express the properly cultic connotation. This means that *"abàd'* and *'saràt'* are often perceived as synonyms. Thus when the Septuagint seeks to render in Greek the cultic nuances it perceives in the forms derived from the roots *"abàd'* and *'saràt'*, it chooses the semantic pair *'leitourgèin/leitourgia'*. Indeed, the angels, which the Hebrew Bible calls *'mesartim'*, become in Greek *'leitourgòi'* (cf. Psalms 103:21; 104:4). To find the relationship between *'leitourgèin/leitourgia'* and *'diakonèin/diakonia'* – which, as recalled earlier the Septuagint does not have – one must wait until Christian literature. Nevertheless it would be naïve to hope to find the notion of cultic service attributed to *'diakonèin/diakonia'* when the Septuagint has fixed it on *'leitourgèin/leitourgia'*. Yet there are some significant instances, especially in the euchological formulas. In the anaphora of the Apostolic Tradition, from an ancient Latin translation of a lost Greek original, the anamnesis goes like this:

> *Memores igitur mortis et resurrectionis eius,*
> *offerimus tibi panem et calicem,*
> *gratias tibi agentes*
> *quia nos dignos habuisti adstare coram te et tibi ministrare.*

Some think that underlying the Latin *'ministrare'* is the Greek *'hieratèuein'*, as attested in the Apostolic Constitutions.[6] I could agree with this, provided that the notion expressed by the Greek *'hieratèuein'* not be restricted only to ministerial priesthood. In effect the anamnesis is open by its very nature, in so far as the subject of its principal verbs is the entire celebrating community. Nothing says that beneath *'ministrare'* one cannot read, if not *'diakonèin'*, then at least *'litourgèin'*.

In the attempt to find some connection, let us turn to the prayers for diaconal ordination, whose theme makes them a privileged context. In the formulary of the Apostolic Tradition, one notes that, in parallel with the Latin version *'ministrare ecclesiae tuae'*, the Ethiopian version says 'so that he may be deacon in your Church'.[7] In the Apostolic Constitutions (8:18),[8] the prayer over the deacon reads like this:

> Almighty God, show your face to this your servant who has been chosen for you for ministry [*eis diakonìan*]. Grant that he, exercising faithfully the service [*leitourgèsanta/ten diakonìan*] entrusted him, may be found worthy of a higher degree.

The sacramentary of Serapion says similarly:[9]

> Father of the Only-Begotten, who have chosen bishops, presbyters and deacons for the liturgy [*eis leitourgìan*] of your catholic Church, you who chose the seven deacons through your Only

118

Begotten, and blessed with the Holy Spirit, constitute this one also a deacon [*diàkonon*] of your catholic Church, and give him the Spirit of understanding and discernment, so that in the midst of a holy people, he may serve in this liturgy [*diakonèsai en te leitourgia tauté*] in purity and without blame.

Let us now consider the diaconal theme as it is projected on to the theology of the Eucharist.

3.2 The Double Diaconal Dimension of the Eucharist

Based on the above lexical research, it can be affirmed that both the notions of *leitourgia* and *diakonia* splendidly express the attitude of the praying community that 'confesses' its Lord. We have already seen that the anaphoric celebration cannot be reduced to a mere effusion of gratitude to God for benefits received, as a superficial reading of the Greek '*eucharistèin*' and the Latin '*gratias agere*' would suggest. The entire Syriac anaphoric tradition attests instead that to celebrate the Eucharist meant to confess the faithfulness of the divine partner and our unfaithfulness. And what is our 'confession' of the Lord if not the highest expression of the Covenant ''*abodà*,' the liturgical *diakonia*?

If the term '*diakonia*', understood in its cultic connotation, and the term '*leitourgìa*' express well the praying community's 'confession' (*eucharistia/gratiarum actio*) of its Lord, the etymology of these two terms suggests interpersonal relationship, not only between the community and God but also between the community and all the present or absent members of the whole Church. Even though the etymological dictionaries say nothing about '*diakonèin*', the prefix '*dia*' is enough to evoke a relationship begun between two unequal partners, first of all between the praying community and God, and therefore between each of us and those whose feet we must wash (cf. John 13:1–15). In the case of '*litourgèin*' interpersonal involvement is clearly attested by its two components. '*Leit-*' refers to the '*laòs*', the people, and '*-ourgèin*' refers to action and service. In short, '*diakonìa*' and '*leitourgìa*' complete the theological picture of the anaphoric confession.

A comparative lexicological reflection might be helpful here. The history of the missions shows us how hard it was for the evangelists to find adequate terminology in the languages of the young churches to express concepts that took centuries to formulate adequately in the languages of the ancient churches. For example, in Madagascar, the first missionaries resorted to forced transliteration – not unusual – to express the concept of liturgy: '*litorzia*', exactly as had been done for the names of the sacraments taken directly from the corresponding French terms (cf. *batèmy, konfimasio, eokaristia, komonio, lamèsa, konfèsy, ordre, mariàzy*). Although some of these terms have by now entered into common usage, others continue to sound exotic, like '*litorzia*'. Luckily today there is also the more Malagasy-sounding expression '*fòmbam-pivavàhana*', which literally means 'prayer ritual' or 'cultic usage'.[10]

The first missionaries, sent in 1648 by Vincent de Paul to the south-east of Madagascar, were more resolute about inculturation. For example the 1657 Catechism, the first document written in Malagasy, already had the expression '*fòmbam-pivavàhana*'. Indeed the first element of this expression carries the notion of service, exactly like the Greek '*diakonìa*' and the Hebrew ''*abodà*'. Likewise, to translate the term 'Mass' into Malagasy, the Vincentian missionaries used the term '*missacabiri*', completely unknown in contemporary Malagasy. Various hypotheses have been suggested for its etymology. One scholar has recently pointed out that this term comes from an Islamic theological term '*takbir*', which means the action of recognizing the greatness of God, or the act of pronouncing the ejaculation '*Allah akbar*' (God is great).[11] The hypothesis is credible, especially given that the first missionaries regularly consulted Islamic scribes to help them inculturate religious language.

3.3 Transformation into 'One Body' as Transformation of the Whole Body

Let us return to the school of *lex orandi* and take up the anaphora of St Basil.[12] I use the version found in the Greek Patriarchate of Alexandria. Let us examine the double epiclesis and the intercessions. In this anaphora, as in all eastern anaphoras, the epiclesis on the offerings[13] comes after the institution narrative and the anamnesis, and immediately precedes the epiclesis on the communicants. The two epicleses are harmoniously linked, even from a literary point of view. Furthermore, the first epiclesis, which asks for the Holy Spirit to be sent on the gifts so they may be transformed into the body and blood of the Lord, is oriented towards the second one, which asks that the ones who are to receive communion receive the gifts connected with it. This firm link is strongly highlighted in Basil, where the two epicleses are so dependent on each other that they make one seamless horizontal paragraph. The text says it thus:

We pray and invoke you, Lord, O lover of humankind, we sinners and unworthy servants who adore you, that in your goodness you may deign to send your Holy Spirit upon us your servants and upon these your gifts that we offer, to sanctify them and manifest them as the holy mysteries of the saints, to transform this bread into the body of our Lord and Saviour Jesus Christ for the forgiveness of sins and for eternal life for those who will take of it, and that this chalice may become the precious blood of the new covenant of our Lord God and Saviour Jesus Christ, for the forgiveness of sins and for eternal life for those who will take of it; Lord, make us worthy to share in your holy mysteries, for the sanctification of our souls, bodies and spirits, so that we may become one body [*hìna genòmetha hen soma*] and one spirit, that we may share in the inheritance of all the Saints, who have pleased you ever since they were in the world.

To paraphrase it very simply, 'Send your Holy Spirit upon US and upon these GIFTS to transform them into the sacramental body so that WE, who are about to communicate, may be transformed into the one ecclesial body.'

After the gathered assembly has asked for eschatological transformation 'into one body', the intercessions expand the same request to include all the other parts of the Church who are not physically at the celebration but who nevertheless are present. The request is expanded because the entire Church is involved in every eucharistic celebration. Consequently, every part of the Church – from the hierarchical Church to the Church in everyday life, to the Church militant, to the Church triumphant – must be mentioned, so that every group and individual has their part in our ongoing transformation into the mystical body. Thus the complex of epiclesis-intercessions-praise by the people (vertical *diakonia/leitourgia*), which was earlier expressed in terms of *eucharistia, gratiarum actio* and confession, becomes supplication on behalf of the people (horizontal *diakonia/litourgia*), all parts of the people, whether present or absent.

Then what does the intercession for the universal Church ask for, that is, for the Pope, the bishop, the presbyters, the deacons and all the people of God? That they be transformed into 'one body', with all that this fundamental question implies for ethics and society, for family and professional life, horizontally and vertically.

The Latin text of the epileptic acclamation in the second eucharistic prayer for children brings this out very well. There every single intercession is followed by the acclamation 'That they may be one body!' By calling this transformation eschatological, I want to highlight how our insertion into the process of ecclesial growth occurs according to the pattern of a transformation already begun but not yet completed. This transformation happens precisely according to the rhythms of our eucharistic celebrations and our sacramental communions.

The intercessions from the anaphora of St Basil make this point explicit. After the first intercession for the universal Church, which asks the Lord to remember his 'holy, one, catholic Church', the intercession for the hierarchical Church goes like this:

First of all remember, Lord, our holy father the Archbishop N., pope and patriarch of the great city of Alexandria: by your grace may he preside over your holy Churches peacefully, with peace, security, glory, health, long life, properly dispensing your word in truth and peacefully shepherding your flock in peace. Remember Lord, the orthodox presbyters, all the order of deacons and of ministers, all those who have professed celibacy, and all your most faithful people.

The human touch is notable in this text; it motivates the assembly to ask, through its patriarch, that he may not only properly dispense the word of truth and shepherd in peace the flock entrusted to him, gifts inherent to his ministry as pastor, but also enjoy health and long life. Alongside the archbishop, who is here designated by the ancient title of 'Pope of Alexandria', are listed the other components of the ecclesial structure: presbyters, deacons, ministers, people. The intercession for the hierarchical Church should never be considered as a clerical intercession. If we take the Church as a pyramid, then how can there be a top without a base? Furthermore, the laws of physics state that the higher the point, the wider the base must be. The base of the ecclesial pyramid is none other than the people of God, mentioned clearly in this prayer.

Next comes the intercession for the Church in the world, which passes in review the various circumstances of the human condition:

Remember, Lord, the salvation of this our city, and of those who live in it. Remember, Lord, the climate and the fruits of the earth. Remember, Lord, the rains and the seeds of the earth. Remember, Lord, the orderly swelling and diminishing of the river waters. Gladden and renew the face of the earth: bathe its furrows, multiply its seedlings; give what is needed for the planting and the harvest. Govern our life: bless the cycle of the year with your benevolence, for the sake of the poor of your people, for the sake of the widow and the orphan, for the sake of the stranger in our midst, for the sake of all of us who hope in you and who invoke your holy name: that all eyes may hope in you, that you may give them food in due time. Fill our hearts with joy and rejoicing, so that, having always and everywhere everything we need, we may abound in every good work to do your holy will.

Some of these supplications may seem strange to wealthier societies who unfortunately no longer know the precariousness of living under

123

the threat of the damage caused by seasonal cataclysms. But, if we try to overcome our Western egocentrism, we realize that at the beginning of the third millennium a good portion of humankind, born in countries constantly under stress, have no difficulty identifying with the faithful of the Church of Alexandria who in every Eucharist repeated, 'Remember those of us who suffer hunger!' What about the intercession that asks God to remember the 'orderly increase of the river waters'? Does this not seem written for us who, because of rash exploitation of the land, risk our lives at every torrent of rain?

Basil's text is meaningful for another reason in particular. The intercessions are not so much intended for the satisfaction of the material needs of those praying, but rather to ensure sustenance for the poor, the orphans and widows, resident foreigners (those who have permission to stay) as well as those foreigners called 'illegals'. In short, God is asked to do his share, to bless the harvest so that those who are not in need can help those who are.

Now let us look at the more detailed and 'human' expression found in the version of Basil's prayer that is currently in use in the Byzantine Churches. The master of the *lex orandi* teaches us that God is not extraneous to any situation and that, principally through our Eucharists, God becomes engaged in our joys and especially in our sufferings. Thus we read:

> Remember, Lord, the people around here; fill the larders and cupboards with every good thing; preserve marriages in peace and harmony; raise the children, educate the youth, fortify the old; console the fainthearted, gather the scattered, lead the stray back to your holy, catholic and apostolic Church; free those afflicted by impure spirits; sail with the sailors; walk with those who are walking; care for the widows, protect the orphans, free the prisoners, heal the sick; remember those who are in the courts, in the mines, in exile, in hard slavery and in any need, trouble and tribulation; remember, O God, all who need your great compassion, those who love and those who hate, and all who have asked us to pray for them, unworthy as we are. Remember too, those whom we have neglected to mention,

whether out of ignorance or forgetfulness or the abundance of names: remember, O God, that you yourself know each person by name, and their ages, and that you have known them from their mothers' wombs. Truly, O Lord, you are attention for the neglected, hope for the desperate, rescuer of the disturbed, safe haven for sailors, physician to the sick; be everything to all of them, you who know each one and their prayer, their home, their need. And Lord, free this flock, the city and the entire region from famine, plague, earthquake, drowning, fire, and sword, from foreign invasion and from civil war.

Turning now to the intercessions in the Alexandrine version of Basil's anaphora, we find the one for the bidding Church followed by the intercession for the saints and the dead:

And because, O King, your only begotten Son has commanded us to communicate with the memory of your Saints, deign once more to remember, Lord, also those who were pleasing to you in this world: the holy fathers, the patriarchs, the apostles, the prophets, the preachers, the evangelists, the martyrs, the confessors, and every just spirit who through faith in Christ has arrived at perfection. In particular remember the most holy, most glorious, immaculate, overflowing with blessings, our Lady, mother of God and ever-virgin Mary; remember your holy and glorious prophet John, precursor, baptist and martyr; remember holy Stephen, protodeacon and protomartyr; remember our holy and blessed father Mark, apostle and evangelist; remember our holy father and wonder worker Basil; remember Saint N., whose memory we celebrate today; and the entire choir of your Saints: through their prayers and intercessions have mercy on us too, and save us for the sake of your holy Name which has been invoked upon us. Likewise remember, Lord, all those belonging to the order of priests who have died, and those belonging to the laity: deign to give rest to their souls in the bosom of the holy fathers Abraham, Isaac and Jacob; remove them from this world and plant them all in green pastures, near restful waters, in a garden of delights, from which pain, sadness and groaning have fled, in the splendour of your saints. Give rest to those whose spirits you have gathered to yourself and make them worthy of the Kingdom of Heaven.

A difference between today's liturgies and those of the past leaps immediately to the eye. While the eucharistic prayers used today ask for growth 'in communion with' the Virgin Mary, the apostles and all the saints for the assembled community, the ancient Eastern liturgies considered the saints as the first among the dead, and were not afraid to ask further eschatological transformation for them, even for Mary. The line between the two categories was not as clear then as our usual theology today leads us to think. Were we to object that the ancients' request seemed superfluous because the canonized saints already enjoy the fullness of the beatific vision, they would answer that precisely because the mystical body is eschatological, it is always possible even for the saints to grow in holiness, which it is always up to God to measure.

After presenting 'those who were pleasing to you in this world', Basil's prayer names in particular the host of canonized saints, that is, those who after an exemplary life of wide influence, have been proposed to us as models: the fathers, the patriarchs, the apostles, the prophets, the preachers, the evangelists, the martyrs and the confessors. A few names are selected from this host of the elect. In first place comes Mary, named with no fewer than seven honorific titles: the 'most holy, most glorious, immaculate, full of grace, our Lady, Mother of God and ever-virgin'. In second position comes John the Baptist, the greatest of those born of women (cf. Matthew 11:11). Then come other saints, which the Eastern formularies tend to accumulate in endless lists.

Once the memorial of canonized saints has been completed, the prayer moves on to remember non-canonized saints, that is, those we usually simply call the dead. Even if they can never be solemnly proposed as models for living, often because their lives were hidden, many of these have left us an example of gospel-living that makes them our family saints. We ask God to 'detach them from this world', not to

126

distance them from those who grieve for them, but rather to 'bind them to each other', that is, to their fathers, their mothers, to all their relatives and friends, to all the members of the human family who have preceded them in the common dwelling. Are not most of our difficulties those of loneliness and division? Is it not the refusal to be 'bound to one another' that torments individual and collective life with misunderstanding, bitterness, tensions of every kind, even war? For the dead we desire full rest: that is why we ask that they may enjoy it 'together'.

One might find the idea of dwelling 'in a lush place, by restful waters, in a paradise of delights' says little to us who, with sophisticated technology, take great pains to contain the discomforts of seasonal changes with every change of the moon. But this is an image that we need to retrieve, because it is so exquisitely human. It is no accident that Genesis represents primordial happiness as a 'paradise of delights' watered by four rivers, in which Adam – to take it literally – was placed (Genesis 2:15). The laudative celebration which is typical of Eastern eucharistic prayers that began by referring to the paradise of delights where Adam was placed, and was transmitted together with the memory of the historical disruption of relationship caused by the first Adam's 'no' and prolonged by an infinite series of other human 'nos' (cf. anaphora of the Apostolic Constitutions), concludes with the paradise of delights where God welcomes Adam and his children (cf. the anaphora of St Basil), the true paradise of which the primordial paradise was but a utopic projection backwards into the past. The intercessions conclude with a final supplication for those present, upon which is built the concluding doxology:

As for us who live as pilgrims here below, preserve us in your faith and guide us to your Kingdom, bestowing your peace upon us in every circumstance so that now and always your most holy, venerable and blessed Name may be glorified, exalted, praised, blessed and sanctified in Christ Jesus and in the Holy Spirit, as it was, is now and will be from generation to generation, for ever and ever.

127

If we want to read the Eucharist not only as vertical *diakonia*, that is as cultic homage which the celebrating community renders to God, but also as horizontal *diakonia*, then we must admit that the epiclesis for 'one body' and the intercessions that extend it to the various parts of the Church constitute the privileged moment for living this dimension. Without the intercessions, how could each member of the Church who is not physically present intervene in the dynamic of our Eucharist, in order to be thus Masses for the great request to be transformed into 'one body'? Is this not the *diakonia* we are called to exercise, following the rhythms of our Masses, for the universal Church, the hierarchical Church, the Church in the world, the Church triumphant, and the Church of our dead, so particularly dear to us?

4. The Eucharist: Vertical *Diakonia* as a Function of the Horizontal *Diakonia*

4.1 The Presided-Over Assembly as the Subject Celebrating Liturgical *Diakonia*

Over the centuries and especially in the medieval period, the liturgy became more and more the property of the ordained clergy and the laity were reduced to being devout but mute spectators. Popular ways of speech, some still current, demonstrate this: 'to hear Mass', and other similar expressions. But the Eucharist is not and cannot ever be private.

Even if the eucharistic prayer must be prayed alone by the presider because of the traditionally presidential nature of the prayer, neverthe-less the laity must be helped to recognize it also as their own. It should not be 'heard' in the same way that the readings are 'heard' when they are proclaimed, because theologically these are two radically different situations. Indeed, the readings are proclaimed for the ears of the listening assembly, and God, through the ministry of the lector, is the speaker. On the other hand, the eucharistic prayer is proclaimed for the ears of God the Father who listens, while the whole assembly, through the ministry of its president, is the speaker. During the entire eucharistic prayer, the ritual assembly is physically listening, but theo-logically, it is speaking. This is why Theodore of Mopsuestia says:

128

Because at this time the presbyter is the common tongue of the Church, for this magnificent liturgy he makes use of adequate words – which are the praises of God – confessing that all praise and glory are due to God.[14]

John Chrysostom speaks at greater length on this question, exhorting the faithful thus:

That which pertains to the eucharistic prayer is also common [to the priest and to the people]. Indeed he does not say the eucharistic prayer by himself [*oudè/eucharistèi mònos*], but also the entire people [says it with him]. Indeed, only after he has received the voice of those who consent that it is right and just to do so does he begin the eucharistic prayer. I say these things so that each one may be attentive, even those who depend on the one who presides, that we all may realize that we are one body, so that we do not differentiate ourselves from one another except as members of the members [cf. I Corinthians 12:12–30; Romans 12:4–5]. In this way we will not cast everything on to the priests [*me to pan epì tous hierèas riptomen*], but we too, as part of the common body, are concerned for all the Church. This in effect makes [them] more secure, and makes us more relaxed.[15]

The teaching of the ancient mystagogues is obviously confirmed in the anaphoric formularies, where the governing verbs regularly occur in the first person plural. Does not the bishop or presbyter say '*gratias agimus*' (*eucharistoùmen*), '*offerimus*' (*prosphèromen*), '*petimus*' (*deòmetha*), not only in his own name but also in the name of the entire community he has been called to preside over? The one presiding does not address the words of the prayer to the liturgical assembly, nor to the eucharistic elements, but the entire assembly addresses the words to God the Father, narrating, through the ministry of the presider, the institution of the eucharistic memorial that the Lord Jesus wanted to leave to his Church on the eve of his passion.[16] Even if canonically the terminology 'to celebrate' and 'to concelebrate' continues to be used by many to refer to the ordained ministry, nevertheless in a rigorous theological sense, it is good to get the faithful used to taking it as their own.[17]

To celebrate the Eucharist, or better to concelebrate it with the priest or bishop in virtue of the common baptismal priesthood, means communicating with the Living One, who gives himself to us under the sign of a lifeless body to allow us to be sacramentally re-presented in the redemptive effectiveness of the one sacrifice. Consequently, we should see ourselves theologically as on pilgrimage each time that we go to communion. We should notice ever more readily the intense movement of our theological feet: while our physical feet keep us in church, our eucharistic feet take us to Calvary to submerge us yet again, together with all the parts of the Church for whom we offer our *diakonia*, in the death of the Lord Jesus before the tomb of the Risen One, so that we may rise with him yet again to a perpetually new relational existence, since our Mass is Calvary and the splendour of Easter morning. That is where we go every time we go to Mass, that is, to use Theodore of Mopsuestia's words, every time 'we do the memorial of the sacrifice'.[18]

What I have been arguing here becomes all the more touching when applied to suffrage for our dead. To the faithful who want to offer a Mass for the dead, we would say, It is right for you to have a Mass celebrated for your dead. You have good reasons for this practice. But you should understand that it is not necessary to have Masses said. Each time that you participate in the eucharistic celebration, you concelebrate it with the priest, together with him you offer the eucharistic memorial, and you ask for your dead the transformation into 'one body' that they, through your 'con-celebration' and your communion for them, ardently desire.

To sum up, it is important to catechize the assembly about the qualitative difference between the receptive listening they are called to during the proclamation of the readings through the ministry of the lector, and the active listening they are called to during the proclamation of the eucharistic prayer through the ministry of the presbyter; in the former they listen, understand and memorize; in the latter they speak to God who at that moment is their direct interlocutor. Because the *lex orandi* places each member of the presided assembly in first rank, at the level of the celebrating subject, so also should they be in first rank when it comes to fulfilling the obligations that flow from the celebration.

4.2 Horizontal *Diakonia* as True Criterion of Vertical *Diakonia*

Many accuse Christians of confining their religiosity to prayer, guaranteeing thereby a convenient fracture between liturgy and life. However, an examination of the anaphoric formularies demonstrates that the vertical and horizontal dimensions penetrate each other, such that one is not found without the other in the same way that one cannot observe the commandment about God without previously observing the commandments about the neighbour. Mastering the *lex orandi* shows us that the eucharistic prayer, which opens us up to God and to others, creates a strong vertical tension which nevertheless would not be authentic if it were not accountable in daily life.

In the intercessions of the anaphora of St Basil, we saw that the assembly addresses very concrete requests to God, asking that we be granted open-handed generosity towards the needy who depend on our support. This reminds us that our eyes must be the ones through which God sees their needs, our ears must be those with which God hears their laments, our hands must be those with which God comes to their help.

Justin wrote in analogous terms. Immediately after mentioning communion under the eucharistized elements, he added:

> Those who have abundance and who want [to give], give freely what each one chooses, and what has been gathered is then deposited with the presider, who in turn helps the orphans and widows, those neglected because of sickness or other reasons, the imprisoned and resident foreigners: in other words, the presider becomes the provider for all who are in any kind of necessity.[19]

Liturgy and ethical commitment, or *lex orandi* and *lex agendi*, constitute the two sides of the one and selfsame reality: without liturgy it is difficult to have true ethical commitment; without ethical commitment, it is impossible to have true liturgy. If this is true for any liturgical action, then it is even more so for the Eucharist, which the tradition of the Byzantine Churches calls 'the Divine Liturgy'.[20] Indeed the transformation into 'one body', which the epiclesis asks for and which intercessions extend and amplify, is both vertical and horizontal. The vertical dimension, which is our tension and attention to God, is properly verified in the horizontal dimension, which is our tension and attention to those whose neighbours we must become. When we come into church, we bear with us all the joys and sufferings of the world, to experience them fully in that special relationship with God and with others which is the eucharistic celebration. Then, leaving church, we carry into the daily rhythm of the world all the commitments assumed and resumed during our Eucharists. If we do not carry our concerns and those of the world when we come into church, there is no point in going. Likewise, if we do not carry our own commitments when we leave church, then it was pointless to enter in the first place, since a Eucharist without the willingness to commit oneself ethically, especially with regard to one's neighbour, is void. Without active commitments, worship is comfortable entertainment, empty ritual, a pretence of worship – in short, negligent *diakonia*.

As individuals and communities, if we do not actively work 'for the cause of the poor, the widows, orphans, and the foreigners in our midst' – as Basil's anaphora reminds us – from Monday to Saturday, then our prayer in church on Sunday is Pharisaical. Then we might be surprised to find ourselves among those Christians that the Malagasy proverb calls '*kristiànina alahàdy, ka mangàlatra akòho alatsinàiny*', which means: 'Sunday Christians who steal chickens on Monday'.

10

The Sacramentality of the Word

Timothy Radcliffe, OP

I feel deeply honoured to be asked to address this International Meeting of the Society of Jesus on 'The Sacramentality of the Word', but I have to confess that when I accepted I had no idea what the title meant. I accepted for two reasons. First of all as a very small expression of my gratitude for all that the Society does and is. For nine years, as Master of the Order, I travelled the world, and frequently I have been filled with admiration for the utter dedication of Jesuits to the preaching of the Gospel, often in situations of danger and deprivation. If ever there is another attempt to suppress the Society, I am sure that the Dominicans will oppose it with much more vigour than the last time!

The second reason I accepted to give this lecture was precisely because I did not know anything about the subject, and so it was a good opportunity to learn something. I quickly discovered that the best book was, of course, by a Jesuit, Paul Janowiak, *The Holy Preaching: the Sacramentality of the Word in the Liturgical Assembly*.[1] The author shows the development of a profound link, in the theologies of Semmelroth, Rahner and Schillebeeckx, between the proclamation of the Word of God, the preaching of the homily and the consecration of the bread and wine. We begin by breaking the bread of God's word for the people, and then we gather around the altar to share the feast of the Word made flesh. Each moment belongs to the speaking of what Karl Rahner calls 'the one whole word of God.'[2] As Schillebeeckx writes, 'the whole celebration of the Eucharist is thus a service of the word, and the whole Eucharist is a sacramental event'.[3] The Eucharist is thus a single transformative sacramental event. Preaching is an intrinsic part of that event, and not just instruction or teaching about the Gospel. It offers a sacramental word.

Janowiak then develops this theology through a fascinating use of new literary theories of the relationship between texts, contexts and readers. This morning I would like to develop a complementary approach, starting from the observation that often the preaching of the word fails to be transformative. Frequently its effect is to put the people of God to sleep, or to drive them to pray that the preacher will stop. How can we develop the theologies of the sacramentality of the preached word when, to be truthful (and *Veritas* is the motto of my Order), many homilies are painfully tedious. I am not just talking about homilies by Dominicans or even Jesuits. One of the definitions of 'to preach' given by Webster's dictionary is 'to give moral or religious advice, especially in a tiresome manner'.

Boring preaching has been a challenge for the people of God since the beginning. Even St Paul droned on so tediously that Eutyches fell asleep and dropped to his death. This has always consoled me in moments of self-doubt. St Caesarius of Arles preached rarely, but when he did the church doors had to be locked so that people could not flee the ordeal. I asked that the doors of this meeting room be locked this morning to stop you escaping, but the organizers would not agree! John Donne, the Anglican preacher and poet, said that the Puritans preached for so long because they would not stop until the congregation had woken up again! So tedious and ineffective preaching has always been a problem. But the history of the Church has been marked by recurrent major crises of preaching. Both the Dominicans and the Jesuits were founded in response to such crises. The thirteenth and the sixteenth centuries were both times of profound social transformation, with the emergence of new ways of being human. The preacher had to discover how to address these new hearers of the word, with their own questions, doubts and aspirations. Otherwise his preaching would be ineffective and his words would not be sacramental.

Now we face another crisis in the preaching of the Gospel. Semmelroth, Rahner and Schillebeeckx have beautiful theologies of the sacramentality of the word, but we must face the fact that our words are not always filled with the power of God. They do not always touch the hearts of our hearers at the beginning of the twenty-first century. Why is this and what are we to do? Dominic and Ignatius reacted by founding new religious orders. You will be relieved to know that I am not going to propose the foundation of yet another religious order!

I will try to answer that question by looking at what sort of an event was the Last Supper. What was its dynamic? How was it transformative? And therefore what might it mean for a preached word to share in its power and be marked by the same dynamism? How might this transforming power touch our contemporaries? What in the contemporary world might hinder the hearing of the Word?

I will suggest that there are three elements or moments in that event of the Last Supper that the preaching of the Church should echo: 1. Jesus reaches out to disciples in their individual puzzlement and confusion; 2. He gathers them into community; 3. He reaches beyond this community for the fullness of the Kingdom.

These are three of the elements that make the Last Supper a transformative event, a 'happening'. The same dynamic must be present in the preaching of the Church if its words are to be sacramental. If not, then we shall have a beautiful theology of preaching, but the preaching will be dead.

1. Beginning in Silence

Theologians may give the impression that the people of God gather for the Eucharist as a warm and united community, bound together by love of God and each other, eager to hear the preaching of the Gospel. But this idealized view is remote from reality. The global, postmodern culture of today, especially in the West, is highly individualistic. Parishes rarely reflect natural communities, especially in the great megacities in which ever more people live; often the people who are gathered to share the Eucharist do not know each other, or even especially wish to do so. In a world that is increasingly secularized, often the words of the Gospel and the teaching of the Church are puzzling and incomprehensible. In all this, one's average parish is like that community of disciples gathered around Jesus at the Last Supper.

The disciples are confused and questioning: 'Lord, why do you wash my feet?' 'Lord, where are you going?' 'Show us the Father and then we shall be satisfied.' They say to each other, 'We do not know

135

what he means' (John 16:18). What is this man talking about? Furthermore, the community of the disciples is deeply divided and about to explode. Judas has already sold Jesus; Peter will deny him within hours; most of the rest will flee. In this little gathering Jesus faces all that divides and destroys human community: fear, greed, hatred, failure, suffering and death. This is not at all a cosy parish community.

Karl Barth said of the enormous *Yes* at the centre of Mozart's music, that it has weight and significance 'because it overpowers and contains a *No*'.[4] This can also be said of the Last Supper. The power of the new covenant that Jesus enacted that night lies precisely in its embrace of all that contradicts it, humanity's great *No* to God. It is a story that includes all our puzzlement and misunderstanding faced with Jesus. It embraces all that destroys human community, all the sin and failure that undermine our common lives. Here God's *Yes* embraces and acknowledges every possible *No*.

Every crisis in the preaching of the Church is a challenge to discover how to face and embrace the *No* of that society. For the Dominicans, the preaching had to be brought out of the monasteries and cathedrals into the new democratic and urban world of the thirteenth century. The word had to be carried into the new universities and the market places, for it was there that the new generation was to be found, and it was there that their questions could be faced. This meant leaving the protection of the cloister and sharing more closely the lives of the people. Blessed Jordan of Rivalto, an early Dominican, told people not to complain about the young friars being not very holy: 'Being here among people, seeing the things of the world, it is impossible for them not to get a bit dirty. They are men of flesh and blood like you, and in the freshness of youth. It is a wonder that they are as clean as they are. This is no place for monks! We are certainly here among you for our own good, but it is much more for your sake that we are here.'[5] Being a preacher implied a certain solidarity with sinners. In fact Humbert of Romans said that the one advantage of a preacher's vocation was that it did not exclude sinners.[6] There is an old Spanish proverb: 'Guard your wife from the friars, but watch your wallet with the Jesuits.' It is part of our qualification to be preachers that we are sinners!

In the sixteenth century, the new crisis of preaching, which led to the foundation of the Society, was due to the ossification of the scholastic way of preaching. The Constitutions of the Society ordained that preaching be not in the scholastic style, because it is 'dry' and 'speculative'.[7] In other words, 'Do not preach like the Dominicans'! Perhaps the most effective Dominican preacher of the epoch was Tetzel, since his preaching of indulgences provoked Luther, and hastened the Reformation, which led to the foundation of the Jesuits. A new preaching was needed, which touched the emotions and led to a conversion of the heart. This was a preaching based on a new understanding of our relationship with Jesus, embodied in the very name of the Society. It was a way of preaching adapted to the new individual that was emerging with the breakdown of medieval hierarchy, typified by that fine product of Jesuit education, Descartes. Ignatius saw the approach to the individual as an intrinsic part of this preaching. He sent his brethren to 'enter gently into the thoughts of a specific individual',[8] 'going in by their door in order to come out by ours'. They were to go out 'fishing', entering into conversation with people, responding to their questions. With both Dominic and Ignatius, we can see that preaching begins with the reaching out to embrace what separated their contemporaries from the Gospel. We start by embracing their *No*, their incomprehension, before the *Yes* can be preached.

How is our preaching to acknowledge and embrace all the doubts and questions of our generation and offer a powerful word? We face the triumph of a postmodern culture of consumerism, of the market place, which has a far more radical and universal grip than anything that the founders of Domincans and Jesuits ever faced. The triumph of this cultural and economic order has been so almost universal that hardly anyone in the world is unaffected. It has subverted nearly all local cultures with its profound individualism and secularism. There are reports of Thai Buddhist monks being seduced by the attractions of consumerism and driving around in Mercedes![9] It marks the hearts and minds of our own Christian communities. We preachers are ourselves contemporary men and women who are radically influenced by it as well.

I am not saying that it is any worse than what preceded it. I do not wish to attack modernity or postmodernity. My point is that, with the near disappearance of Christian culture, we must radically enter into the doubts, puzzlement and failures of contemporaries if we are to preach a word that is efficacious. This is a kenotic act, of reaching out to humanity in its distance from the Gospel. But it is more necessary than ever before, because that distance is embedded in the culture that is not only universal but our own. We must face these doubts within ourselves, for we are modern men and women. The temptation of the preacher is to know the answers from the beginning and to share from the riches of our knowledge and expertise. But this must be resisted. We must discover ourselves as like the disciples around the table at the Last Supper, puzzled, confused and wondering what is happening. We must let the Gospel reduce us to silence, resistant to our ownership. We must hear it with all the doubts and questions of our contemporaries. We must beg for illumination. We must be mendicants for a word. Of course it is true that when we do preach, we will probably produce one of our standard sermons. Most of us have five or six themes that can be adapted for nearly any Gospel text! But that same old sermon will come as a gift, with some hint of surprise and freshness, and not as an expression of our mastery and expertise.

All the Gospels begin in silence:[10] Luke with the astonished silence of Zechariah; Matthew with the puzzled silence of Joseph; Mark with silence of the wilderness and John with the plenary silence from which the Word comes. Our words of good news too must begin in silence, as we, with our contemporaries, struggle to make sense of what is happening, just like the disciples at the Last Supper.

2. Gathering In

So the first moment in the dynamism of the Last Supper is Jesus' embrace of all that is resistant to communion, all the puzzlement, the confusion, the sin and the failure of humanity. The second is the gathering in of the disciples into communion. This is especially evident in John. He gives them a new commandment, that they are to love one another; he calls them his friends; he promises that they will be one as he and the Father are one. So our words will be sacramental in making communion.

A French Dominican who was celebrating a funeral after the Second World War discovered that all those who had fought in the resistance were seated on one side of the church, and all those who had collaborated on the other. The coffin was in the middle. He refused to begin the Eucharist until they crossed the divide to embrace one another. From the beginning of the Order, preaching was linked to reconciliation and peace making. In the thirteenth century, most cities in northern Italy suffered from deep internal divisions, as factions fought for power. The Franciscans and Dominicans were peacemakers,[11] preaching what was known as 'The Great Devotion' in 1233. Often the climax of the sermon was the ritual kiss of peace between enemies. It was precisely as preachers that they ordained the release of prisoners from prison, the forgiveness of debts and the reconciliation of enemies. The preached word gathers into communion. This is its sacramental power.

My most powerful experience of this was in Argentina. When I was due to preach to the Dominican Family I had not realized that it was Malvinas Day, when the whole of Argentina pledges itself to win back these islands from the British. The streets were filled with Argentinean flags. But my brothers had brought a little British one for me! By chance I had chosen to preach on non-violence. I concelebrated with the Provincial of Argentina and we prayed for all the dead. It was a graced moment of deep healing for us all.

How can our preaching gather into communion? This begins with telling the truth. At the Last Supper Jesus tells the disciples the truth. One of them will betray him; they will all flee and be scattered; he will suffer and die; he will rise again and the Holy Spirit with be sent. 'Because I have said these things to you, sorrow has filled your hearts. Nevertheless I tell you the truth' (John 16:6); 'Sanctify them in the truth; thy word is truth' (John 17:17). There is no communion without truth. It is in the truth that we meet each other face to face. The new covenant is born in this new truth telling.

The preacher must first of all tell the truth about human experience, its joy and sorrow. This is symbolized in the very bread and wine we bring to the altar. Geoffrey Preston, OP wrote:

Think of domination, exploitation and pollution of man and nature that goes with bread, all the bitterness of competition and class struggle, all the organized selfishness of tariffs and price-rings, all the wicked oddity of a world distribution that brings plenty to some and malnutrition to others, bringing them to that symbol of poverty we call the bread line. And wine too – fruit of the vine and work of human hands, the wine of holidays and weddings. This wine is also the bottle, the source of some of the most tragic forms of human degradation: drunkenness, broken homes, sensuality, debt. What Christ bodies himself into is bread and wine like this, and he manages to make sense of it, to humanize it. Nothing human is alien to him. If we bring bread and wine to the Lord's Table, we are implicating ourselves in being prepared to bring to God all that bread and wine mean. We are implicating ourselves in bringing to God, for him to make sense of, all which is broken and unlovely. We are implicating ourselves in the sorrow as well as the joy of the world.[12]

Our preaching will only gather in the people of God, if we honestly name their sorrows and joys. We have to be seen to speak truthfully, to tell things as they are. Do people recognize their lives in our words? Our congregations include young people struggling with their hormones and the teachings of the Church, married couples wrestling with crises of love, the divorced, old people facing retirement, gay people feeling on the edge of the Church, sick and dying people. Does their pain and happiness find some space in our words? Do they recognize the truth of their experience in what we say?

I believe that the crisis of preaching today is in part a crisis of truthfulness. Barbara Brown Taylor, a well-known Episcopalian preacher, reports the complaint: 'I wish preachers did not lie so much.'[13] It is not so much that preachers tell blatant lies. It is rather that sometimes we fear to grapple with the complexity of human experience. We fear to live the tension of the encounter of the experience of people with the Gospel or with the teaching of the Church. If we really acknowledge the joys and the sorrows of humanity, then we will find ourselves lost for easy words. Our ecclesiastical language will appear threadbare and inadequate. We may find ourselves drawn into discussions that alarm us. We may become involved in controversy that may split the community. We may open 'cans of worms' and be accused of 'rocking the boat'. And so for the sake of peace and unity, it may appear safer to keep quiet. Thus we lose that bold truthfulness of the early preaching, the *parrhesia* of the apostles (Acts 4:29; 28:31). But there is no true communion except in the truth.

Telling the truth is more than accurately reporting the experience of our people. It is letting the story of Jesus disclose the true meaning of our lives. Jesus says to the disciples at the Last Supper: 'If they persecuted me, they will persecute you; if they kept my word, they will keep yours also...' (John 16:20f.). Bringing to word the joys and sorrows of the people of God is acknowledging the Christ who now lives and dies in them. In the word of Mary Catherine Hilkert, OP, we must name the grace and the dis-grace at work in our world.[14] When Afro-American congregations in the United States are looking for a pastor, they ask the question: 'Can the reverend tell the story?'[15] The first task of the preacher is to be able to tell the story of Jesus. If that is told properly then it is our story too. The congregation will recognize in it their struggles, their victories and defeats, their agony and their ecstasy. They are his body. This is exactly what the evangelists did when they wrote their accounts of the Last Supper. John's account gives a space to all that his community has lived. Their story is part of the story.

If we test what we say against the reality of people's lives, then maybe our homilies will be more modest. The temptation of preachers is to make great and vague claims that must make our hearers smile to themselves. I dread the ecclesiastical indicative, 'Married couples, living in complete unity and perfect love, express the love of Christ.' Really? Try asking some of my friends! Our words will be more powerful if we say less. An old Eskimo woman was asked why the songs of her tribe were so short. She replied, 'Because we know so much.'[16] We talk too much because we listen too little. As Barbara Brown Taylor wrote, 'In a time of famine typified by too many words with too much noise in them, we could use fewer words with more silence in them.'[17]

So then, if our words are to be sacramental, eucharistic, then they

141

must gather people into communion. We can see from the Last Supper that this requires that we speak truthfully. The disciples say to Jesus, 'Now you are speaking plainly, not in any figure' (John 16:29). But this truthfulness is more than an accurate description of what other people live. We cannot describe their joys and sorrows from outside. We must find with them the words in which to tell the story. Our preaching must be the fruit of our conversation, in which the people recognize the echo of their own voices.

Wittgenstein wrote that 'to imagine a language means to imagine a form of life'.[18] There is only a common life where there is a common language. When a husband and wife live together for many years, their communion comes to fruition in a shared way of speaking; they share a vocabulary, a stock of jokes and memories. They develop their own dialect. This language is the fruit of their communion. Dominicans and Jesuits do the same thing. From Tokyo to the Amazon, I discovered a communion with my brethren in a shared way of talking. The preacher gathers the congregation into communion by actively trying to make a common language with the people, to which they contribute, and which resonates with their words, experiences and stories.

In St Augustine's sermons, one can see him wrestling with the congregation. He argues with them, and they shout back. He makes jokes, he provokes them; they cheer and boo. Their encouragement makes him take off. Often he appears to fail, and sometimes he even sulks and refuses to preach at all.[19] In this interplay the common language of the community is being born. They are like a husband and wife evolving their common tongue. John Donne said that 'True Instruction is making love to the Congregation, and to every soule in it.'[20] In a similar way, our words will only be transforming, sacramental, if they are born of such a conversation, a love-making. We must actively reach out to hear and give a space for those whose voices are not usually heard. Who are the people who are silent in our congregations? Often it is the women and ethnic minorities. Do we talk about them? Do we talk to them? Or do we allow their voices to mould the language that we speak, so that a new discourse is born? Then our preaching will gather into communion.

3. Reaching out for the Kingdom

I now turn to a final element of the dynamism of the Last Supper, which is that Jesus reaches out into the future, towards the Kingdom. John's account of the Last Supper is marked by a paradox that is hard to capture in a few words. On the one hand, it is the fruition of Jesus' community with the disciples. The whole narrative has led to this moment of intimacy. He calls them his friends, he promises that the disciples will be one, and that the Father and he will come and make their home with them. Yet at the same time, it is, in a sense, the end of this common life with him. They are about to lose him as a man among them. Never again will they sit at table with Jesus and eat and drink with him. When they meet the Risen Christ, he will scatter them to the ends of the earth. So within the dynamic of the new covenant, this final meal is a beginning and an end. It is a gathering and a dispersal. It is the climax of their friendship and it points beyond it. It is the moment for speaking the truth, and yet when the truth cannot be as yet spoken. It is a provisional consummation.

This paradox marks every Christian Eucharist. Gathered around the altar, our community is a sign of the Kingdom. We are the friends of God. But this same Eucharist challenges us to break down the walls around our little community and welcome in those who are excluded. Every Eucharist is the sacrament of our home in the Lord, and yet breaks down the walls that we build to keep out strangers. This is the necessary paradox of being both Roman and Catholic, both a particular historical community and the sacrament of a community which transcends us and stretches out to embrace all of humanity. It is a tension that will mark every Eucharist until the Kingdom, when the sacraments will cease and the Church will be no more.

Our preaching will be powerful, sacramental, if it is marked by this same tension. We have seen that the preacher builds community, gathers in the lost and the stray. As Donne said, he makes love to his congregation. On the other hand, he challenges that congregation for its exclusions. It is a sacrament of the Kingdom, but the universal embrace of the Kingdom challenges it in turn. The preacher invites us to find identity within the Church, but then subverts every identity that has been secured. This was the drama of the little Jewish Church in its early years. It had barely been born when it had to lose its identity to welcome in the Gentiles. Three hundred years later, the Church was finally accepted as truly Roman, and then it had to lose that identity and embrace the barbarians. This is the drama that has been repeated throughout the history of the Church. Just when we have made of the Church a comfortable home, we are challenged to give hospitality to strangers.

This is the ever-repeated drama of the Church's preaching. For example, for the early Spanish conquistadors in the Americas, the Eucharist was the deepest expression of their identity, for they were Christians far from home. Yet when, on the First Sunday of Advent, 1511, the Dominican Antonio de Montesinos preached in Hispaniola, he challenged this precious identity. Did they not understand that these indigenous people whom they were enslaving were their brothers and sisters in Christ? 'Are they not human? Do they not have rational souls? With what right do you make war upon them? Are you not obliged to love them as yourselves?' His compatriots experienced this preaching as subversive, as destructive of who they were. This same sermon both gathers them into communion and yet challenges the communion they have achieved. Until the Kingdom, all identities are provisional.

We have seen that the preacher makes communion by speaking the truth. He must name the grace and the dis-grace. He gathers us together, placing upon the altar all our joys and sorrows, bringing to word the beauty and the pain of our human lives. To do this, the preacher must speak truthfully. But there are other moments when he reaches for the Kingdom, for 'what no eye has seen, nor ear heard, nor the human heart conceived, what God has prepared for those who love him' (I Corinthians 2:9). Then clarity is not possible. He is preaching what is beyond our words. He has reached the limits of language. This is where language breaks down. Truthfulness demands of the preacher here not boldness but humility. The mystery defeats our words. Herbert McCabe, OP, wrote: 'Our language does not encompass but simply strains towards the mystery that we encounter in Christ. The theologian uses a word by stretching it to breaking point, and it is precisely as it breaks that the communication, if any, is achieved.'[21]

This is essentially a poetic task, which is why the greatest preachers have always been poets. Poets live at the limits of what we can say, on the frontiers of language. The poet reaches out for a fullness of meaning and communion that is beyond literal statement. Seamus Heaney, the greatest living poet of the English language, says that poetry offers 'a glimpsed alternative',[22] beyond the contradictions of experience. In situations of conflict, such as Heaney's Northern Ireland, it is poets who can evoke that place of peace where all divisions are overcome, 'an elsewhere beyond the frontier of writing where "the imagination presses back against the pressure of reality"'.[23]

This is another reason for the crisis of preaching today. The poetic imagination is marginal within our dominant scientific culture. This tends towards a deadening literalism. In most traditional societies, poetry, myth, song and music were central to the culture. In our society these have often been reduced to entertainment. The hunger for the transcendent is still there in the human heart. As St Augustine said, it is restless until it rests in God. But in our postmodern society it is harder for the preacher to evoke that ultimate human destiny which transcends our words. Few preachers are poets. I am not. But if the preaching of the word is to flourish, then we need poets and artists, singers and musicians who keep alive that intuition of our ultimate destiny. The Church needs these singers of the transcendent to nurture her life and her preaching.

I asked many people what was the most powerful sermon of the twentieth century, and a surprising number immediately claimed that it was Martin Luther King's famous speech, 'I have a dream.' This was given at the height of the Civil Rights movement in August 1963. It was more than a political manifesto; it evoked an eschatological vision of universal peace, of 'that day when all of God's children, black men and white men, Jews and Gentiles, Protestants and Catholics, will be able to join hands and sing in the words of the old Negro spiritual, "Free at last! Free at last! Thank God Almighty, we are free at last!"' It was not a sermon but it empowered thousands of sermons. Whose words open up the transcendent for us? Especially after 11 September, in a world in danger of coming apart, we need poets, singers of the transcendent. We need artists who can bring us to the edge of what can be said. Their words can feed and enliven all our preaching.

4. Conclusion

We have a beautiful theology of the sacramentality of the word. This claims that there is an intimate coherence between the proclamation of the Word of God, preaching and the sharing of Christ's body and blood. We break the bread of God's word, and then feed on the Word made flesh. This theology is founded on claims about the efficacy of that preached word. It is powerful and transformative, sanctifying us in the truth. The question that I wished to explore was this: how can this fit with the present crisis of preaching in the Church? So much preaching is in fact dull and inefficacious.

My claim is that our preaching will only be powerful and transformative if it reflects the dynamism of the Last Supper. If we wish to understand how our preaching might be sacramental, then we must understand that sacramental moment which founded the Church. I looked at three moments in that drama which our preaching must enact if it is to share its power:

Jesus reaches out to the disciples in their puzzlement, confusion and failure. This is the beginning of our preaching. We must dare to embrace the silence and the doubts of our contemporaries. This is above all true in the present global culture, which penetrates almost all human hearts with its values, including our own. Jesus gathers the disciples into communion. This necessitates telling the truth. We too must make communion by truthfully bringing to word the joys and sorrows of our world. Jesus stretches forward to the Kingdom, which lies beyond our grasp of our words. We need the help of poets and artists if we are to do this.

There is a rhythm to these moments, like the tempo of breathing. We reach out to the people, gather them in and then reach out to the Kingdom, like lungs that are emptied, filled and then emptied again. Humanity's history is breathing, from the gift of breath to Adam, to Christ's yielding of his last breath on the cross, to the breathing into us of the Holy Spirit. Our preaching will be sacramental, efficacious if

146

it reflects the rhythm and measure of humanity's breathing, gathering in and expelling out, giving us life, and oxygen for our blood.

Notice finally that this dramatic event of the Last Supper moves us from the silence of incomprehension to the silence of the mystery, from an empty silence to a plenary silence. We go from the silence of the disciples who understand nothing, to the silence of those who cannot find words for what they have glimpsed. The preacher lives within that space, begging for words. It is the gift of God's grace, what the early Dominicans called the *gratia praedicationis*, that propels us from that silence of poverty to that *pleroma*. And now I too must be silent!

11

The Liturgy of the World: Ecumenical and Inter-Religious Dialogue and its Challenges for Christian Worship in the Postmodern Age

Francisco F. Claver, SJ

Many years ago there was a book authored by the great Jesuit theologian Karl Rahner – I don't remember its title – which was quite a hit with those of us in our Jesuit formation. It described the Jesuit vocation as 'a mystical running to the world'. My young Jesuit companions liked that book particularly because it gave holy justification to what they were doing a lot of then: getting out of house as often as they could manage to, ever running to the outside world in pursuit of their vocation. But, truth to tell, I don't think it mattered much whether the running was done mystically or not.

In preparing this text on Rahner's 'liturgy of the world', I read Michael Skelley's *The Liturgy of the World: Karl Rahner's Theology of Worship*. What he says about the Liturgy of the World is pretty much along the lines of that 'mystical running to the world' which I just mentioned. What God is doing in the world – that is the liturgy Rahner speaks of and we his people must respond to it in a similar liturgy. Christian liturgy must partake of that Liturgy of the World, must in fact be an acting out of that same Liturgy.

If our vocation is indeed a mystical running to the world, what is it we are supposed to do in the world in our running to it? I would suggest that, simply put, it is to dialogue with the world. And if God is in that world, dwells in it, continues to work in it, to sustain it, to bless it, then ultimately it is to dialogue with God himself, to come face to face with him in his Liturgy of the World.

'Dialogue' has been a much used and abused word in our post-Vatican II Church. Indeed, I know some bishops and religious superiors who get positively apoplectic when they hear the word. Dialogue is often an excruciating listening to monologues for them – monologues which they can't easily abort for fear they would be accused of a superior's gravest modern sin: that he or she is 'lacking in dialogue'. Yet dialogue is so essential, not just for superiors and subjects, not just for us in the Church as we try, hopelessly, it often seems, to change outdated ways of thinking and doing, but also and more basically for us as ordinary human beings as we try to lead lives that make sense in what often seems to be a senseless world. Everything we do has to be dialogue, for we are essentially dialogic beings. That's a direct consequence, I would think, of our being *animalia socialia*. And we are 'social animals' because we possess speech, intellect, judgement – the *sine qua non* conditions of dialogue.

Enough of my philosophy of dialogue. In this essay, I'd like to do what I think I've been doing since I squeezed through my last seminary exam, and that is, trying to be pastoral, looking at things from a pastoral angle, acting always as much as possible as an ordinary parish priest. And how do I define 'pastoral work'? Not just in the classical sense of *cura animarum*. That too, of course, but I'd take *animae* not only as disembodied spirits but as fully embodied ones too, having care for people in all aspects of their lives – care for what happens to them because of ideas, events, actions (theirs and those of others) – a concern in the Lord for anything that happens to them that will make them more human or less human, more spiritual or less spiritual. It is a definition, I must say, that was imposed on us by Vatican II. My context is that of the Philippines.

1. *Gaudium et Spes*

Let me start with a document from Vatican II that pointed us in the direction we took. The 'we' here, I'd like you to know, is not a pompous episcopal 'we': it means a whole community of parish priests, pastoral workers, unlettered farmers, tribal folk, manual labourers, people trying, wanting to be Church – people whom I had the privilege

149

of working with, agonizing with, to plumb the meanings of things we didn't understand too clearly about the Church we sought mightily to be in the post-Council years. The document I refer to here is *Gaudium et Spes: The Church in the Modern World*. It is the one document of Vatican II that led us – nay, forced us – to take the pastoral perspective as I defined it above. Its very first paragraph says everything. You are all familiar with it, but let me read it in full anyway:

The joys and the hopes, the griefs and the anxieties of the people of this age, especially those who are poor or in any way afflicted, these too are the joys and hopes, the griefs and anxieties of the followers of Christ. Indeed, nothing genuinely human fails to raise an echo in their hearts. For theirs is a community composed of men and women. United in Christ, they are led by the Holy Spirit in their journey to the kingdom of their Father and they have welcomed the news of salvation which is meant for all people. That is why this community realizes that it is truly and intimately linked with humankind and its history.

Ours is a Church – 'a community that realizes it is truly and intimately linked with humankind and its history'. Is that true? We tried to make it so in God-forsaken Bukidnon, *our* little world, and things started to happen. Let me say what some of those things were.

First, when the Church – and by Church I mean its rank and file membership, its hierarchy and clergy too – begins to have a real concern for the problems of people in all areas of human life (not just for their narrowly spiritual well-being, nor just in order to later 'convert' them into institutional Christianity), priorities will shift from a narcissistic focus on 'churchy' matters to what I said when I described what I meant by pastoral: having a concern for what happens to people when new ideas, social changes, oppressive governments, wars, revolutions, physical disasters like earthquakes, droughts, crop failures, typhoons, volcanic eruptions and the like impinge on their lives and we ask what these do to their spirit, their humanity. Actually when we started to ask that question, we suddenly realized the Philippines was the natural disaster capital of the whole world, and that is why

Filipinos are among the most religious – and superstitious – of people, although the Irish might possibly beat us hands-down in that category! But even such a realization was integral to that pastoral approach: something happens too to those who take it.

Secondly and consequently, going beyond concern, the Church starts doing what that concern requires: it gets heavily involved in the social apostolate. And here I must say the social apostolate as we got into in the early 1970s was not exactly what Father General Ledochowski used to talk about in the 1930s and 1940s, bidding the Society of Jesus to engage in it. Not the usual kind, that is, that we were doing for the most part in our social institutes – speculative, intellectual, philosophical analysis of social problems – but the dirty-hands type: *doing* the apostolate, getting involved with actual issues of justice, poverty, human rights, everything and anything that gives rise to grave inequities among people. And when we did, we began to see there is more to the Social Teaching of the Church than just correct doctrine. We had to become a Church of the poor.

Becoming such a Church – that was the third thing that happened. But what did that mean in a country like the Philippines where the poor are the majority of the population and traditional Jesuit work was in education, hence with the rich who could afford the kind of education we gave in our universities and schools? The readiest place we could do the kind of social apostolate *Gaudium et Spes* was urging the Church to do was in our mission parishes in Mindanao, although in time our schools too went beyond merely teaching their students the Church's social doctrine to getting them involved in live social issues. Working with labour in the Manila area was not possible then. Father Walter Hogan had tried and he had been thrown out by the ecclesiastical powers-that-be, deprived of faculties, after being involved in strikes against the University of Santo Thomas and the Coca-Cola Company! Being a Church of the poor meant for us being *for* the poor in their aspirations for a better and more human life and more importantly being *with* them in the decisions and efforts they made to realize those aspirations.

Fourthly and finally, this led to what liberation theologians in Latin America were already proposing then, that is, that the Church put itself in fact and not just in spirit on the side of the poor by working for their liberation from all kinds of social evils. The Marxists' model of the good and just society and their way of attaining it all of a sudden became attractive to many a priest, nun, seminarian, not to mention young university students. That put the Church of the Philippines through the wringer as it suffered through a most painful period during which it tried threshing out what we used to call the faith-ideology problematic.

In our attempts at becoming a Church of the poor, we followed what Communists do – do an 'analysis of the situation', of social and political structures especially, find out what is wrong with them, come up with a vision of social change, draw up a programme of reform. We became expert at this only to realize something that is essentially wrong with Marxist analysis. And I'm not referring to what we traditionally demonize Marxism for, its 'atheistic materialism'. What we saw wrong with the analysis Marxists were doing was more basic: its insufficient consideration of cultural factors. Social structures – economic and political structures particularly – have to be analysed and corrected, yes, but as every budding anthropologist will tell you, culture provides the rules and laws whereby those structures operate. Those rules, those laws, they are to be found in the cultural values that guide people in their interactions with one another, and any scheme of social reform must consider whether they abet or hinder the change that is sought. The would-be reformer must then harness them, re-direct them, even counteract them if they negate necessary change, all, of course, in a way that respects the dignity of people.

What followed next was a kind of socio-cultural analysis to supplement the structural, realizing that the joys and hopes, the griefs and anxieties of people are not generically human but specifically so, and it is culture that makes for their specificity. For culture is a particular way of being human.

We still needed to go further. If we were to make people's life concerns our own, we would need to do so as men and women of faith, allowing that faith to guide us in our endeavours. And this is where the social encyclicals became most relevant and helpful. Human analysis *cum* faith – that is, trying to see things as God sees them in order to do things as God would do them. Spiritual discernment is at the heart of this process. And when that discernment is done not just by theologians and Church functionaries but by ordinary men and women in the grass-roots communities of the Church that we call basic ecclesial communities (BECs), interesting things begin to happen as together we moved towards reform.

As we reflected on reform within societal structures we sought peaceful, non-violent means of bringing about change. Active non-violence (ANV) began to capture our collective imagination. For all the evil President Marcos worked on the Philippines, we have to thank him for forcing the Church to look more closely at what its action for justice and peace should be. Here was a government justifying dictatorial rule to reform society. And there were the Communists offering ideas of their own on how to do the same. They were at loggerheads on many crucial issues in their reform agenda, but both were one in their recourse to violence as their main means of reform. And most ironical: both could – and did – quote the Church's traditional teaching on the just war, on the moral use of violence as a last resort, to defend their use of violence. ANV, irrational as it may seem in contrast to the rigorous rationality of the just war position, proposed itself as *our* 'third way'. And it worked, if the peaceful People Power Revolution of 1986 meant anything at all. It brought down the Marcos government non-violently and it showed that a revolution unto blood wasn't the only way to meet a situation that justified – or seemed to justify – a last resort solution.

Even before then, the Alinsky method of confronting social problems was being practised by many socially active groups. It had been developed in the urban ghettoes of Chicago by Saul Alinsky and is an issue-oriented approach to solving social problems. The people of a community are trained to focus on a burning issue in their community and put all their energies and powers of creative imagination into solving it. It is an effective method, but then what happens when there are no more issues? You invent them! That was a difficulty some of our parish communities had to face early on. And that is when they saw and felt the need for deepening their faith. For in their discerning, they realized issues alone were not sufficient to sustain them in their work over the long run. Neither was a secular ideology, even a mesmerizing one as the Marxists were offering. Something else, something deeper and more spirit-sustaining, was needed: a spirituality built on religious faith. And for that, they had recourse to the Bible, in the process becoming an even more discerning faith community.

Something else happens to people when communal spiritual discernment becomes an ordinary part of their being a Church community. If discernment is basically an attempt to see things as God sees them, this cannot be done unless the discerning community gets in touch with the Holy Spirit – the Spirit of knowledge, understanding, wisdom. And that in turn cannot be done unless one prays, unless a whole community prays. This is where liturgy comes in when whole communities practise communal faith-discernment.

2. Worshipping in Engagement with the World

One of the great things that came out of Vatican II was the impetus for the development of the local church. It is a development that takes place necessarily when a church becomes involved with people in the way *Gaudium et Spes* demands. For as I said, people's human problems are deeply cultural in nature. The church becomes so involved in those cultural problems that it will inevitably become a local church. This 'local' church grows in its own self-identity and is gradually empowered to preach and do the Gospel of Christ in a way that is pertinent to and respectful of a people's culture, enriching not destroying it. And in the process, that local church is itself enriched. Herein lies the whole problematic of inculturation, since a genuinely local church is an inculturated church.

I have always been intrigued by the part that liturgy played and still plays in the process of inculturation and in the development of an authentic local church. As we look back to the immediate aftermath of Vatican II and ask ourselves what disturbed people most about it – or, conversely, what was most heartening – it was the reform of the liturgy initiated by the Council. In my opinion, one seemingly insignificant aspect of the liturgical reform was, in fact, the most crucial: the shift from Latin to the vernacular.

Consider the consequences. When you allow people to pray in their own language, the next thing they will do will be to think of and reflect on their faith using their own language, to express that faith according to native mental categories, cultural categories. What follows is the beginning of indigenized theologizing since theology is, after all, a reflection in faith on faith. Further, if they can do theology in their own way, then consequently they will next endeavour to structure themselves as faith communities in their own way, organize themselves, evangelize, live their faith in their own way. This was one factor in the rise of BECs. Dangerous? Yes – but only if you overlook the centrality of faith in these communities, regard them as purely human groupings, treat them as such.

This reality was brought home to me powerfully on one confirmation trip I made to a village when I was still Bishop of Bukidnon. The pastor who invited me to do the confirmations in his parish told me that he would accompany me if I would stop by to collect him at the parish house. When I arrived at his residence, he informed me that he was unable to join me since he hadn't found any substitute to replace him for a regularly scheduled parish Mass; it was a Sunday. I left in a cantankerous mood as I had no idea how to get to the chapel where the confirmations were to take place. I found it somehow and prepared everything myself, went through the start of the Mass still in a bad mood. When we arrived at the homily I launched into my usual catechesis on the sacrament of confirmation. At one point, I asked a rhetorical question, following it with what I thought was a dramatic pause. All of a sudden, a wise old woman sitting right in front of me started to give ('cackle out' is probably the more correct term) the answer to my question and share her thoughts on the sacrament. I was taken aback at first and then I remembered that the congregation was a functioning BEC and like most of our BECs, they were used to Sunday liturgies without a priest and sharing ideas on the readings was standard procedure in their worship. I got into the spirit of that congregation and what followed was a most instructive and lively exchange on what a confirmed faith meant to the people. Thinking back to the event, I feel it was one of the best sermons I ever preached!

What that little incident underlines was what I started to say above.

A faith community is not just a human community made up of individual women and men interacting with one another in worship. It is that, certainly, but it is also something else. There is one other inter-actor, a divine one without whose presence and activity the community cannot call itself Church: the Holy Spirit, the Spirit of Jesus. 'I will send you my Spirit, I will be with you till the end of time.' Strange – or not at all strange? – but when lay people are allowed to play a fuller role in the Church, doing what they should have been doing all along in their vocation as laity, one is compelled to believe there is in truth such a person in the Blessed Trinity as the Holy Spirit – his promised presence is felt almost tangibly in the kind of worship the BECs habitually conduct.

I must confess that I am not sure how liturgists would judge the kind of exchange we had in that little village chapel – a 'dialogue homily'? One that is proscribed by the Congregation for Divine Worship and the Discipline of the Sacraments? In our official (Roman) liturgy the preacher alone is supposed to preach the Word of God – do a monologue, that is, a holy one but still a monologue as far as the assembly is concerned. Oh, yes, the Spirit is there too, but that Spirit is rather monopolized by the preacher. In that little chapel I spoke of, the 'dialogue homily' was participated in not just by the presider and the assembly but also by the Holy Spirit. Taken together, they were and are the Church. I am afraid that this is a fact which we have not in reality fully believed. Indeed, if we had believed it, we would not have acted for so long as though the Holy Spirit spoke only through the magisterium – a practical heresy, if there ever was one.

I spoke above of the Congregation for Divine Worship. Somehow the mere mention of it makes me think of diocesan liturgical commissions. Back when we started grappling with the main idea of *Gaudium et Spes*, I noticed something about diocesan liturgical commissions in the Philippines and how they were working (or not working) precisely as commissions. The more established (read 'conservative') dioceses all had proper liturgical commissions. And one thing we couldn't avoid seeing about them: they were breaking their heads about how to come up with 'relevant' liturgies – *relevant*, those of you old enough to remember, was one of those in-terms then – and often their end products, or, better, productions, tended to be just the opposite: theatrical, well-choreographed, yes, but often quite artificial and hence irrelevant. Dioceses, on the other hand, that were into BECs and social action often didn't have such commissions, but the liturgical life of the people was nonetheless quite alive, and noticeably so. The reason? The liturgy of the former was mostly concocted from above and was quite divorced from the life of *hoi polloi*; that of the latter, issuing from below, literally from the churning guts of the poor and suffering masses that made up their communities, tended to be vibrant liturgies of life because issuing from real life.

This was all happening when Marcos was at the height of his power, and the Communist movement was also at its peak. An interesting development was that Marcos wanted to suppress the BECs and the Communists wanted to infiltrate them. The reason was because they were 'relevant' to the bad political situation. More traditional bishops, for that reason, simply wrote them off as too activist, too political, and forbade them in their dioceses. Some had a change of heart later when they realized that there was actually more real praying and discerning being done in the BECs than in regular parish communities. As I mentioned above, when a faith community takes seriously the life conditions of the poor in their midst, it tries to do something about the evils the poor suffer, enters into their world, becomes part of it, but always in a discerning way. And this it cannot do except in continuous dialogue with the world and with the Spirit infusing that world. Dialogue with the former leads to action; dialogue with the latter to prayer. So a word about dialogue is appropriate here.

3. Dialogue

Looking back now over the close to 40 years since the end of Vatican II and assessing the pastoral work we've been doing since then as a result of it – here I speak only for our part of the world, not for yours – several observations can be made. We see that where we were faithfully pastoral according to the definition of 'pastoral' that we started out with, we had no other way to go but in the direction we went: making the world of the poor and the afflicted our own which pushed us into dialogue with that world. This world was not made up of Catholics and Christians alone, but also of others coming from different cultural and religious traditions. And we had to do this while being church all the while, keeping our identity as Church. In the so-called Third World, that direction led quite inevitably to the building of BECs, small faith communities that also had to be thoroughly pastoral in their orientation, their action, and their being.

More and more we were pushed further into dialogue with the world of the poor – that was in the beginning. Later we wondered why we had to be pushed at all. We discovered how being pastoral in the Vatican II mode was inherently dialogical. We had to be a Church of dialogue – from top to bottom, *ad intra* to the extent that we were part of the Church Universal, *ad extra* as far as we were obliged to follow the mandate of Christ and preach his Gospel to every creature.

On the *ad intra* part, there wasn't much we could do about the top (except to pray and sometimes make a nuisance of ourselves – at least with the Papal Nuncio) but even those exceptions were dialogue too. At the grass-roots level, that is where there was plenty we could do. And that's where we worked with the Church at the base, with the people of God at the lowermost ranks of the Church.

On the *ad extra* part, this meant ecumenical and inter-religious dialogues, not on the high level of theological discourse, but in what the Asian bishops in 1974 encouraged us to enter into: 'the dialogue of life'. Going into that kind of dialogue, we found it so much easier co-operating with Protestants in works of justice rather than arguing about possible theological differences in regard to the biblical understanding of justice. With them the common source of our working together was Christ himself and his Gospel morality. Nor were there great difficulties with those of other traditions (Buddhist, Hindu, Animist, et al.) in discovering common motivations and rationales in working for justice. What we call (condescendingly?) *semina Verbi* in their traditions were unquestionably there. We have to ask, though, why we think those common moral values are only *semina* and not the *Verbum* himself (as I think Rahner would have no difficulty saying) – the Word does speak in and through the Liturgy of the World.

An apology is in order at this point. I am supposed to address the

158

topic of ecumenical and inter-religious dialogue as a challenge to the future of Christian worship in its postmodern context. I am not going to say anything more on the subject than I have just done now. My reason: such dialogues will not prosper, not to say begin, unless we accept that the Church by its very nature, is dialogic, and unless we truly believe that the Word, the *Verbum*, speaks to us in and through the Liturgy of the World. It is a world which includes all kinds of people, cultures, religions, and if we are indeed true believers, we should always be ready to hear what he is trying to say to us in that Liturgy.

Making much of the dialogical character of the Church and all we have to do as Church must be the mother of all generalizations about that institution. Back in 1969 the all-India Conference took place in Bangalore, a gathering of all the dioceses of the Church in that vast sub-continent. It took three general ideas from Vatican II, namely, dialogue, participation and co-responsibility, and proposed these as the main themes around which Church renewal in India should revolve. The event was, we were told, truly Pentecostal. The results, however, were not quite that, as some Indian bishops themselves confessed. The reason, at least it seemed to us from the outside, was that there was no real follow-up on the gains made; or, as sociologists would put it, no 'institutionalization of charisma'.

Those three ideas from Bangalore were adopted in the Philippines by the bishops of Mindanao. In 1971 all the dioceses (not just bishops but also representatives from the laity, the religious, the clergy) on the island came together and mapped out a programme of co-operative renewal for themselves, institutionalizing themselves into a regional conference which has been meeting without fail every three years since. The effects have been quite revolutionary for the Church in that part of the country. Of course, they had to be revolutionary when you consider that a pre-Vatican II Church was generally non-dialogical and non-participatory and there was no such thing as (or at least very little of) shared responsibility in its doing of mission. When you come down to it, those three ideas, if their dynamisms are worked out fully, cannot but be subversive of the old Church and are in fact architectonic for the new: a church of communion, the model of Church that is now

159

being acknowledged widely as the prime one for the post-Vatican II Church.

Those of you who are old enough to have lived through the years immediately following the end of the Council in 1965 will remember that aside from the switch from Latin to the vernacular in the liturgy, the most visible changes brought about by the Council were in the new Church structures it introduced: the synod of bishops, national conferences of bishops, diocesan and parish pastoral councils, senates of priests. These were supposed to be structures of dialogue within the Church, of participation and shared responsibility. I leave it to you to judge if in your experience these structures have been working out as they were originally envisioned to be. I suspect, however, that those three thematic ideas of dialogue, participation and co-responsibility have not yet been fully internalized in the Church and the new structures have been for the most part operating with the old mindsets of a pre-Vatican II Church with the result that they still often are by and large structures of – to put it bluntly – domination and control.

It is instructive to compare how communication – dialogue is basically communication – took place in the old Church and how it is supposed to take place in the new. Those Council-mandated structures we just referred to were meant to make for two-way and direct communication between Pope and bishops (the Synod of Bishops), bishops among themselves (national conferences), bishops, clergy and laity (diocesan pastoral councils), priests and people (parish pastoral councils). In the old, it was one-way from top to bottom, and feedback was indirect. So we get this paradigm of communication and dialogue: the laity want to complain about their priests, they go to the bishop; priests want to complain about their bishop, they go to the Pope; bishops want to complain about the Pope – they go to God! It sounds funny, yes, but we are not yet out of the old system of *delationes* – having recourse to higher levels in the Church when we have complaints to make in the lower.

Synods and pastoral councils are governed by provisions of Canon Law. So much of what the Council says about dialogue, participation, co-responsibility are kind of strait-jacketed by those provisions – especially, to mention just one problem area, the consultative-delibera-

160

tive disjunction in the way decisions are made in the Church. BECs and BEC-type bodies in the Church, on the other hand, are not, at least up till now, burdened by constricting Church law and they are hence freer to follow through where the spirit of those three Vatican II ideas lead them. *Spirit* with a small *s*? I'd rather think *Spirit* with a big *S* is more like it.

But more basic than those thematic ideas from Vatican II, is, I think, what was said at the very beginning of this paper about us humans being essentially dialogical beings. And if we are such, that is so because our God is a dialogical God and he deals with us in a dialogical way, always has, if salvation history is any guide. (We divide that history into the Old and the New Covenants – and a covenant by its very nature is, I take it, a dialogic undertaking.) It strikes me that if BECs are more alive as faith communities than others in the Church in our part of the world, it is precisely because they are open to dialogue, *ad extra*, *ad intra*, in many other ways, are vehicles of dialogue themselves, engage in the dialogue of life with other people, with God himself, and from that fact alone we come to the conclusion our work with them is precisely to develop and form an authentically dialogic people.

4. Ecclesiology and Spirituality

To form a dialogic people – that is quite a tall order for a Church that has not been, we all know, a paragon of dialogue. It is a long process of conversion we have to go through, and the process, thank God, has been under way since Vatican II. But we still have a long way to go. To come to that conclusion (the conclusion, that is, that our pastoral task is to build a dialogical Church), I did not have to spend all that time speaking of our experience of social involvement and base communities. But Asians are supposed to do things in a round-about way and I thought I'd write as a quintessential Asian. Now it is time to explicate some ideas present in this essay. I choose to focus on only two: ecclesiology and spirituality.

On the first, *ecclesiology*: we need to ask a fundamental question: What is your theology of the Church, your defining vision of the Church? Perhaps this is a stupid question to ask of liturgists. But what

I'm asking is your operative ecclesiology, what you actually work from in all you do, not one that may be intellectually and doctrinally correct and up-to-date as theologies go, but having no real influence on what you actually do as liturgists. We've had this problem again and again with bishops (and bishops not just in the Philippines). We see how many of them, priests too and laity, for that matter, will claim they fully subscribe to Vatican II ideas of Church, yet from their pastoral pro-grammes we see clearly they operate mainly from the model of Church as Institution (and Institution in a decidedly pre-Vatican II mould), very differently from bishops who act in conformity with other Church models like Servant, Herald, Communion, Sacrament, Community of Disciples, to use Avery Dulles' models – and carry out pastoral pro-grammes that try to faithfully reflect their stated theology of Church. One wonders whether this problem with bishops and their operative ecclesiologies would also be a problem with liturgists.

On the second, *spirituality*: a consequence of one's theology of the Church is one's spirituality. So we ask: What is yours? Back in 1987, John Paul II wrote *Sollicitudo Rei Socialis*. In it he spelled out what he meant by the virtue of solidarity. Not a third way between Marxist collectivism and liberal capitalism, he took pains to explain. He had difficulty, though, giving a name to what he had been talking about. But he gave one anyway, and he said that what he was offering was 'a moral theology' – a let-down to an excellent exhortation, I thought. Our unlettered farmers in Bukidnon would have had no trouble calling his 'moral theology' a spirituality of solidarity, or simply the spirituality of the Gospel spelled out more explicitly for the work of justice in the understanding that the values that guide a person in his religious and moral life make up his spirituality.

So I pose this question to liturgists: Is our spirituality enough for the task of building up a dialogical Church, the task too of developing liturgies that will reflect and advance that kind of Church? Or is something lacking? Does our spirituality need rethinking, redirecting? Back in the early 1970s the question was being bandied about by some Jesuits working in the social apostolate. We never seriously posed the question to ourselves in Bukidnon. For us work-horse parish priests in the late 1960s and early 1970s, there was no problem. We thought the kind of pastoral orientation and spirituality that *Gaudium et Spes* was requiring of us was no different basically from what the Spiritual Exercises of St Ignatius or other schools of Christian spirituality had provided us with. So to the question about whether our spirituality was connected with the world or not, our answer was an unequivocal and resounding *yes*. But that was possibly because, as I described ourselves above, we were simple, uncomplicated parish priests – still are.

5. The Challenge

If there is any challenge at all inherent in what I have argued here, I see none other than the problem which Karl Rahner posed so many years ago: that our liturgy, official and unofficial, in the Church and out, be fully grounded in, be attuned to and expressive of, what he calls the 'Liturgy of the World'. There can be no other way of doing the Church's liturgy. But that way of doing liturgy, I'm afraid, requires 1. a theology that provides a vision of what kind of Church will fully effect that liturgy and 2. a spirituality that will move us to achieve as well as we can that vision in our life and work.

The Church has provided both the vision and the spirituality. The task remains effectively to implement that vision and spirituality and how to let that vision and spirituality emerge from the lives of believers in each local church – even when those local churches are not comfortable with your theology of Church or spirituality. But that, I am afraid, is your problem!

12

On the Road to Liturgical Unity: An Anglican Response to Bishop Francisco Claver

Canon Donald Gray

In his encyclical *Ut Unum Sint* Pope John Paul II made reference to movements in the wider church 'corresponding to the liturgical renewal carried out by the Catholic Church' which have brought the Eucharist to the centre of their worship each Sunday.[1] Although my own church, the Church of England, had always intended, from the introduction of the first Book of Common Prayer in 1549, to have the Lord's Supper as the lynch-pin of worship on the Lord's Day, patterns of worship grew up which tended to obscure this apostolic principle.[2] The high-church Oxford Movement in the mid-nineteenth century recalled many parishes to more strict observation of the rubrics.[3] However it is a later movement which can most accurately be described as corresponding to the liturgical renewal carried out by the Catholic Church.

This movement was an attempt to bring together the people of God in each parish around the Lord's Table on the Lord's Day at an hour when they could all make their communion (fasting communion being then an inviolable rule in many places). Yet there was more to these endeavours than a desire to unite the parish in a single act of eucharistic worship week by week. Its pioneers believed that, in its eucharistic worship, the church in that place was being empowered for its social and political witness in the world outside the confines of the church building. They believed worship should not be for spiritual self-improvement or devotional delectation but a strengthening for tasks in the world. Often the Parish Eucharist (as it was called) was followed by a Parish Breakfast, slowing down the headlong homeward congregational dash. Then, during the week they held the Parish Meeting; not an administrative assembly but a gathering for planning the church's community action and outreach.[4] Such a programme and understanding of the profound interdependence of the liturgical movement and social action was the hallmark of the American liturgical agenda in its glory days. Fr Keith Pecklers has said, 'The liturgical movement needed the multi-faceted social action movement for the credibility of its own message.'[5] He quotes from a paper given by John J. Egan at Boston College in 1983:

> What the best of the social activists taught us was what the best of the pastoral liturgists practiced: that the primary object of our concern must be the *whole* person, the person considered not merely as a statistical victim of systematic injustice or even as merely a subject of the Church's sacraments; but the person in their whole existence, with a personal history and a world of relationships all their own.[6]

All of which came to my mind as I read Bishop Claver's challenging and thought-provoking lecture. An approach such as that of Claver provokes an immediate ecumenical 'hear, hear.' We too would want to emphasize, as does Vatican II, the supreme importance of the local church, and acknowledge that a vital and living liturgy plays a fundamental part in developing the authentic local church. Yet, that church is divided at the very point where it should be united. Pope John Paul again in *Ut Unum Sint*:

> We constantly need to go back and meet in the Upper Room of Holy Thursday, even though our presence together in that place will not be perfect until the obstacles to full ecclesial communion are overcome and all Christians can gather together in the common celebration of the Eucharist.[7]

We have moved some way along the road to liturgical unity – but there is still a way to go. One point of tremendous encouragement lies

165

in the fact that, although we still cannot share the eucharistic elements, we are now united in the Ministry of the Word. The publication in 1992 of *The Revised Common Lectionary (RCL)*[8] based primarily on the *Ordo Lectionum Missae* of 1969 was a gigantic step forward in ecumenical liturgical co-operation. The *RCL* has become a major ecumenical document. Christians gather to praise God each Sunday and their common praise is shaped by a common lectionary.[9] Its publication, and subsequent wide adoption by Anglican, Reformed and Protestant Churches, has achieved one of the objectives set out in the *Ecumenical Directory* of 1993,[10] leaving the tantalizing prospect of some further official levels of inter-communion as an urgent objective for all those who take seriously the mission of the Church to the world.

It was a recognition that the manifest weakness of the Church, advertised by its divisions, was affecting the integrity of its witness that brought together the great missionary societies and agencies in the early days of the twentieth century, particularly on occasions such as the seminal 1910 Edinburgh Conference.[11] Surely it must equally be 'for the world' and the integrity of present-day missionary tasks that the last barriers in divided Christendom must be removed, and removed soon.

Bishop Claver illustrated his lecture from significant experience in the Philippines and emphasized the challenges which will inevitably confront a church which is willing to take the risk of entering into dialogue, creating a 'spirituality of solidarity', with the people and the place where God has set us. The particularity of those pastoral challenges varies for each of us, but urbanization of the world continues apace and the growth of our cities progresses unabated. The temptation for many churches has been to retreat into the more comfortable and rewarding pastures of suburbia leaving, at the best, only a rump in the forbidding and unresponsive urban deserts.

On a global scale the era known as the industrial society has given place to something new, a report of an Anglican Commission on Urban Priority Areas declared in 1985.[12] New anonymous housing estates, high-rise tenement buildings, together with urban deprivation of all kinds have created an underclass of multi-deprived urban dwellers in cities all over the world, East and West. The Commission said that a new strategy and reassessment of priorities was urgently needed for the Church. On the subject of liturgy they commented that the (then) new 1300-page Church of England *Alternative Service Book* was 'a symptom of the gulf between the Church and ordinary people'.[13]

Any new strategy, both liturgical as well as pastoral, needs to be not only imaginative but also fundamentally incarnational, if it is to succeed. We must never forget that the Church and its sacraments have been spoken of as 'the extension of the Incarnation'. The Anglican divine Bishop Jeremy Taylor (1613–67) claimed that it was an expression derived from the Fathers:

> The Sacrament of the Lord's Supper being a commemoration and exhibition of this death which was the consummation of our redemption by His body and blood, does contain in it a 'visible word', the word in symbol and visibility and special manifestation. Consonant to which doctrine, the fathers by an elegant expression called the blessed sacrament 'the extension of the incarnation'.[14]

There are those who have accepted and worked out this incarnational principle sacrificially. Let me give you just one example, and not from my own church. East Harlem, where *West Side Story* was set, failed to respond to the ministry of many different ecclesial groupings until three ministers of the East Harlem Protestant Parish adopted the incarnational principle:

> The three summed up this basic conviction in the one word *identification*. Identification would mean living in the same kind of apartment and amid the same garbage as others in East Harlem. It would mean taking their families along, and exposing their children to the same temptations as the children who lived next door. It would mean being always at the disposal of the people with whom they sought identity, always having an open door, always responding to a visitor's knock, however late in the night it might come; it would mean, in other words, an abandonment of privacy and a free welcome into their family circle for

the drug addicts and the drunks and the friendless and the thieves. Identification with East Harlem would mean looking down the dismal streets and saying, 'This is my home; this is where I belong.'

This was, of course, what Christ had done on the first Christmas Day when he came right down into the dirt of the stable in order to be *with* men, to share with them their loneliness, their tensions, and their rats, and from that position to offer his Good News. No doubt this was a way that might lead his disciples beyond Christmas Day to the darkness of Good Friday; but it might also be the one sure way that would lead to Easter Sunday.[15]

If the Eucharist is the extension of the Incarnation then all the guests of God at the Holy Table, from whatever church tradition, go from there to be, in the words of St Teresa of Avila, Christ in the world:

> Christ has no body now in earth but yours
>> no hands but yours,
>> no feet but yours.
> Yours are the eyes through which Christ's compassion
>> is to look out into the world.
> Yours are the feet with which He is to go about
>> doing good.
> Yours are the hands with which He is
>> to bless men now.[16]

It has been truly said that the *Ite Missa Est* is not a dismissal, it is a command.[17]

13

Liturgy in a Religiously Plural World: Muslim and Christian Worship in Dialogue

Daniel Madigan, SJ

In this response to Cisco Claver's paper I want to offer some brief reflections on two particular issues raised by the topic. The first is the very complex question of how we do liturgy in religiously plural contexts. Then I want to follow that with some things we can learn about liturgy from our inter-religious encounters. In that I will draw on my experience prinicipally with Muslims.

1. Liturgy in Dialogical Contexts

Perhaps the greatest risk we run when we plan liturgy for inter-religious settings is that it becomes an exercise in mutual observation and analysis rather than worship. We often create an amalgam of gestures, symbols, texts and movement and then we watch each other pray – often critically, sometimes open to learn. It is no simple task to develop a liturgy in such a context because a major element in what makes a liturgy 'work' as worship is precisely its familiarity, its groundedness in the community's tradition and collective memory. No invented amalgam of traditions can carry this off, nor is it easy to see how a liturgy that avoids the specificities of any particular tradition could truly serve as liturgy.

The default approach to common liturgy tends to lean heavily on texts. Unfortunately this often leads us to a very cerebral approach to what we intend to be an act of common worship, touching the body and the spirit as well as the mind. We create a parade of religious ideas from different traditions, searching for texts with common themes, original ideas or recognizable echoes. This can be a valuable exercise, but it is not worship.

Furthermore we tend to make category mistakes when it comes to the use of scripture. The texts of the different traditions play quite diverse roles in our religions, yet we act as though scripture were a universal concept. That is far from true. To take an example, the place of scriptural recitation in the Muslim tradition could be considered analogous to the role of the Eucharist in the Christian tradition. Since for Muslims the Qur'an is the very Word of God that has taken shape in our world and in our history, the recitation functions as a re-presentation of the primordial moment of revelation, the real presence of God's speech. What is heard is not a report of the Word, but the Word itself as the believer makes present once more those same sounds once conveyed by God to the Prophet. Even if that believer is not able to translate those sounds or make sense of the words she is using, nonetheless the 'sacrament' of the Word is real. It does not require too much of a stretch, when we consider our concept of the Word-made-flesh, to see the analogy, *mutatis mutandis*, between what Qur'anic recitation means for Muslims and what the Eucharist means for Christians.

To take the point one step further, I recently overheard a Muslim scholar borrowing the Christian term 'sacrament' to explain to two other Muslims what the act of studying Torah means to Jews. He could see the complexity of the question of the role of scripture in our various traditions. Perhaps the question we need to ask ourselves when faced with the prospect of multi-religious liturgy is what is it that moves each of us into the sphere of communion, of encounter with the divine as it addresses itself to us? In short, what is sacramental for us? For Muslims it is the act and art of recitation; for Jews perhaps the communal study of Torah; for Christians it is without doubt the Eucharist and other sacraments.

Undoubtedly Christians believe in a certain sacramentality of the Word, but it seems to me that we do so in a rather derivative sense, very different from the way in which the Qur'an or the Vedas, for example, function in their respective communities. The words of scripture we know to be the work of the community. They have been chosen and treasured precisely because they put us in contact with the Word-made-flesh. They cannot substitute for it. Other words making similar claims – they have come to be called *apocrypha* – were rejected by the community because they failed to yield that insight into, and create that bond with, the Jesus that the community experienced and in whom they believed.

So what are we to do in these multi-religious contexts where some form of liturgy seems called for? We can take a Quaker approach and be silent together, avoiding the problems that inevitably arise when we put words to our prayer. This can be very effective in certain circumstances, but not everyone is comfortable in such silence, and not every ambience lends itself to the creation of it.

Another alternative is to celebrate one community's form of worship and hope that that group's experience of worshipping will open a way into worship for the others. This also has its drawbacks. In the Christian tradition there is a process of initiation which leads towards the full celebration of Eucharist, or even to the presence throughout the Eucharist as a non-communicant. To have people of other religious traditions as onlookers at the Eucharist, as is often done on official occasions even in Rome, seems somehow out of place. On some occasions I have found myself wishing the Mass were still muttered in Latin rather than having the eucharistic prayer prayed aloud to the puzzlement and even consternation of the Muslim worthies who have been invited for the occasion. With its language of body and blood, that prayer has an intimacy that makes it inappropriate as a public inter-religious proclamation. A liturgy of the Word might serve better, but again we run into the question of how scripture is used and seen.

From another side, participating in some measure in the worship of one particular community can seem to work. Many Christians find themselves drawn to pray in a mosque behind a group of Muslims performing their ritual prayer together. Some have even been invited to join the line of worshippers and perform the various prostrations and other gestures with them. This can be a profound experience. However, like intercommunion, it is also an ambiguous gesture. It has sometimes caused great hurt among Christians in the Middle East when a well-known priest has joined the Muslims in their ritual.

At the inter-religious gathering to pray for peace in January 2002 in Assisi, the various religious groups prayed separately, meeting together both before and after in order to offer reflections and make declarations. (There was due to be a period of silence together, but this was passed over, perhaps because of time constraints and the noisy environment.) However, using such avoidance to solve the question of inter-religious worship cannot be a definitive answer. Our worshipping together is the objective of our unity, precisely because we understand that worship of the creator is so closely tied to recognition of the creature. John asks us rather pointedly how we can claim to love the God we cannot see when we do not love the brother or sister we do see (John 1:20–21). A disunited worship will always be incomplete because it bespeaks an as yet imperfect love.

It may be that in this connection is the answer to our difficulty. Recognition of the creature will draw us to worship the creator so we begin with that recognition – perhaps in ritualized form, but even more basically and more importantly in non-ritual activity, which might eventually find its way into ritual and explicit worship. What I am suggesting is that, rather than beginning with the presumption that we can find a meaningful way to worship together, we should first be seeking non-liturgical ways of being together in an awareness of the presence of God. We should count these moments as in their own way liturgical.

Let me offer an example. The day after overhearing that Muslim scholar speak of the sacramental nature of study for the Jewish community, I went with two professors (who are also rabbis) and the wife of one of them to visit the family of one of our Muslim students near Istanbul. We sat under the trees outside the small summer house, picking cherries and mulberries as we chatted, using the various languages and translations we could manage to muster between the eight of us. It was unavoidable that we would talk about religion at least part of the time because the father of the family was a retired high-school religion teacher. Never having had a rabbi in his house before – let alone two at once – he could not miss the opportunity to ask about various things that had puzzled him over the years. The honest courtesy of the inquiries, the warmth of the hospitality and the unostentatious care taken to ensure that the meal could be readily shared by all combined to make the evening truly memorable. At the end of the meal the father invited the three Jews present to pray the grace. Then my student asked me to sing the Taizé *Magnificat* that is used after meals in the community where she lives in Rome. The family followed this with their own prayer in Arabic. For all of us, it was a moment of profound gratitude for a rare glimpse of unity among believers. However, it was a moment long prepared by studying together, by simple contacts in the university, by years spent by all parties in trying to understand the tradition of another, or the others. That small unrehearsed 'liturgical' moment that seemed so perfectly to express the reality of our friendship as believers of related but diverse traditions was the goal towards which we strive, not the point from which we begin. We could sense in one another at the end of that evening desire to worship, to give thanks. It was, in the literal sense of the word, 'eucharistic'.

If our inter-religious worship is to have any sense as praise and thanksgiving, then it probably has to come after the simple living and working together in which we discover a motive for gratitude and a desire to praise the God who made all this and brought us together in human solidarity.

2. Learning from our Dialogue Partners

The second thing I want to discuss is what I have learned about liturgy from my partners in dialogue – in my case mostly from Muslims. It is a great pity and, indeed, a gross injustice that almost the only images of the Muslim ritual prayer seen by people in the West are the accompaniment to television news reports of bombings, attacks and radical Islamic groups. Imagine the outcry if a report about the Catholics of the IRA were illustrated by images of the Mass.

The ritual itself is carried out in silence except for the occasional brief formula of praise used to enable a group to synchronize their movements when a group prays together shoulder to shoulder. Even for one person alone, the ritual is physically dramatic. In large assemblies it is strikingly expressive of community. The postures are physically demanding and even their boldness does not seem to cause self-consciousness. This is often in contrast with many of our liturgies in which movement and gesture have been reduced to an embarrassed minimum, the involvement of the body sacrificed to an ever greater reliance on words to substitute and explain symbols now so vestigial that they cannot speak for themselves.

It is very obvious in Muslim worship that those who participate are not spectators but worshippers. The community prays in what seem to be straight ranks. However, since all those lines are directed towards one point on the globe, they form in fact concentric circles of enormous dimensions – world dimensions. In many Christian liturgies we too often witness a move away from the assembly as co-celebrants towards community as audience. This can happen even in situations where there is a great deal of involvement of the people in various liturgical ministries. It can lead to a sense of 'the cast' in the sanctuary and 'the audience' in the pews – especially when we 'roll the credits' at the end of the liturgy and give a round of applause to the choir, the organist, the cantor, the liturgy committee, and on and on.

With the possible exception of the Friday sermon, Muslim worship is non-clerical. The obligation to perform this ritual five times a day is incumbent upon the individual whether there is a community and a leader or not. One witnesses among those Muslims who fulfil the obligation a striking sense of individual responsibility even if the time and place are less than ideal. The imam (literally 'the person in front') is the facilitator of the community's common worship in the most minimal way. Virtually anyone who knows what he is doing can perform the role. He performs the same actions as the other worshippers and says the same words, just setting the pace and giving the audible cues for those ranged behind him.

The relegation of women to a position out of sight – where they will not prove an immodest distraction to the ever-susceptible male – offers a dramatic demonstration of *de facto* exclusion even if the obligation to pray is also incumbent on women. Seeing such exclusion in an unfamiliar setting alerts one to the ways in which women are excluded

174

in so many ways from Catholic worship, even more so *de facto* than even the narrow regulations require. In most parts of the world the involvement of women in the liturgical ministries currently open to them lags well behind the law that allows it.

The experience of others' beliefs and others' ways of worship yields insights by way of contrast or similarity, but at the same time it is precisely in our encounter with the other that we come to know our own specificity and uniqueness. Through my dealings with Muslims I have been forced to think a great deal about how we speak of the 'Word of God' and how we treat it in the liturgy. It is perhaps ironic that in the religion we identify as so bound to the sacredness of the book, there is no role at all for a physical book in the ritual. Scripture is present in oral form, but not even publicly. Rather it is recited silently or *sotto voce* by the worshipper. Christians, on the other hand, for whom the Word of God is first and foremost enfleshed rather than encoded, often find themselves reverencing the physical book of the scriptures in a way that suggests a much more literal and mechanical approach to inspiration than our theology would normally accommodate. In religiously plural situations this can be rather misleading – especially for Christian minorities in Muslim contexts. There the dominant theology of the Word-made-book or Word-made-recitation can subtly supplant a truly Christian belief in the Word-made-flesh.

For all the attractive simplicity and dramatic directness of Muslim ritual, it will usually strike a Christian as somehow foreign – and not just in the sense that it is exotic and 'oriental'. The Muslim worshipper is the *'abd*, 'servant' or 'slave'. The word for worship is *'ibâda,* coming from the same root meaning. Ultimately for a Christian worship must take its tone from Jesus' declaration that we are no longer slaves, but friends – guests whose feet he will wash – or from Paul's insight that we are the adopted daughters and sons of the household. It is something we need to be reminded of again and again, since as George Herbert puts it in his poem 'Love', beginning 'Love bade me welcome', our souls draw back, 'guilty of dust and sin'. We come into God's presence, but prefer to remain shamefaced servants rather than accept

175

that we are honoured guests. When it comes to worship, the Christian must hear the final lines of that haunting poem:

'You must sit down,' says Love, 'and taste my meat.'
So I did sit and eat.

Conclusion

During the international meeting of Jesuit liturgists, Robert Taft proposed three major theses: '1. Liturgy is at the very centre of the redemptive work Christ exercises through the ministry of the Church; 2. A community that does not pray together regularly cannot claim to be Christian; 3. Anyone who does not celebrate and live the liturgy of the Church according to the mind of the Church, cannot pretend to be true to the Church.' Taft's theses, of course, are not limited to Jesuit liturgy. Indeed, they apply to all of Christian worship even though his third point might sound more exclusively Catholic. From his theses, several affirmations can be made.

Firstly, as the work of Christ, liturgy is God's gift to the Church. In other words, God doesn't need the liturgy, we do. As such, Christian worship invites the community to tap into this divine activity in order to ascertain what God is doing within us and within the Church as it worships *now*. What is God teaching us? What is God asking us to do? How and where is God calling us to welcome the stranger or free the prisoner here and now? This vision of discerning God's movements within worship is consistent with Ignatian spirituality, but it pertains to all of Christian liturgy.

Secondly, Christian worship is fundamentally communitarian in scope. Private prayer and meditation flow out of the common, but common prayer always takes precedence. Gathered together in holy assembly, the Christian community discovers who it is and recovers its collective memory, as Wendelin Köster's essay reminded us. Postmodern influences like individualism offer their own challenges in this area, but the fact remains that the Christian community is less than complete when any one of its members is absent. That is why the sick are visited by a community member with the eucharistic food carried from that assembly. It is also why delegates at the Rome meeting seriously called

177

into question the pratice of 'private' Mass where some Jesuits continue to celebrate the Eucharist alone in private chapels, even on Sundays.

Thirdly, there is a tradition of 2000 years which provides the basis, the form and structure for our liturgy. Happily, in the twentieth century, Christian liturgists of all different denominations returned to the same biblical and patristic sources, and discovering the same form and structure, adopted and reformed a similar liturgy for all the churches. Today the liturgical structure for Sunday Eucharist is virtually identical whether the worshipping assembly happens to be a Church of England parish in Lincolnshire, a Lutheran parish in Stockholm, a Methodist church in Atlanta, or a Roman Catholic community in Harare. This is very good news, indeed. We Christians share a common liturgical tradition, as Canon Donald Gray reminded us, and with the Revised Common Lectionary we even preach on the same lessons. This common tradition also reminds us that we cannot 're-invent the wheel' every Sunday, creating new ritual forms *ex nihilo* under the guise of 'liturgical creativity'. What makes ritual work is precisely the fact that ritual is repetitive behaviour; one doesn't have to think about what to do next because we know what to do.

That being said, delegates at the international meeting on Jesuit liturgists also delineated some important elements which will need consideration as we ponder the future of Christian worship. One fundamental area is that of liturgical inculturation. Now more than ever, we recognize the fact that we belong to a 'world church' as theologian Karl Rahner said so many years ago. Underlying such a concept is both a harmonious union of peoples and churches which share a common baptism and profession of faith and also a deep respect for cultural diversity. As such, this 'world church' is multi-faceted and its liturgical future will be seriously compromised if inculturation is not at its heart. As Peter Phan noted in his text, gone are the days of absolute uniformity as equatable with catholicity. The Gospel of Jesus Christ needs to be incarnated uniquely in each culture so that evangelization can take place. The Sunday Eucharist itself provides a privileged venue for evangelization, but will only be an effective instrument to the extent that the worship expresses and symbolizes the lives of those who gather to celebrate. Respect for our identity as a world church will include ever greater attention to popular religion with its various forms of non-liturgical devotions especially in Latin America, and to inter-religious dialogue with Muslims and other people of faith who seek God 'with a sincere heart'.

A second area is that of liturgical preaching, which will require serious attention as we consider the future of liturgy. By and large, Anglican and Protestant preachers are far ahead of their Roman Catholic counterparts in this regard both in the quality of the preparation and in the delivery. Of course, there are exceptions on both sides, but the truth remains that too often, Catholic preaching fails to intersect with the problems in people's lives. On the one extreme, more traditional preachers feel obliged to communicate doctrine in the homily as if it were a catechism class, while more progressive homilists tend to trivialize the scriptural text with banal examples from everyday life or poorly timed jokes. Neither approach is ideal if our preaching is to be itself sacramental. Timothy Radcliffe's insistence on a contemplative listening and on greater attention to poetry is essential, as is his insistence on honesty – both within the preaching and in what is asked of its hearers.

The issue of clerical concelebration and its foundation in the theology of priesthood was a third area which the delegates addressed. Greater study will be needed if we are to better understand the ecclesial symbol of concelebration with respect to (a) the diversity of ministries within the liturgical assembly; and (b) baptismal priesthood shared by all members of the Church. This is significant especially when the number of clergy concelebrating outnumbers that of the laity in the pews. We shall never arrive at the root of these problems if we do not first plumb the depths of this theology of priesthood – or perhaps we should say 'divergent existing *theologies* of priesthood'.

The overarching theme of this meeting was the future – an analysis of the present situation so as to move towards the future in the context of postmodernity with all of its inherent challenges. From all that has been said, what is at stake is the credibility of the Church's worship and indeed, of the Church itself. With church members who are increasingly astute theologically, they will not tolerate poor preaching or presidency at the Lord's table, nor will they tolerate condescension in any form. This was made abundantly clear in the recent lay response to the clergy sexual scandals in North America when US and Canadian Catholic laity called for a greater voice; some even withheld their financial contributions to their churches or dioceses. We know statistically that large numbers of Roman Catholics (more than 100,000 each year) leave the Church in Latin America because they are made to feel more at home in small, fundamentalist churches than they are in their own parishes which are too large and anonymous. Moreover, we also know of increasing numbers of Catholics who find themselves excluded – 'beyond the pale' – because of lifestyles or situations which are considered unacceptable by the Church. What to do? While we do not wish flippantly to disregard Church teaching, we must honestly admit and confront the gap between ideal and the real, not unlike that same gap which existed in Jesus' own day, recognizing that these members of the body of Christ are present with us in our Sunday assemblies and deserve our welcome and respect as Christ would have us do. Quite simply, failure to be hospitable will result in more and more empty churches, as is increasingly the case in Western Europe. On the contrary, welcoming the stranger, the marginalized or the outcast is to put Rahner's 'Liturgy of the World', and even more fundamentally the Gospel, into practice.

Related to the issue of liturgical hospitality is that of increased and ever-greater ecumenical liturgical co-operation. This means that much more is needed than gathering together during the Week of Prayer for Christian Unity to hold joint evensong, or a shared Bible Vigil at holiday times. We need to think and act ecumenically; to pray for one another's bishops and communities at the Sunday Eucharist, and to rejoice that there is infinitely more which unites us than divides us – even as we remain sadly divided at the eucharistic table.

Finally, for Jesuit community worship as in all Christian worship, we need to recover the sense of awe and mystery with greater attention to silence and the non-verbals, as Cardinal Danneels reminded us. Liturgy is an art form where the heart and emotions are engaged at the deepest levels. In the past and still in the present, liturgy has been viewed too often as a purely intellectual activity. On the contrary, liturgy is art, and this is best seen in the use of liturgical symbolism.

When liturgical symbols are well used and reverenced they don't need to be explained. The sign of the cross does not need an introduction before it is enacted; it *is* an introduction. The importance of water does not need to be explained before the presider sprinkles the assembly with baptismal water. Something is wrong if symbols fail to communicate or function liturgically. In this regard, those in the West have much to learn from the East; our use of symbols is in great need of refurbishing.

At the conclusion of their meeting, Jesuit liturgists committed themselves to ongoing study and further reflection on specific topics mentioned above. (Some more peculiarly Jesuit topics have not been included here.) In the meantime, as they look towards the future and evaluate their own liturgical practices, it is their hope that these essays will stimulate the ongoing liturgical reforms within other Roman Catholic communities and, indeed, within all the Christian churches.

Notes

Chapter 2

1. John Paul II, *Proclaiming Christ*, 9 & 13.
2. Margaret R. Miles, *Seeing and Believing: religion and values in the movies* (Boston, MA: Beacon Press 1996) 25.
3. In 1986–7, the Australian bishops commissioned a national enquiry into communications. This excellent report argues for the Church to understand and budget for a high profile participation in Australia's media. The report demonstrates the level of media activity the dioceses were undertaking. Such an optimistic report could not be tendered today. See Paul Duffy, SJ, *To Bring Good News: evangelisation and communications* (Report of the National enquiry into the Communications Apostolate 1987).
4. Quoted in John Paul II, *Ut Unum Sint* (1995) 19.
5. The idea that the Church is now a competitor with the media in our culture is explored in detail in Jay Newman, *Religion vs. Television* (Westport, CT: Praegar 1996), especially chapter four.

Chapter 4

1. I indicate, where available and known to me, translations of the works cited in the notes.

Abbreviations used:

ARSI = *Acta Romana Societatis Iesu.*

Bertrand, *Politique* = D. Bertrand, *La politique de S. Ignace de Loyola. L'analyse sociale* (Paris 1985).

BHG = F. Halkin, *Bibliotheca hagiographica Graeca* (Subsidia hagiographica 8a, 3rd ed. Brussels 1957).

Bouyer, *Liturgical Piety* = L. Bouyer, *Liturgical Piety* (Liturgical Studies, Notre Dame 1955).

Cattaneo, *Culto* = E. Cattaneo, *Il culto cristiano in occidente. Note storiche* (Bibliotheca *Ephemerides Liturgicae*, Subsidia 13, Rome 1978).

CSJ = *Constitutions of the Society of Jesus.*

DOL = International Commission on English in the Liturgy (= ICEL), *Documents on the Liturgy 1963–1979. Conciliar, Papal, and Curial Texts* (Collegeville 1982), ICEL English translation of official Latin text of Catholic magisterial documents concerning the liturgy. References are to paragraph numbers in the margin.

EDIL = R. Kaczynski (ed.), *Enchiridion documentorum instaurationis liturgicae*, Bd. I: 1963–1973 (Turin 1976), official Latin text of Catholic magisterial documents concerning the liturgy. References are to paragraph numbers in the margin.

Klauser, *Short History* = Th. Klauser, *A Short History of the Western Liturgy. An Account and Some Reflections*, trans. J. Halliburton (2nd ed. Oxford/NY/Toronto/Melbourne 1979) = trans. of *Kleine abendländische Liturgiegeschichte* (Peter Hamstein Verlag 1965).

LMD = *La Maison-Dieu*.

OCA = Orientalia Christiana Analecta.

O'Malley, 'Priesthood' = J. W. O'Malley, 'Priesthood, Ministry, and Religious Life: Some Historical and Historiographical Considerations', *Theological Studies* 49 (1988) 223–57.

Schurhammer, *Xavier* = G. Schurhammer, *Francis Xavier. His Life, His Times*. Vol. I: *Europe (1506–1541)*, trans. M. J. Costello (Rome 1973).

SSJ = Studies in the Spirituality of Jesuits (The Seminar on Jesuit Spirituality, St Loius).

Taft, BEW = R. F. Taft, *Beyond East and West. Problems in Liturgical Understanding*. Second revised and enlarged edition (Rome 1997) = *Oltre l'oriente e l'occidente. Per una tradizione liturgica viva*, trans. Sara Staffuzza (Pubblicazione del Centro Aletti 21, Rome 1999).

Taft, *Hours* = id., *The Liturgy of the Hours in East and West. The Origins of the Divine Office and its Meaning for Today*. Second Revised Edition (Collegeville: The Liturgical Press 1993) = *La Liturgie des Heures en Orient et en Occident. Origine et sens de l'Office divin* (Mysteria 2, Turnhout: Brepols 1991) = *La Liturgia delle Ore in Oriente e in Occidente. Le origini dell'Ufficio divino e il suo significato oggi*, 2a edizione revisionata con nuova traduzione di Sara Stafuzza (Rome: Ed. Lipa 2001).

Taft, *Precommunion* = id., *A History of the Liturgy of St John Chrysostom*, vol. V: *The Precommunion Rites* (OCA 261, Rome 2000).

Tanner 1-2 = N. P. Tanner (ed.), *Decrees of the Ecumenical Councils*, 2 vols. (London/Washington, DC 1990).

WL = *Woodstock Letters*.

2. 'Principle and Foundation', *The Spiritual Exercises of St Ignatius* §23.

3. Although there are Jesuits belonging by birth or adoption to Eastern Catholic Churches, my remarks are perforce limited to Latin-rite Jesuit liturgy. On that topic, see the seminal work on liturgy in the Society: J. E. Weiss, *Jesuits and the Liturgy of the Hours: The Tradition, its Roots, Classical Exponents, and Criticism in the Perspective of Today* (University of Notre Dame doctoral dissertation, Sept. 1992), unfortunately available thus far only in University Microfilms International dissertation service format. In addition, see: P. Cas-

perz, 'Liturgical Prayer and the Ignatian Exercises', *New Blackfriars* 54 (1973) 72-80; F. Cavallera, *Ascétisme et liturgie* (Paris 1913); P. Cioffi & W. Sampson, 'The Society and the Liturgical Movement,' WL 88 (1959) 238-247; J. Gelineau, 'The Liturgical Spirit of the Exercises', WL 89 (1960) 241-260; G. Ellard, 'St Ignatius Loyola and Public Worship', *Thought* 19 (1944) 649-670; G. & A. Ellard, 'The Laymen's Retreat and the Liturgy', WL 81 (1952) 13-23; G. E. Ganss, 'Ignatian Research and the Dialogue with the Contemporary American Mind', WL 93 (1964) 158-161; J. Leo Klein, *American Jesuits and the Liturgy* (SSJ 11/3, May 1979); M. Nicolau, 'Liturgia y Ejercicios', *Manresa* 20 (1948) 233-274; J. Schumacher, 'Ignatian Spirituality and the Liturgy', WL 87 (1958) 14-35; D. Stanley, 'Our Jesuit Response to the Word of God in the Liturgy and the Spiritual Exercises', unpublished paper read at the Liturgy Day, Weston College, Weston, MA, 9 April 1964; Keith Pecklers, SJ, unpublished 1997 essay 'Liturgy in the Houses of the Society of Jesus'. See also the Jesuit Generals' letters on liturgy cited below in notes 44, 69, 81.

4. Much of the material in this section is resumed from my earlier writings: R. F. Taft, 'The Liturgical Year: Studies, Prospects, Reflections', *Worship* 55 (1981) 2–23, reprinted in id., BEW chapter 1, and in M. E. Johnson (ed.), *Between Memory and Hope: Readings in the Liturgical Year* (A Pueblo Book, Collegeville 2001) 3-23; Taft, *Hours,* esp. chapter 21; id., 'Teologia della Liturgia delle ore', Pontificio Istituto Liturgico Sant'Anselmo, *Scientia Liturgica. Manuale di liturgia,* ed. A. J. Chupungco, vol. 5: *Tempo e spazio liturgico* (Casale Monferrato 1998) 150–165 = 'The Theology of the Liturgy of the Hours', in: *Handbook for Liturgical Studies,* vol. V: *Liturgical Time and Space,* ed. A. J. Chupungco (A Pueblo Book, Collegeville 2000) 119–32.

5. Jn 1:1, 14.

6. II Cor 5:17, Gal 6:15, Rom 8:19ff, Rev 21–2.

7. I Cor 15:45, Rom 5:14.

8. I Cor 5:7; Jn 1:29, 36; 19:36; 1 Pet 1:19; Rev 5ff.

9. Mt 26:28; Mk 14;24; Lk 22:20; Heb 8–13.

10. Col 2:11–12.

11. Jn 6:30–58; Rev 2:17.

12. Jn 2:19–27.

13. Eph 5:2; Heb 2:17–3:2, 4:14–10:14.

14. Col 2:16–17; Mt 11:28–12:8; Heb 3:7-4:11.

15. Lk 4:16–21; Acts 2:14–36.

16. See, for example, Pius XII's 20 Nov. 1947 Encyclical *Mediator Dei* on the Sacred Liturgy §§16–20.

17. 'Just as surely as we have borne the image of the man of dust, we shall also bear the image of the man of heaven' (I Cor 15:49; cf. Phil 2:7–11, 3:20-21; Eph 4:22–24), the Risen Christ, 'image of the invisible God, the first-born of all creation' (Col 1:15; cf. II Cor 4:4), who conforms us to his image through the gift of his Spirit (II Cor 3:15; Rom 8:11ff., 29). For St Paul,

'to live is Christ' (Phil 1:21), and to be saved is to be conformed to Christ by dying to self and rising to new life in him (II Cor 4:10ff, 13:4; Rom 6:3ff; Col 2:12–13, 20, 3:1–3; Gal 2:20; Eph 2:1ff.; Phil 2:5ff, 3:10–11, 18, 21) who, as the 'last Adam' (I Cor 15:45), is the definitive form of redeemed human nature (I Cor 15:21–22; Rom 5:12–21; Col 3:9-11; Eph 4:22–24). Until this pattern is so repeated in each of us that Christ is indeed 'all in all' (Col 3:11), we shall not yet have 'filled up what is lacking in Christ's afflictions for the sake of his body, that is, the church' (Col 1:24). For we know 'the power of his resurrection' only if we 'share his sufferings, becoming like him in his death' (Phil 3:10).

18. For St Paul liturgy and Christian life are one. Never once does Paul use cultic nomenclature – liturgy, sacrifice, priest, offering – for anything but a life of self-giving, lived after the pattern set by Christ: see for example Rom 1:9, 12:1, 15:6; Phil 2:17, 4:18; 2 Tim 4:6; Heb 13:11–16. When Paul does speak of what we call liturgy, i.e. church services, as in I Cor 10–14; Eph 4; or Gal 3:27–28; he makes it clear that its purpose is to build up the Body of Christ into that new temple and liturgy and priesthood, in which sanctuary and offerer and offered are one. For it is in the liturgy of the Church, in the ministry of Word and Sacrament, that the biblical pattern of recapitulation of all in Christ is returned to the collectivity, and applied to the community of faith that will live in him.

19. *Sermon 74 (De ascensione 2)* 2, PL 54:398. I translate Leo's 'sacramenta' as 'liturgical ministry' because when the Fathers referred to 'sacraments' they did not have in mind our list of seven sacraments, a list not fixed before the Middle Ages, but understood 'sacramenta' in the sense of the entire visible ministry of the Church as portrayed in *Sacrosanctum Concilium*, the Vatican II *Constitution on the Sacred Liturgy*, and in Pius XII's *Mediator Dei*, both cited below.

20. Citing a phrase from the old Roman Secret for the 9th Sunday after Pentecost: DOL §2; EDIL §2.

21. *Encyclical Letter of His Holiness Pius XII on the Sacred Liturgy*. Vatican Library Translation (Washington DC: NCWC, n.d.).

22. I.e. if Ignatius had known the term 'liturgy' in the sense in which we use it today, which is, in fact, of recent vintage.

23. On this system, see Taft, *Hours* 297ff; H. G. J. Beck, *The Pastoral Care of Souls in South-East France during the Sixth Century* (Analecta Gregoriana 51, Rome 1950) 66–79; G. W. O. Addleshaw, *The Early Parochial System and the Divine Office* (Alcuin Club Prayer Book Revision Pamphlets 15, London n.d.); P. Salmon, *The Breviary through the Centuries* (Collegeville 1962) 6ff.

24. Quotations from Klauser, *Short History* chapter 3.

25. Even small towns had their bishop and a large number of lower clergy – in some places as many as one in 20 of the population. Two churches in 15th century Breslau had 236 priests between them: J. A. Jungmann, *Pastoral*

Liturgy (New York 1962) 66; trans. from *Liturgisches Erbe und pastorale Gegenwart* (Innsbruck/Vienna/Munich 1960); Italian trans. *Eredità liturgica e attualità pastorale* (Rome 1962).

26. Taft, *Hours* 298. This system of church organization lasted in some parts of Western Europe until the 10/11th century. Of course there were also country chapels beyond the towns, served by presbyters sent out from the cathedral. But only the cathedral had a baptistry, and all major feasts were celebrated only at this main church. Even in larger cities like Rome, where there were numerous suburban churches, the unity of the one eucharistic and ecclesial community was maintained by such practices as the *fermentum* or carrying a particle of the Eucharist from the one Sunday papal or 'cathedral' Mass to the outlying communities as a sign of their communion in the one Eucharist of the *basilica senior*, the episcopal church. See R. F. Taft, 'One Bread, One Body: Ritual Symbols of Ecclesial Communion in the Patristic Period', in *Nova Doctrina Vetusque: Essays in Early Christianity in Honor of Fredric W. Schlatter, SJ* ed. by Douglas Kries and Catherine Brown Tkacz (American University Studies, Series VII, Theology and Religion vol. 207, New York: Peter Lang 1999) 23-50; id., *Precommunion* 398ff; and the further references in these works.

27. As early as the Council of Chalcedon (451), canon 6 forbids the ordination of ministers 'absolutely,' i.e. not for a specific ministry: Tanner 1:90. On the shift away from this pristine communitarian concept of ecclesial ministry, see *inter alia* C. Vogel, 'Une mutation cultuelle inexpliquée: le passage de l'eucharistie communautaire à la messe privée', *Revue des sciences religieuses* 54 (1980) 231-50.

28. Taft, *Hours* 298. They were called minsters in Anglo-Saxon England, baptismal churches (*plebes baptismales*) in Gaul, or simply *plebes* in Italy, from which we have the Italian *pieve*, still used for parish churches in some parts of central Italy and which, like minster in England, is at the origin of many place names. Historians refer to these churches as 'first foundation' parishes, to distinguish them from the later break-up of urban dioceses into parishes 'of the second foundation' by the middle of the 12th century. Unlike the latter, which were served by one presbyter, 'first foundation' parishes were organized just like the cathedral churches, except that the superior was not a bishop but a prelate called chorbishop (from the Greek *chora*, a rural habitation), provost, custos, archpriest or abbot, depending on the area in question. There, too, the body of clergy shared a quasi-common life and celebrated the offices in common.

29. Cattaneo, *Culto* 295.

30. Ibid. 295–6.

31. Klauser, *Short History* 98–9. This practice began in Gaul under Eastern influence probably in the 8th century, but was not introduced into Rome until c. 1000. On the whole question see J. A. Jungmann, *The Mass of the Roman*

Rite. Missarum sollemnia, 2 vols. (New York 1951, 1955) 1:82–3, 152, 2:137–8, 141; and much more extensively, especially for the early and Eastern evidence, and with additional recent bibliography: R. F. Taft, 'Was the Eucharistic Anaphora Recited Secretly or Aloud? The Ancient Tradition and What Became of It', paper to be read at the St Nersess Seminary 40th Anniversary Symposium *Liturgy in Context: Worship Traditions of Armenia and the Neighboring Christian East,* New York, 25-8 September 2002, to appear in the Congress Acta.

32. Cattaneo, *Culto* 307.

33. Ibid. 308-9; A. Franz, *Die Messe im deutschen Mittelalter. Beiträge zur Geschichte der Liturgie und des heiligen Volkslebens* (Freiburg im B. 1902/ Vienna 1963) 46ff.

34. See the descriptions in Klauser, *Short History* chapter 4, and Bouyer, *Liturgical Piety* chapter 1. Already in 1450 the Cardinal legate Nicholas of Cusa (1401–64), travelling through Germany, complained that Jesus instituted the Eucharist to be eaten, not to be looked at: Klauser, *Short History* 71; P. Browe, *Die Verehrung der Eucharistie im Mittelalter* (Rome 1967) 170ff.

35. The Little Office of the Blessed Virgin and, except on greater feasts, the entire Office of the Dead were added to the normal Office of the Day, along with the Penitential Psalms after Prime and the Gradual Psalms before Matins, plus all sorts of prayers and intercessions for various intentions: W. J. Leonard, SJ, *The Letter Carrier* (Kansas City 1993) 350–51 (cited in note 47 below); Klauser, *Short History* 96. The office, thus overblown, was sterile even for monastics, as the Black Monks of England lament at their chapter in 1277: '...because of the length of the Office which causes disgust and extinguishes devotion, study, once the glory of the Order, has become obsolete.... Therefore, many people distinguished for dignity, knowledge and morals keep away from the Order and contemptuously refuse to enter it': W. A. Pantin, *Documents Illustrating Activities of the General and Provincial Chapters of the English Black Monks* (The Royal Historical Society, Camden Third Series XLV, London 1931) 64ff.

36. See canon 22 of the Council of Vienne in 1311/12, cited in Cattaneo, *Culto* 296-7.

37. See Klauser, *Short History* chapter 4.

38. Bouyer, *Liturgical Piety* 1ff. As late as *Mediator Dei* §25 (1947), Pius XII still felt the need to counteract this view of liturgy.

39. This was not, of course, the theology of the best in medieval Catholic scholasticism, like the teaching of St Thomas Aquinas, for whom sacraments are *mysteria fidei:* 'Verbum operat in sacramentis non quia dicitur sed quia creditur.' Martin Luther taught basically the same thing in his *Commentary on Romans.*

40. Indeed, as has been shown, many of the popular devotions in use at the time of the early Society were in fact surrogate forms of the Divine Office –

something like an attempt to 'recathedralize' the Liturgy of the Hours – developed to fill the void left when the overgrown Hours had become so formalistic and monasticized that they had lost all usefulness as popular cathedral prayer. See Th. Schnitzler, 'Stundengebet und Volksandacht', in J. A. Jungmann (ed.), *Brevierstudien. Referat aus der Studientagung von Assisi 14.-17. September 1956* (Trier 1958) 71–84, esp. 75ff, and the additional literature 72–73, cited by G. V. O'Connor, 'What is Common Prayer?' 3 (unpublished paper made available to me by the author, one of my former students, and cited with his permission). On the relationship between the Divine Office and popular devotions, see also the very acute reflections of C. Dehne, 'Roman Catholic Popular Devotions', in J. Gallen (ed.), *Christians at Prayer* (Liturgical Studies, Notre Dame/London 1977) 83–99.

41. This turning away from a liturgy distant from the people in favour of the flowering of interior private prayer is already apparent in the great 14th century Rhenish and Flemish mystics, especially the Dominican friars Meister Ekhart (c. 1260–1327), Tauler (c. 1300–61), Suso (c. 1295–1366); and the Fleming Ruysbroeck (1293–1381). We see the same phenomenon in the *Devotio Moderna* of Grote and Kempis. See Taft, *Hours* 301–4.

42. Klauser, *Short History* 120ff.

43. Cited in J. Leclercq, *Alone with God* (London 1962) 111.

44. Bouyer, *Liturgical Piety* 2. In his 'pilgrim years' Ignatius himself read the Passion while attending mass: J. Brodrick, *Saint Ignatius Loyola. The Pilgrim Years 1491–1538* (New York 1956) 104 note 2.

45. Similarly, the first ex professo official Jesuit teaching on liturgy, the letter of 5th and longest-reigning (33 years and 11 months: 10 Feb. 1581–31 Jan. 1615) General Claudio Aquaviva, treats the Mass and the breviary as entirely a matter of interior piety, without a hint of their communal, ecclesial nature: 'Epistula R.P.N. Claudii Aquavivae ad Provinciales Societatis de Officii Divini Recitatione ac Celebratione Missae', *Epistolae Praepositorum Generalium ad Patres et Fratres Societatis Iesu*. Tomus Primus complectens epistolas priorum sex Praep. Generalium, editio altera (Rollarii Typis Iulii De Meester 1909) 326–37.

46. J. de Guibert, *The Jesuits, Their Spiritual Doctrine and Practice. A Historical Study*, trans. W. J. Young (St Louis 1972) = *La spiritualité de la Compagnie de Jésus: esquisse historique* (Ouvrage posthume, Rome 1953) 53–9.

47. Vatican II *Constitution on the Sacred Liturgy* §112, DOL 112; EDIL 112. Here too, however, we must note that Ignatius had in mind the liturgical chant of his time, when the Office 'of portentous length...was prolonged still further by accretions of several kinds... It was of unconscionable length; its texts were padded out by tropings; the melismata of its chants were hypertrophied; it abounded in prolix sequences (over a hundred occurred in the course of a year), and the ceremonies had a complexity and duration which we

of the twentieth century could hardly imagine. A Conventual Mass lasted anything up to three hours.' All this 'occupied most of the day and half the night': Leonard, *The Letter Carrier* (note 35 above) 350–51, citing Clifford Howell without reference to the source.

48. Of course under the influence of what Philip Endean, SJ, has called our 'Jesuit fundamentalism', in *Who do You Say Ignatius Is? Jesuit Fundamentalism and Beyond* (SSJ 19/5, November 1987), Jesuits who are not professional historians are unaccustomed to treating Ignatian sources with the modern historico-critical methods we apply to any corpus of literature, even the Bible. And so we tend to read into Ignatius' vocabulary and teaching our modern meanings without futher ado, comfortable in the security that we know what Ignatius really thought and taught, and all we have to do is follow it, thereby turning Jesuit life into a sort of Ignatian Kempis, *The Following of St Ignatius.* See also the reflections of J. Veale, 'Dominant Orthodoxies', *Milltown Studies* 30 (1992) 43–65; and J.W. O'Malley, 'de Guibert and Jesuit Authenticity', WL 95 (1966) 103–10.

49. Rom 8:34; Heb 9:11–28.

50. Rev 1:17–3:22 and *passim.* That this contemporary, active, Risen Christ present in the Church through his Spirit was the chief focus of the New Testament Church can be seen in the earliest New Testament writings, the authentic Pauline epistles, which say next to nothing about the historical details of Jesus' life.

51. On imagination in medieval Catholic monastic culture, see J. Leclercq, *The Love of Learning and the Desire for God. A Study of Monastic Culture* (New York 1974) 93–5.

52. On the meaning of historicism see R. F. Taft, 'Historicisme: une conception à revoir', LMD 147 (1981) 61-83 = id., 'Historicism Revisited', *Studia liturgica* 14, nos. 2-3-4 (1982) 97–109, reprinted as chapter 1 of id., BEW. Devotional historicism leads to what Jungmann described as the shift from Easter piety to Christmas piety, in which the Jesus of devotion is the Jesus of his historical past, while Jesus as Son of God retreats into the Trinity, and the middle – Jesus the incarnate risen mediator interceding for us before the throne of the Father, the only Jesus still with us today, and the only basis for true liturgical piety – drops out. So when people think of Jesus as man they have in mind the human historical Jesus of the past, and Jesus as God is Jesus in the Godhead. They fail to realize that they are one and the same, and that the *only* Jesus of today is not the Baby Jesus of the Christmas crib but the adult Risen Christ: Jungmann, *Pastoral Liturgy* (note 25 above) 1–101.

53. In Ignatius we see this combined, ironically, with an extremely limited, premodern sense of historico-cultural evolution and change. The foundational documents of the Jesuit Institute are a curious mélange of extraordinarily farsighted and flexible principles joined to a mass of ridiculously detailed

legislation on administrative and economic issues that could not possibly stand the test of time and in fact has not.

54. Rom 6:3-11; Gal 2:20; II Cor 1:5, 4:7ff; Col 2:20; Eph 2:5–6. I am following here D. Stanley, *A Modern Scriptural Approach to the Spiritual Exercises* (Chicago 1986) 210–11.

55. That explains the popularity of early Jesuit books of piety among Protestants. For both, prayer was not something, like the Divine Office, accomplished in set forms and at set times: see T. H. Clancy, *An Introduction to Jesuit Life. The Constitutions and its History through 435 Years* (St Louis 1979) 127–8, 148. Ignatius has often been accused by those ignorant of his writings and spirit of setting down restrictive, strait-jacket methods of prayer. Nothing is further from the truth. No founder of a religious order or congregation in history more resolutely refused to make any legislation whatever concerning the prayer of his formed religious, beyond the general norm of constant union with God (CSJ §§342–5, 582). '…In what pertains to prayer, meditation, …fasts, vigils, and other austerities or penances, it does not seem expedient to give them any other rule than that which discreet charity dictates to them…' (CSJ §582). Ignatius' *Spiritual Exercises* contain numerous methods of prayer, but their very number shows them to be merely a selection of possibilities to be used in so far as they are helpful. Ignatius' constantly repeated norm in all such matters is to stress whatever is conducive to the end sought, under the direction of the spiritual guide or superior, and always avoiding excess in austerities.

56. In deciding to reduce the burden of liturgy in favour of apostolic mobility, Ignatius showed himself a man of great vision. What shows how historically conditioned the actual practice of such legitimate spiritual insights must always be is his decision to gain time and mobility by eliminating the daily common office. It would not have crossed a 16th century Latin Catholic's mind to eliminate daily 'private' Masses instead. But in the light of liturgical history, that would have been the far more traditional option. So Ignatius' choice was totally Latin, totally medieval. Before the Western Middle Ages no one would have dreamt of preferring daily private Mass to the common Hours on weekdays. If such an affirmation leaves you perplexed, that only shows that we, too, are the victims of our own clichés. There is much more historical evidence for the obligation of daily morning and evening prayer, in common and incumbent on all, laity as well as clergy and religious, than there is for the obligation of Sunday Mass. That does not change until the Middle Ages, and even then it changes only in the West. But by the time of St Ignatius, this had long been forgotten. Mass was the high point of Ignatius' day, and he took an hour at it: Schurhammer, *Xavier* 485. He attended Mass daily but did not himself celebrate Mass every day (ibid. 483 note 112).

57. For what we know of the Pachomian tradition, see Taft, *Hours* 62–5. This insight on religious reformers reducing the burden of liturgy I owe to

Joseph Gelineau, SJ. Here is what he wrote (or said) according to my notes: 'Reformers and true spiritual guides, like Pachomius or Benedict, always reduced, lessened the weight of ritual.' I have preserved the citation but lost the reference.

58. The same was operative in the East: St Nil Sorskij radically simplified the Russian-Orthodox monastic vision of his Clunaic-like contemporary Iosif Volokolamskij, and the same phenomenon can be observed today in the small skete tradition on Mt Athos, as distinct from the great cenobitic monasteries and the more losely organized lavras.

59. On this breviary see Taft, *Hours* 311. This was the first breviary designed explicitly for private recitation, which was an unheard of innovation. Right up through the Council of Trent (1545–63), I know not a single synodal decree that obliges private recitation of the Office or approves such recitation as the norm. Up until the 16th century, official Church legislation, at least, continues to view private recitation of the Office as an exception, permissible only when necessary. Trent itself, in Session 21 (15 July 1652), Decree on Reform, canon 4 (Tanner 2:729–30), refers to the public Office in parishes but never to private recitation. In spite of the official line, however, by the time of Trent the early and medieval notion of the public Office in common as the only one normative for all had died under the pressure of new forms of spirituality and apostolic and religious life. On the whole question, see Taft, *Hours* chapter 18. Because of illness, Ignatius received the pope's permission to use the shorter Quiñones breviary or substitute other prayers. He was so afflicted with tears when reciting the Office that it took an inordinate amount of time, and he finally had to be dispensed from the obligation in 1539: Schurhammer, *Xavier* 451, 484.

60. On these 16th to 20th century reforms, see Taft, *Hours* 311–17; for an assessment of the Vatican II reform of the Hours, see note 104 below.

61. As far as the liturgy was concerned, initially, at least, monks did what everyone else did: they celebrated or attended the liturgy on Sundays and feast days or other special occasions such as when a monk was being waked. See for instance Cyril of Scythopolis (c. 512–58), *Life of St Euthymius* 29, 33 (= BHG 647); *Life of St Sabas* (439–532) 18, 20, 24, 36 (= BHG 1608); *Life of St John the Hesychast* (†559) 7 (= BHG 897); *Life of St Cyriacus* 5 (= BHG 463): E. Schwartz (ed.), *Kyrillos von Skythopolis* (Texte und Untersuchungen 49.2, Leipzig 1939) 46–7, 51, 102, 105, 108, 123, 206, 225; English trans. in Cyril of Scythopolis, *The Lives of the Monks of Palestine*, trans. R. M. Price, annotated by J. Binns (Cistercian Studies Series 114) Kalamazoo 1991, 42–3, 48, 111, 114, 117, 132, 225, 248. Cf. Taft, BEW 102. Despite the romanticism of Benedictine-revival literature of the Western liturgical movement, with its references to the daily monastic conventual Mass as 'the summit of the Divine Office' – see for instance J. Dubois, 'Office des heures et messe dans la tradition monastique', LMD 135 (1978) 62ff. – daily Eucharist has nothing

whatever to do with the daily Divine Office, and played no part in monastic life in the early period. Cf. A. de Vogüé, *La Règle de s. Benoît,* VII (Sources chrétiennes hors série, Paris 1977) 240ff.; Taft, *Hours* 334 and *passim;* id., BEW 99ff. Indeed, some early monks were so anti-liturgical that their disdain for the sacramental life of the Church caused serious preoccupation. For example, some Syriac texts attributed to St Ephrem (c. 306–73) go so far as to imply that monastic asceticism even replaces the eucharistic liturgy: cited in Syriac and English translation by A. Vööbus, *History of Asceticism in the Syrian Orient,* vol. 2 (Corpus Scriptorum Christianorum Orientalium 197, Subsidia 17, Louvain 1960) 311. One can note a similar diffidence towards the external, sacramental life of the Church elsewhere in the Syriac literature, e.g., in the late 4th century *Liber Graduum,* Memra 12, Patrologia Syriaca 3:284–303, cf. A. Kowalski, *Perfezione e giustizia di Adamo nel Liber Graduum* (OCA 232, Rome 1989) 216–17; in the writings of John the Solitary (second half of 4th century): Jean le solitaire (Pseudo-Jean de Lycopolis), *Dialogue sur l'âme et les passions des hommes,* traduit du syriaque sur l'édition de Sven Dedering par I. Hausherr (OCA 120, Rome 1939) 101–2; and John of Apamea (late 5th/early 6th century): W. Strothmann, *Johannes von Apamea* (Patristische Texte und Studien 11, Berlin 1972) 79–80. See R. Murray, *Symbols of Church and Kingdom. A Study in Early Syriac Tradition* (Cambridge 1975) 129, 262–76 *passim.* The same approach can be seen in Anastasius of Sinai (fl. 640–700), *Quaestion 2,* PG 89:344-52; Palladius (c. 363–c. 431), *Historia lausiaca* (written c. 419), chapters 25.2–5, 26.2, 27.2: Palladio, *La Storia lausiaca,* testo critico e commento a cura di G. J. M. Bartelink, traduzione di Marino Barchiesi (Vita dei santi 2, Milan 1990) 134–42. A similar indifference – even disrespect – towards Church and sacraments is reflected in the antics of the 'holy fools' who sought humility and contempt by aberrant behaviour: Leontius of Neapolis *Life of St Symeon the Fool,* written in Cyprus in 642–9 but set in the Syrian city of Emesa during the 6th century: D. Krueger, *Symeon the Holy Fool. Leontius's 'Life' and the Late Antique City* (Berkeley/Los Angeles/London 1996) 4ff. The fool's violently disruptive behaviour during Sunday services is a case in point: Léontios de Néapolis, *Vie de Syméon le fou et vie de Jean de Chypre,* Édition commentée par A. J. Festugière en collaboration avec Lennart Rydén (Institut français d'archéologie de Beyrouth, Bibliothèque archéologique et historique, tome 95, Paris 1974) 79–80, 133; cf. V. Déroche, *Études sur Léontios de Néapolis* (Acta Universitatis Upsaliensis, Studia Byzantina Upsaliensia 3, Uppsala 1995) 194–5. See also *Vita* 190 of St Andrew the Fool, PG 111:836CD. I develop this material at length in my forthcoming study: 'Changing Rhythms of Eucharistic Frequency in Byzantine Monasticism', paper delivered at the Pontificio Ateneo S. Anselmo Monastic Institute Fiftieth Anniversary Symposium *Classic Texts and Themes of the Christian Monastic Tradition (Yesterday – Today – Tomorrow),* 27 May – 1 June 2002, to appear in the Symposium Acta.

62. On the whole question see R. F. Taft, 'Christian Liturgical Psalmody: Origins, Development, Decomposition, Collapse'. One of Two Keynote Lectures: *The Differing Natures of Jewish and Christian Liturgical Psalmody – The Kavanagh Lectures in Liturgy and Liturgical Art*, at the Conference: *Up with a Shout. The Psalms in Jewish and Christian Religious, Artistic and Intellectual Traditions. From Historical and Theoretical Studies to Practice and Performance*. Sponsored by The Institute of Sacred Music at Yale University, New Haven, to appear in the *Acta*. On chant and psalmody and monastic opposition to it, the basic work is still J. Quasten, *Musik und Gesang in der Kultur der heidnischen Antike und christlichen Frühzeit* (Liturgiegeschichtliche Quellen und Forschungen 25, Münster 1930) = *Music and Worship in Pagan and Christian Antiquity*, trans. B. Ramsey (National Association of Pastoral Musicians Studies in Church Music and Liturgy, Washington, DC 1983); and, most recently, S. S. Froyshov, 'La réticence à l'hymnographie chez les anchorètes de l'Égypte et du Sinaï du 6ᵉ au 8ᵉ siècles', in: A. M. Triacca & A. Pistoia (eds.), *L'hymnographie. Conférences Saint-Serge – XLVIᵉ Semaine d'études liturgiques, Paris 29 juin – 2 juillet 1999* (Bibliotheca Ephemerides Liturgicae, Subsidia 105, Rome 2000) 229–45. See also the invaluable anthology of patristic texts on the topic: J. McKinnon (ed.), *Music in Early Christian Literature* (Cambridge Readings in the Literature of Music, Cambridge/New York/New Rochelle/Melbourne/Sidney 1987). Concerning Ignatius' rejection of chant, see note 47 above.

63. Lk 18:1, 21:36; Eph 6:18; Col 4:2; I Thess 5:16–18.

64. E. Dekkers, 'Les anciens moines cultivaient-ils la liturgie?' in A. Mayer, J. Quasten, B. Neunheuser (eds.), *Vom christlichen Mysterium. Gesammelte Arbeiten zum Gedächtnis von Odo Casel, O.S.B.* (Düsseldorf 1951) 97–114 = revised and resumed under the same title in LMD 51 (1957) 31–54 = trans. 'Were the Early Monks Liturgical?' *Collectanea Cisterciensia* 22 (1960) 120–37. See also Friedrich Wulf, 'Priestertum und Rätestand', *Geist und Leben* 33 (1960) 109–18, 246–61; and the discussion in Taft, *Hours* 362–3.

65. Clancy, *Introduction* (note 55 above) 86–7 and the literature he cites on p. 359 note 36.

66. This represented a fundamental reorientation of religious life. The early monks were occupied with their own salvation, not with anyone else's. Furthermore, their monastic obedience was for self-denial and personal perfection, whereas Ignatian obedience is for *soli Deo gloria* and apostolic disponibility.

67. O'Malley, 'Priesthood', 226–7, referring to D. Knowles, *From Pachomius to Ignatius. A Study in the Constitutional History of the Religious Orders. The Sarum Lectures 1964–5* (Oxford 1966).

68. See J.W. O'Malley, *The First Jesuits* (Cambridge MA/London 1993) chapters 2ff.

69. Tanner 1:193; O'Malley, 'Priesthood', 235–6.

70. M. J. Buckley, *Mission in Companionship of Jesuit Community and Communion* (SSJ 11/4, September 1979) 11. This seminal treatment of Jesuit community shows that for Ignatius the key word was 'communion', not 'community', and that the Jesuit's community is the whole Society, not the local community (ibid. 16). On this, see now the letter to the whole Society of Fr General Peter-Hans Kolvenbach, 'Sur la vie communautaire', ARSI 22 (1999) 276–89, esp. §§2–4. It was precisely because Jesuit life *was not* to be one of community living in the conventional sense that the Ignatian novitiate was structured around a series of 'experiencias' or trials *outside* (CSJ §§65–77, 82), and was not meant as an apprenticeship in conventual living: see the remarks of Ganss in Saint Ignatius of Loyola, *The Constitutions of the Society of Jesus*. Translated with an Introduction and a Commentary by G. E. Ganss, SJ (The Institute of Jesuit Sources, St Louis 1970) 96 note 7, 98–9 note 11.

71. See Bertrand, *Politique* 374ff.

72. Eventually, of course, the Society had to fit itself into the existing canonical framework of the Church's religious life, just as the Catholic Church could not rest until it had squeezed Benedictine and Eastern-Catholic monasticism into its system of religious orders, calling Benedictines 'The Order of St Benedict' (OSB), and Byzantine Catholic monks 'The Order of St Basil the Great' (OSBM). But in the East, monks are just monks, and they do not belong to the Order of St Basil or of anyone else – rather, *Basil belonged to their order*, the order of monks *tout court*. In the East, to be a monk is a consecration conferred, not a juridical act called 'taking vows'. Being a monk is an 'order' one enters not by vows one *takes* but by a consecration one *receives*, just like being a deacon is an order, and not a juridical structure to be forced into someone else's procrustean bed.

73. O'Malley, *The First Jesuits* (note 68 above) chapter 4. In the first Jesuit community in Rome, Mass was offered outside the house, not at home: Schurhammer, *Xavier* 490.

74. O'Malley, 'Priesthood', 240. This ministry was carried out with 'energetic and hardheaded pragmatism... Whatever seemed to "produce fruit" in souls, whatever met a need, was pursued with creativity and method' (ibid. 238). See also id., *To Travel to Any Part of the World: Jerónimo Nadal and the Jesuit Vocation* (SSJ 16/2, March 1948) esp. 6–16.

75. O'Malley, 'Priesthood', 239. In Ignatius' rush 'to help souls' in need of ministry, O'Malley says it is the 'herald' and 'discipleship' models of the Church that predominate over the model of the Church as sacrament, to use the construct of A. Dulles, *Models of the Church* (Garden City 1978) cited ibid.

76. Session 24 (11 Nov. 1563), Decree on Reform canon 4, Tanner 2:763; cf. O'Malley, 'Priesthood', 244.

77. A situation that still exists in much of Orthodox Christianity, *pace* the paeons of praise by starry-eyed Western romantics who have read a couple of books by Schmemann or Meyendorff.

78. O'Malley, 'Priesthood', 245.

79. Brodrick, *St Ignatius* (note 44 above) 102-4.

80. Details in de Guibert, *The Jesuits* (note 45 above) 197–8, 201, 206–7, 556–7.

81. In this context it is worth noting something little known: 21st Jesuit General J. Ph. Roothaan (1829–53) and the Jesuits in Rome at that time were major supporters of the Benedictine monastic and liturgical renewal in France and Italy, and in particular of the Solesmes renewal under Abbot Dom Prosper Guéranger (1805–75), which many consider the beginning of the modern Liturgical Movement: see C. J. Ligthart, *The Return of the Jesuits. The Life of Jan Philip Roothaan,* trans. J. J. Slijkerman (London 1978) 232–8.

82. Recognizing this, 27th Jesuit General J.-B. Janssens (1946–64) sought to bring Jesuit thinking and practice into line with that of God's Church in his 'De Nostrorum in Sacra Liturgia Institutione Instructio atque Ordinatio,' ARSI 13 (1959) 636–75, summarized by C. J. McNaspy, 'The Apostolate: Jesuits and the Liturgy', *Worship* 35 (1961) 298–301. But not even Fr Janssens succeeded in overcoming traditional Jesuit ambivalence regarding the liturgy. See also the much shorter 8 Dec. 1932 letter of General W. Ledochowski to the Provincials of Italy, 'De spiritu sacrae liturgiae in nostris templis et operibus in Italia impensius promovendo' (in Italian) ARSI 7 (1932–4) 227–31. In this context it is interesting to reflect on community life in the Society, which in the 53 years since I entered has always been considered more of a problem than a given, a lived reality. The fact that we have not solved this problem either, at least not everywhere, despite all our 'friends in the Lord' rhetoric, is not unconnected with the problem of liturgy: those who have no real community life together have perforce no real community – i.e. liturgical – prayer together. On Jesuit community life, see the letter to the whole Society of Fr General Kolvenbach (note 70 above) *passim,* and p. 285 §6 on the role of community Eucharist in Jesuit community life.

83. Information from my late confrère Bernhard Schultze, SJ, regarding the German Jesuit scholasticate in exile at Valkenburg in Holland before World War II.

84. *Consuetudinarium Assistenciae Americae Societatis Iesu* (1938, place of publication not indicated), cited in O'Connor, 'What is Common Prayer?' (note 40 above) 8.

85. Nor is this just a thing of the past: the 9 Dec. 1979 Jesuit directives for the parish apostolate, 'Directivae quaedam de apostolatu paroeciali', ARSI 17 (1977–9) 881–902 (text in French, English and Spanish) say nothing about liturgy!

86. As my late teacher and confrère Edward J. Kilmartin, SJ, has shown, Roman Catholic manual theology promotes a view of the presbyterate and priesthood that is questionable. The inevitable effect of this on how Jesuit priests view themselves, their vocation, and the role of liturgy, especially the

Eucharist, in their lives, is obvious. So we need a renewed theology of priesthood operative in our formation. Much of this has been treated trenchantly in K. Rahner & A. Häußling, *The Celebration of the Eucharist* (New York 1968). On Kilmartin's theology see E. J. Kilmartin, *The Eucharist in the West. History and Theology*, ed. R. J. Daly (A Pueblo Book, Collegeville 1998) *passim*, esp. chapters IV, VII, XI; and most recently, J. M. Hall, *We Have the Mind of Christ. The Holy Spirit and Liturgical Memory in the Thought of Edward J. Kilmartin* (A Pueblo Book, Collegeville 2001); On Jesuit priesthood see also J. W. Harmless & D. L. Gelpi, *Priesthood Today and the Jesuit Vocation* (SSJ 19/3, May 1987).

87. I am not talking about the training of the head, our theological education in liturgical theology, nor about the practical process of learning how to preside at liturgy, but the spiritual training of the heart. There is also the lesser but none the less real issue of the liturgical indiscipline of some Jesuits. This can lead to problems for the Society when such abuses come to the attention of the hierarchy, leading to disciplinary actions ultimately interfering with far more important issues for the Society's work than the fact that some fool thinks he has the right to say Mass vested only in shorts and a T-shirt.

88. Individual cases apart, this defective formation is never made up for in later years with one exception: the only group of Jesuits I know of personally who truly live an adequately *liturgical* spiritual life are those trained in the Byzantine Russian tradition at the 'Russicum' or Pontifical Russian College in Rome. That is because the exceptionally strong Russian liturgical tradition has shown itself stronger than our liturgically impotent Jesuitness.

89. DOL §§1155, 1176, 1816; EDIL §§421, 432, 2876.

90. Private Mass requires the presence of at least one of the faithful: DOL §1176; EDIL §432; CIC canon 906. Solitary Mass is allowed only 'for a just and reasonable cause' (canon 906), but commentators deny that personal convenience or preference fulfils this requirement: Robert A. Wild, SJ, Chicago Provincial, circular letter 'Jesuits Today and Common Eucharistic Worship', 5 November 1982, lines 35–7.

91. Ibid. lines 32–45.

92. *Spiritual Exercises* §97. On this concept, see Bertrand, *Politique* 592ff.

93. DOL 26l; EDIL §553 see also General Congregation 31 (1965–6) Decree 14:10 §224; General Congregation 32 (1974–5) Decree 11:12, 35 §§210, 235: *Documents of the 31st and 32nd General Congregations of the Society of Jesus. An English Translation of the Official Latin Texts of the General Congregations and of the Accompanying Papal Documents* (The Institute of Jesuit Sources, St Louis 1977).

94. DOL §26–7; EDIL §26–7.

95. On the whole question see Taft, BEW chapter 6.

96. To confront this theology the essential work is Rahner-Häußling, *Celebration of the Eucharist* (note 86 above). With regard to the Eucharist, as

with all sacraments, the important thing is that it be done, not that I do it. Curiously, this mania to 'exercise one's priesthood' involves only the Eucharist: one does not find Jesuits prowling the corridors of their communities daily looking for someone to baptize, confess or anoint!

97. DOL §1276; EDIL §945. This is repeated by General Congregation 31, Decree 14:10, §224 (cf. English edition of decrees cited in note 93 above).

98. *Eucharisticum Mysterium* loc. cit.

99. At Manresa Ignatius began to recite the Little Office of the Blessed Virgin daily. On Ignatius' devotion to the Hours, see P. Dudon, *St Ignatius Loyola*, trans. W. J. Young (Milwaukee 1949) 59, 100 = id., *Saint Ignace de Loyola* (Paris 1934); Schurhammer, *Xavier* 484; also St Ignatius, 'Rules for Thinking with the Church' 3, *The Spiritual Exercises of St Ignatius* §355.

100. Bertrand, *Politique* 373–9.

101. Nor was the abandonment of choir original to Ignatius and the early Jesuits. As I have shown (Taft, *Hours* 302), these ideas were in the air, and several orders founded around the same time as the Jesuits adopted similar norms, as did the Dominicans of Andalusia, who accepted a benefaction for a new priory under the condition that they dedicate themselves to pastoral ministry and not be bound to choir: M. Scaduto, *Storia della Compagnia di Gesù in Italia*, vol. III: *L'epoca di Giacomo Lainez. Il governo 1556–1565* (Rome 1964) 211.

102. '...quedando libertad de tener coro quando y donde les paresciere mayor seruicio de Dios. Solamente se quite la obligación': Dubiorum Series Tertia, in *Monumenta Historica Societatis Jesu*, vol. 63 = *Monumenta Ignatiana* series 3, vol. I: *Sancti Ignatii de Loyola Constitutiones Societatis Jesu. Monumenta Constitutionum Praevia*, ed. A. Codina (Rome 1934) 310; cited by Weiss, *Jesuits and the Liturgy* (note 3 above) 139. This excellent Notre Dame doctoral dissertation, written under my direction, is easily the best study on the Society and the Hours.

103. I trace this process in Taft, *Hours* chapter 18.

104. For a critique of the Vatican II reform of the Roman Office, see R. F. Taft, 'The Divine Office: Monastic Choir, Prayer Book, or Liturgy of the People of God? An Evaluation of the New Liturgy of the Hours in its Historical Context', in: R. Latourelle (ed.), *Vatican II. Assessment and Perspectives Twenty-five Years After (1962–1987)*, 3 vols. (New York & Mahwah, NJ: Paulist Press 1989) vol. 2:27–46 (adapted in id, BEW chapter 14) = 'L'Office divin: choeur monastique, livre de prière, ou liturgie du peuple de Dieu?' in: R. Latourelle (ed.), *Vatican II. Bilan et perspectives vingt-cinq ans après (1962–1987)* (Recherches – nouvelle série 15, Montréal 1988) 33-52 = 'El oficio divino: coro monástico, libro de oración o liturgia del pueblo de Dios? Una evaluación de la nueva liturgia de las horas en su contexto histórico', in: R. Latourelle (ed.), *Vaticano II: Balance y perspectivas. Veinticinco años después (1962–1987)* (Salamanca 1989) 460–81.

105. DOL §3450; EDIL I, §2273.
106. DOL §§3451-3, 3455-7; EDIL §§2275, 2274-7.
107. Page 2 of text. I am grateful to Fr Pecklers for providing me with a copy of this essay.
108. Jesuit resistance to change in liturgical practice via ritual appeals to St Ignatius is ironic in the light of the ease with which Jesuits have abandoned without qualms other basic Ignatian constitutional principles such as the gratuity of ministries (*General Examen* CSJ §4), accepting parishes and the cure of souls (CSJ §324), the intellectual apostolate, regarding which, for instance, the *Constitutions* of 1541, not only forbid parishes but order 'no lectures or studies in the Society'. Cited by Fr General Kolvenbach in 'The Jesuit University in the Light of the Ignatian Charism', Address to the International Meeting of Jesuit Higher Education, Rome, 27 May 2001, (§6) who refers to the Society 'Changing course so many times in a few years' (§8). Like biographers, who allow a subject's later years to colour what they think went before, we do the same with Ignatius and the early Society.
109. On this, see the recommendations in the letter of Fr General Janssens cited above, note 82.

Chapter 5

1. John Paul II, quoting the 1995 Extraordinary Assembly for the Synod of Bishops, says: 'Inculturation means the intimate transformation of authentic cultural values through their integration in Christianity and the insertion of Christianity in the various human cultures,' (*Redemptoris Missio*, 52). For the English text of this encyclical, see *Redemption and Dialogue: Reading* Redemptoris Missio *and* Proclamation, ed. William Burrows (Maryknoll, NY: Orbis 1993) 5–55. The book also contains a commentary on the encyclical by Marcello Zago, ibid., 56–90.

2. As Vatican II puts it: 'The Church learned early in its history to express the Christian message in the concepts and language of different peoples and tried to clarify it in the light of the wisdom of their philosophers: it was an attempt to adapt the Gospel to the understanding of all men and the requirements of the learned, insofar as this could be done. Indeed, this kind of adaptation and preaching the revealed Word must ever be the law of all evangelization. In this way it is possible to create in every country the possibility of expressing the message of Christ in suitable terms and to foster vital contact and exchange between the Church and different cultures' (*Gaudium et Spes*, 44). English translation from *Vatican Council II: The Conciliar and Post Conciliar Documents*, ed. Austin Flannery (Collegeville, MN: Liturgical Press 1984).

3. *RM*, 52: 'Inculturation is a slow journey, which accompanies the whole of missionary life. It involves those working in the Church's mission *ad gentes*,

the Christian communities as they develop, and the Bishops, who have the task of providing discernment and encouragement for its implementation.' In his Discourse to the Bishops of Zaire, 12 April 1983, John Paul II said that 'satisfactory progress in this domain [inculturation] can only be the fruit of a progressive growth in faith, linked with spiritual discernment, theological clairty, a sense of the universal Church' (no. 5).

4. The theological literature alone, not to mention the literary, artistic and philosophical, on postmodernity, has grown by leaps and bounds. For our purposes two introductions are especially helpful: Stanley J. Grenz, *A Primer on Postmodernism* (Grand Rapids, MI: Eerdmans 1996) and Paul Lakeland, *Postmodernity: Christian Identity in a Fragmented Age* (Minneapolis: Fortress Press 1997). The former work contains a useful bibliography on postmodernity (197–202). Generally, the term *postmodernism* refers to the cultural mood and intellectual ideas that are contrasted to those of modernism (here the preposition *post* is taken not only in the chronological sense but also as a rejection – at least partial – of modernism). *Postmodernity* refers to the epoch or era in which postmodern ideas and values shape the outlook of a particular society.

5. For the early uses of the term *postmodernism*, see Margaret Rose, 'Defining the Post-Modern', in *The Post-Modern Reader*, ed. Charles Jencks (New York: St. Martin's Press 1992) 119–36.

6. The following reflections on postmodern architecture, art, theatre, fiction, and various expressions of popular culture are derived from Stanley Grenz, *A Primer on Postmodernism*, 22–38 and Paul Lakeland, *Postmodernity*, 1–7. For general descriptions of postmodern culture, see Steven Connor, *Postmodernist Culture: An Introduction to Theories of the Contemporary* (Oxford: Basil Blackwell 1989) and Walter Truett Anderson, *Reality Isn't What It Used to Be: Theatrical Politics, Ready-to-Wear Religion, Global Myths, Primitive Chic, and Other Wonders of the Post-modern World* (San Francisco: Harper & Row 1990).

7. On postmodern architecture, see Charles A. Jencks, *The Language of Post-Modern Architecture* (London: Academy Editions 1984).

8. See Antonin Artaud, 'The Theater of Cruelty: Second Manifesto', in *The Theatre and its Double*, trans. Victor Corti (London: Calder & Boyers 1970) 81–7. Artaud called for an abandonment of the older script-centred style of theatrical performance and the distinction between actors and the audience. He advocated free performance which includes improvisation of light, colour, movement, gesture and space.

9. On postmodern literature, see Ihab Hassan, *The Dismemberment of Orpheus: Towards a Postmodern Literature* (New York: Oxford University Press 1971) and Brian McHale, *Postmodernist Fiction* (New York: Methuen 1987).

10. S. Grenz, *A Primer on Postmodernism*, 15. P. Lakeland describes the postmodern sensibility as 'nonsequential, noneschatological, nonutopian,

nonsystematic, nonfoundational, and, ultimately, nonpolitical' (*Postmodernity*, 8).

11. S. Grenz, *A Primer on Postmodernisn*, 43.

12. Here is not the place to discuss postmodern philosophy. For a survey of postmodern philosophy, beginning with the critique of René Descartes and Immanuel Kant, through Friedrich Nietzsche's nihilistic rejection of the Enlightenment concepts of truth and value, the emergence of hermeneutics in replacement of metaphysics (Friedrich Schleiermacher, Wilhelm Dilthey, Martin Heidegger, and Hans-Georg Gadamer), the 'linguistic turn' (language as game in Ludwig Wittgenstein, language as social construction in Ferdinand de Saussure, the dissolution of the self in structuralism), to the philosophers of postmodernism (Michel Foucault's theory of knowledge as power, Jacques Derrida's deconstruction of logocentrism, and Richard Rorty's pragmatic utopia), see S. Grenz, *A Primer on Postmodernism*, 83–160. Paul Lakeland distinguishes three types of postmodern philosophy: 'radical postmoderns' (e.g. Foucault, Derrida, Rorty, Georges Bataille, Julia Kristeva and Luce Irigaray); 'nostalgic postmoderns' (e.g. Heidegger, Allan Bloom, Theodor Adorno and Alasdair MacIntyre); and 'late moderns' (e.g. Jürgen Habermas, Charles Taylor and Jean-François Lyotard) and discusses how postmodernism approaches three issues: subjectivity, relativism, and otherness. See his *Postmodernity*, 12–38.

13. See Jean-François Lyotard, *The Postmodern Condition: A Report on Knowledge*, trans. Geoff Bennington and Brian Massumi (Minneapolis: University of Minnesota Press 1984).

14. For reflections on postmodern science, see P. Lakeland, *Postmodernity*, 36–8.

15. For a history of the concept of culture, see Alfred A. Kroeber and Klyde Kluckhohn, *Culture: A Critical Review of Concepts and Definitions* (Cambridge, Mass.: Papers of the Peabody Museum of American Archeology and Ethnology, Harvard University 1952). For a brief overview, see Kathryn Tanner, *Theories of Culture: A New Agenda for Theology* (Minneapolis: Fortress 1997) 3–24. Tanner surveys the meaning of 'culture' as it was used in France, Germany and Great Britain before its current usage in anthropology. For a presentation of Vatican II's understanding of culture and its development, including the notion of culture in John Paul II, see Michael Paul Gallagher, *Clashing Symbols: An Introduction to Faith and Culture* (New York: Paulist Press 1998) 36–55.

16. For a development of this concept of culture, see Kathryn Tanner, *Theories of Culture*, 25–37.

17. See Robert Schreiter, *The New Catholicity: Theology Between the Global and the Local* (Maryknoll, NY: Orbis 1997) 49–50.

18. For the following reflections on the postmodern concept of culture, see Peter C. Phan, 'Religion and Culture: Their Places as Academic Disciplines in

the University', in *The Future of Religions in the 21st Century*, ed. Peter Ng (Hong Kong: Centre for the Study of Religion and Chinese Society 2001) 321-53.

19. See Pierre Bourdieu, *Outline of a Theory of Practice* (Cambridge: Cambridge University Press 1977); James Clifford, *The Predicament of Culture* (Cambridge, Mass.: Harvard University Press 1988); George Marcus and Michael Fischer, *Anthropology as Cultural Critique* (Chicago: University of Chicago Press 1986); Ulrich Beck, *Risk Society: Toward a New Modernity* (London: Sage 1992); Homi K. Bhabha, *The Location of Culture* (London: Routledge 1994); Jonathan Friedman, *Cultural Identity and Global Process* (London: Sage 1994); Mike Featherstone, *Undoing Modernity: Globalization, Postmodernism and Identity* (London: Sage 1995).

20. For a detailed articulation of these six objections against the anthropological concept of culture, see Kathryn Tanner, *Theories of Culture*, 40–56.

21. The phrase is from R. Schreiter, *The New Catholicity*, 54.

22. Serge Gruzinski, *La Colonisation de l'imaginaire: Sociétés indigènes et occidentalisation dans le Mexique espagnol XVIe–XVIIIe siècle* (Paris: Gallimard 1987). English translation, *The Conquest of Mexico* (Cambridge: Polity 1993).

23. See Michel Foucault, *The Archaeology of Knowledge*, trans. A. M. Sheridan Smith (New York: Pantheon Books 1972); *Discipline and Punish: The Birth of Prison*, trans. Alan Sheridan (New York: Vintage Press 1975); *Critique and Power: Recasting the Foucault/Habermas Debate*, ed. Michael Kelly (Cambridge, Mass.: MIT Press 1994); *Madness and Civilization: A History of Insanity in the Age of Reason*, trans. Richard Howard (New York: Vintage Books 1988); *Language, Counter-Memory, Practice: Selected Essays and Interviews*, ed. Donald Bouchard and trans. Donald Bouchard and Sherry Simon (Ithaca, NY: Cornell University Press 1977); *Power/Knowledge* (New York: Pantheon Books 1987); *Politics, Philosophy, Culture: Interviews and Other Writings*, ed. Lawrence D. Kritzman and trans. Alan Sheridan (New York: Routledge 1988).

24. For a discussion of the historical development of globalization, see the works of Immanuel Wallerstein, *The Modern World-System I: Capitalist Agriculture and the Origins of the Europen World-Economy in the Sixteeenth Century* (New York: Academic 1974) and *The Modern World-System II: Mercantilism and the Consolidation of the European World-Economy, 1600–1750* (New York: Academic 1980); Anthony Giddens, *Modernity and Self-Identity: Self and Society in the Late Modern Age* (Stanford: Stanford University Press 1991); and Roland Robertson, *Globalization: Social Theory and Global Culture* (London: Sage 1992). In general, Wallerstein attributes an exclusively economic origin to globalization, while Giddens sees it rooted in four factors, namely, the nation-state system, the world military order, the

world capitalist economy and the international division of labour, and Robertson highlights the cultural factors in globalization.

25. For a brief discussion of globalization, see Robert Schreiter, *The New Catholicity*, 4–14. Social scientist Arjun Appadurai lists five factors that have contributed to the 'deterritorialization' of contemporary culture: 'ethnoscape' (the constant flow of persons such as immigrants, refugees, tourists, guest workers, exiles), 'technoscape' (mechanical and informational technologies), 'finanscape' (flow of money through currency markets, national stock exchanges, commodity speculation), 'mediascape' (newspapers, magazines, TV, films), and 'ideoscape' (key ideas such as freedom, welfare, human rights, independence, democracy). See his 'Disjuncture and Difference in the Global Economy', *Public Culture* 2/2 (1990): 1–24.

26. On these three tendencies or cultural logics dubbed as antiglobalism, ethnification and primitivism, see Robert Schreiter, *The New Catholicity*, 21–5. For a lucid exposition and critique of postmodernism, see Dale T. Irvin, 'Christianity in the Modern World: Facing Postmodern Culture and Religious Pluralism', in *The Future of Religions in the 21st Century*, ed. Peter Ng, 253–66. For Irvin, postmodernism is liable to three temptations: facile acceptance of the processes of consumerism and commodification, disdain for tradition and memory, and reduction of the historical past to its Western cultural form.

27. Congregation for Divine Worship and the Discipline of the Sacraments, *Inculturation of the Liturgy within the Roman Rite*, 36. The official Latin text is 'De Liturgia romana et inculturatione. Instructio quarta ad exsecutionem Constitutionis Concilii Vaticani Secundi de Sacra Liturgia recte ordinandam (ad Const. Art. 37-40)', published in *Notitiae* 30 (1994) 8–115, dated 29 March 1994. Its English text, under the title *Inculturation of the Liturgy within the Roman Rite*, was published by Vatican Press, 1994. Henceforth, *Varietates Legitimae*.

28. *Varietates Legitimae*, 36.

29. Congregation for Divine Worship and the Discipline of the Sacraments, *On the Use of Vernacular Languages in the Publication of the Books of the Roman Liturgy*, 20. The official Latin text of this Fifth Instruction is: 'De usu linguarum popularium in libris liturgiae romanae edendis,' published on 28 March, 2001. Its English translation is available at USCC Publishing of the United States Conference of Catholic Bishops. Henceforth, *Liturgiam Authenticam*.

30. It is interesting to note that *Liturgiam Authenticam* affirms that this *recognitio* 'is not a mere formality, but is rather an exercise of the power of governance, which is absolutely necessary' (80). The instruction further says that the *recognitio* 'expresses and effects a bond of communion between the successor of blessed Peter and his brothers in the Episcopate.' The question is

of course whether there is not a better and more collegial way to express communion between the Pope and the bishops.

31. For a critical survey of postmodern theology, especially under the themes of God, Christ and church, see P. Lakeland, *Postmodernity*, 39–86.

32. For general evaluations of *Varietates Legitimae*, see Nathan Mitchell, 'The Amen Corner', *Worship* 68 (1994) 369–77; Julian Saldanha, 'Instruction on Liturgical Inculturation', *Vidyajoti* 60 (1996) 618–21; David Power, 'Liturgy and Culture Revisited', *Worship* 69 (1995) 225–43; and D. Reginald Whitt, '*Varietates Legitimae* and an African-American Liturgical Tradition', *Worship* 71 (1997) 504–37.

33. *Varietates Legitimae* sees the goal of inculturation as a clear expression of the meaning of the 'holy things' in both texts and rites so as to enable the faithful 'to understand them with ease and to take part in the rites fully, actively and as befits a community' (no. 35). The limit of inculturation is set by the necessity to 'maintain the *substantial unity* of the Roman rite' (no. 36). The authorities overseeing liturgical inculturation are the Apostolic See (that is, through the Congregation for Divine Worship and the Discipline of the Sacraments), and 'within the limits fixed by law', Episcopal Conferences and the diocesan bishop (no. 37).

34. What *Varietates Legitimae* affirms is that liturgical inculturation should not result in 'the creation of new families of rites' (no. 36). The Latin original says: 'novas familias rituales', so that the better translation would be: 'new ritual families'. By 'ritual families' are meant the three canonically recognized liturgical traditions, namely, the *Ambrosian*, the *Hispano-Mozarabic* and the *Roman* ritual families of the liturgical patrimony of the canonical Latin rite. Thus there should not be a new 'ritual family' in addition to the three current ones. Any liturgical innovation of the Roman ritual family through inculturation, even the 'more radical' one, must remain within the Roman ritual family. It is to be noted that Vatican II left open the possibility of the development and recognition of new *ritual families* which can appear within any of the 21 recognized canonical rites forming the six basic liturgical traditions of the universal Church (i.e. Alexandrine, Antiochene, Armenian, Chaldean, Constantinopolitan and Roman) and even of a new *canonical rite*, although since 1963 no new canonical rite has been recognized. For helpful clarifications, see D. R. Whitt, '*Varietates Legitimae* and an African-American Liturgical Tradition', 248–54.

35. For a brief discussion of Vatican II's concept of culture, see M. P. Gallagher, *Clashing Symbols*, 36–43. For discussions of John Paul II's understanding of culture, see S. Bevans, *Models of Contextual Theology*, 42–6 and R. Schreiter, *The New Catholicity*, 22–3; 52–3.

36. See J. Saldanha, 'Instruction on Liturgical Inculturation', 619.

37. See John Coleman, 'Pastoral Strategies for Multicultural Parishes', *Origins* 31/30 (January 2002) 498–501.

38. J. Coleman, 'Pastoral Strategies for Multicultural Parishes', 498.

39. Note the condescending expression of 'concessions granted' in the quotation.

40. On popular religion and liturgy, see Peter C. Phan, 'The Liturgy of Life as the "Summit and Source" of the Eucharistic Liturgy: Church Worship as the Symbolization of the Liturgy of Life?' in *Incongruities: Who We Are and How We Pray*, ed. Timothy Fitzgerald and David A. Like (Chicago: Liturgy Training Publications 2000) 5–33; idem, 'Culture and Liturgy: Ancestor Veneration as a Test Case', *Worship* (2002) forthcoming; idem, 'Popular Religion and Liturgical Inculturation: Perspectives and Challenges from Asia', *Proceedings of the NAAL* (2002) forthcoming; and the whole issue of *Liturgical Ministry* vol. 7 (Summer 1998) which is devoted to popular religiosity, with informative essays by James L. Empereur ('Popular Religion and the Liturgy: The State of the Question'); Patrick L. Malloy ('Christian Anamnesis and Popular Religion'); Mark R. Francis ('The Hispanic Liturgical Year: The People's Calendar'); Keith F. Pecklers ('Issues of Power and Access in Popular Religion'); and Robert E. Wright ('Popular Religiosity: Review of Literature').

41. Nathan Mitchell has noted this 'schizophrenic atmosphere' of *Varietatis Legitimae* – 'appearing to *affirm* a principle while later *rescinding* it' – at least in three areas: in its position regarding inculturation as a double movement of mutual enrichment, its attitude towards central supervision and episcopal collegiality, and its affirmation of the necessity of the Roman Rite and the diversity of liturgical families. See his 'The Amen Corner', 375–6.

42. Note that the Instruction opposes only the *replacement* of biblical readings, chants or prayers by texts from other religions. It does not pronounce on the *addition* of these to the liturgy. As J. Saldanha suggests, 'the rescinding of the prohibition of the use of non-biblical readings in the liturgy in India is long overdue.' See his 'Instruction on Liturgical Inculturation', 621. As to the necessity to avoid, 'even in appearance', any suggestion of religious syncretism, it must be pointed out that the danger can be avoided by enlightened catechesis, and not the refusal to make use of places of worship, liturgical objects and vestments, gestures and postures that are found in other religions.

43. 'Preference should be given to materials, forms and colors which are in use in the country' (no. 43).

44. *Varietates Legitimae* distinguishes three situations for liturgical inculturation. 1. The first is that of countries that do not have a Christian tradition or countries where the use of the Roman Rite, brought in by missionaries, is recent (presumably Asia and Oceania). Here liturgical inculturation is said to bring to the peoples the riches of Christ and welcome their cultural riches into the liturgy so that a mutual enrichment may result. 2. The second is that of countries with a longstanding Western Christian tradition and with a well-established use of the Roman Rite (presumably Europe and the Americas). Here liturgical inculturation is said to be limited to the measures of adaptation

already envisaged in the liturgical books and considered sufficient. 3. The third is that of countries, both with or without a Christian tradition, where there is a growing culture marked by indifference or disinterest in religion. Here it is said that inculturation is not the appropriate approach but 'liturgical formation' and 'most suitable means to reach spirits and hearts' (nos. 6–8). Given the fact that postmodernism, with its indifference (not necessarily hostility) to religion, is the hallmark of contemporary Europe and North America, and is rapidly spreading throughout the world through globalization, for *Varietates Legitimae* to say that the inculturation of the Christian faith is not the appropriate means of evangelization for the third situation is either to have a very jejune notion of inculturation (akin to adaptation, which it has in principle rejected) or to restrict it to a very small geographical area.

45. Earlier, the Instruction has drawn attention to the need to take into account the problems posed by the co-existence of several cultures, especially as the result of immigration (no. 7).

46. Nathan Mitchell recognizes eight valuable points in *Varietates Legitimae*: it affirms that inculturation is a two-way street, enriching a culture by inculturating the Gospel into it and enriching the Gospel with the insights of that culture; it sees parallels between the Incarnation and inculturation; it affirms that faith does not require renunciation of one's culture; it affirms that liturgical inculturation is a gradual process; it highlights the historical evolution of the Roman Rite; it promotes the preservation of all liturgical families of both East and West; it affirms the radical inclusiveness of worship; and it sees the Sunday assembly's full eucharistic worship as the normative ritual. See his 'The Amen Corner', 374.

47. For his bibliography up to 1997, see 'Bibliography of Anscar J. Chupungco', in *Liturgy for the New Millennium: A Commentary on the Revised Sacramentary. Essays in Honor of Anscar Chupungco*, ed. Mark Francis and Keith Pecklers (Collegeville: Liturgical Press 2000) 165–8. The most important works for our purpose are: *Toward a Filipino Liturgy* (Manila: Benedictine Abbey 1976); *Cultural Adaptation of the Liturgy* (New York: Paulist Press 1982); *Liturgies of the Future: The Process and Methods of Inculturation* (Mahwah, NJ: Paulist Press 1989); *Liturgical Inculturation: Sacramentals, Religiosity, and Catechesis* (Collegeville: Liturgical Press 1992); *Shaping the Easter Feast* (Washington, DC: The Pastoral Press 1992); *Worship: Beyond Inculturation* (Washington, DC: The Pastoral Press 1994), reissued in 1995 as *Worship: Progress and Tradition*; *A Church Caught between Tradition and Progress* (Notre Dame, IN: Notre Dame Center for Pastoral Liturgy 1995); as editor, *Handbook for Liturgical Studies*, 5 vols. (Collegeville: Liturgical Press 1997–2001).

48. See the first two chapters of *Cultural Adaptation of the Liturgy*, titled 'A History of Liturgical Adaptation' (3–41) and 'The Magna Carta of Liturgical Adaptation' (42–57) respectively. See also the first chapter of *Liturgies of the*

Future, and the first four chapters of *Worship: Beyond Inculturation* on the early cultural settings of baptism, Eucharist, orders, and music.

49. A. Chupungco, 'Liturgy and the Components of Culture', in *Worship and Culture in Dialogue*, ed. S. Anita Stauffer (Geneva: Lutheran World Federation 1994) 153.

50. *Cultural Adaptation of the Liturgy*, 62.

51. *Cultural Adaptation of the Liturgy*, 81.

52. *Cultural Adaptation of the Liturgy*, 84.

53. Chupungco studies the use of various terms such as 'indigenization', 'incarnation', 'contextualization', 'revision', 'adaptation' and 'inculturation'. See *Liturgical Inculturation*, 13–26. In a later work, he even suggests that one should go 'beyond inculturation', as the subtitle of his later book *Worship: Beyond Inculturation* seems to imply.

54. See *Liturgical Inculturation*, 27–31.

55. *Liturgical Inculturation*, 30.

56. A. Chupungco, 'Liturgy and the Components of Culture', *Worship and Culture in Dialogue*, ed. S. Anita Stauffer (Geneva: Lutheran World Federation 1994) 157.

57. *Liturgical Inculturation*, 37.

58. *Liturgical Inculturation*, 45.

59. A. Chupungco, 'Two Methods of Liturgical Inculturation', in *Christian Worship: Unity in Cultural Diversity*, ed. S. Anita Stauffer (Geneva: Lutheran World Federation 1996) 78–9. There seems to be a slight change of emphasis in Chupungco's later writings. In this essay, some four years after *Liturgical Inculturation*, Chupungco places creative assimilation before dynamic equivalence, and no longer says that it is not the ordinary method of liturgical inculturation. On the contrary, the method of creative assimilation is 'ideal in those instances where the liturgical rite is too austere and sober, if not impoverished. In the liturgy people need to see, feel, touch, taste, act' (81). Which is to say, most of the instances, and therefore the Roman Rite, which is characterized by 'sobriety, directness, brevity, simplicity, and practical sense' (*Liturgical Inculturation*), is totally inappropriate outside of the Latin/Roman world!

60. *Liturgical Inculturation*, 50.

61. *Liturgical Inculturation*, 51.

62. *Liturgical Inculturation*, 52.

63. *Liturgical Inculturation*, 53.

64. *Liturgical Inculturation*, 94: 'There will be occasions when a local Church will experience the need for new sacramentals, for new forms of God's continuing presence in the rhythm of daily life outside the sphere of the sacraments.'

65. *Liturgical Inculturation*, 99–100: 'Through the process of inculturation, liturgy and popular religiosity should enter into the dynamic interaction

and mutual assimilation in order to be enriched with each other's pertinent qualities. For local Churches with long-standing popular religious practices it would seem that inculturation is the only available solution to the problem of liturgical alienation and also the best method to transform popular religiosity into an authentic vehicle of the gospel.'

66. *Liturgical Inculturation*, 169–71. Chupungco puts it pithily: 'An inculturated catechesis presupposes an inculturated liturgy' (169).

67. A. Chupungco, 'Liturgy and the Components of Culture', 155.

68. The FABC was founded in 1970 during the visit of Paul VI to Manila, Philippines. It is a voluntary association of episcopal conferences in South, South-east, East and Central Asia. It functions through a hierarchy of structures consisting of the Plenary Assembly, the Central Committee, the Standing Committee and the Central Secretariat with its seven offices (evangelization, social communication, laity, human development, education and student chaplaincy, ecumenical and inter-religious affairs, and theological concerns). The decisions of the Federation are without juridical binding force; their acceptance is an expression of collegial responsibility. For a collection of the Final Statements of FABC's plenary assemblies as well as assorted documents of FABC's various institutes, see *For All Peoples of Asia: Federation of Asian Bishops' Conferences. Documents from 1970 to 1991*, ed. Gaudencio Rosales and C. G. Arévalo (Maryknoll, NY: Orbis 1991) and *For All Peoples of Asia: Federation of Asian Bishops' Conferences. Documents from 1992 to 1996*, vol. 2, ed. Franz-Josef Eilers (Quezon City, Philippines: Claretian Publications 1997). These volumes will be cited as *For All Peoples of Asia*, followed by their respective years of publication. Later documents of the FABC are available from FABC, 16 Caine Road, Hong Kong.

69. *EA*, 20.

70. See *For All Peoples* (1992) 12–25; 53–61 and 274–89.

71. *For All Peoples* (1992) 14. It says further: 'The local church is a church incarnate in a people, a church indigenous and inculturated. And this means concretely a church in continuous, humble and loving dialogue with the living traditions, the cultures, the religions – in brief , with all the life-realities of the people in whose midst it has sunk its roots deeply and whose history and life it gladly makes its own' (ibid.).

72. *For All Peoples* (1992) 287–8. For a development of this ecclesiology, see Peter C. Phan, '*Ecclesia in Asia*: Challenges for Asian Christianity', *East Asian Pastoral Review* [*EAPR*] 37/3 (2000) 220–26. See also S. J. Emmanuel, 'Asian Churches for a New Evangelization: Chances and Challenges', *EAPR* 36/3 (1999) 252–75.

73. The Final Statement of the Seventh Plenary Assembly of the FABC *A Renewed Church in Asia: A Mission of Love and Service*. FABC Papers, no. 93 (FABC: 16 Caine Road, Hong Kong Road, 2000) 3.

74. For a clear exposition of the communion ecclesiology in Vatican II, see

Joseph Komonchak, 'The Theology of the Local Church: State of the Question', in *The Multicultural Church*, 35–49.

75. John Paul II, *Redemptoris Missio*, 28. For the English translation, see *Redemption and Dialogue: Reading* Redemptoris Missio *and* Dialogue and Proclamation, ed. William Burrows (Maryknoll, NY: Orbis 1993).

76. The Declaration of the Congregation for the Doctrine of the Faith *Dominus Jesus*, 22 (6 August 2000) warns that 'it would be contrary to the faith to consider the Church as *one way* of salvation alongside those constituted by the other religions, seen as complementary to the Church or substantially equivalent to her, even if these are said to be converging with the Church toward the eschatological Kingdom of God.' The operative words here are 'complementary' and 'substantially equivalent'. Obviously, it is theologically possible to hold that non-Christian religions are 'ways of salvation' without holding the view implied in those two expressions. Furthermore, it does not seem necessary to affirm, as the Declaration does, that '[if] it is true that the followers of other religions can receive divine grace, it is also certain that *objectively speaking* they are in a gravely deficient situation in comparison with those who, in the Church, have the fullness of the means of salvation' (no. 22) since 1. what is ultimately important, from the point of view of salvation, is that the person receives divine grace, no matter where and how, and 2. it does not do the Christians much good to have 'the fullness of the means of salvation' and not in fact make effective use of them. As Augustine has observed, there are those who are in the church but do not belong to the church, and those who are outside of the church but do belong to it. At any rate, such expressions as used by the Declaration are nowhere found in Vatican II.

77. Michael Amaladoss, *Making All Things New: Dialogue, Pluralism, and Evangelization in Asia* (Maryknoll, NY: Orbis 1990) 59.

78. The Pontifical Council for Inter-Religious Dialogue and the Congregation for the Evangelization of Peoples, *Dialogue and Proclamation*, 42 (19 May, 1991). The English text is available in *Redemption and Dialogue*, ed. William Burrows, 93–118. See also *For All Peoples* (1997) 21–6.

79. See *For All Peoples of Asia* (1992) 14–16; 22–3; 34–5; 107; 135; 141–3; 281–2; 307–12; 328–34; 344; *For All Peoples of Asia* (1997) 196–203.

80. As Archbishop Oscar V. Cruz, Secretary General of the FABC, said at the Seventh Plenary Assembly: 'The triple dialogue with the poor, with cultures, and with peoples of other religions, envisioned by FABC as a mode of evangelization, viz., human liberation, inculturation, interreligious dialogue.' See *A Renewed Church in Asia: Pastoral Directions for a New Decade*. FABC Papers, no. 95 (FABC: 16 Caine Road, Hong Kong, 2000) 17.

81. *A Renewed Church in Asia: A Mission of Love and Service*, 8.

82. One of FABC's important texts on liturgical inculturation is found in

Theses on the Local Church: A *Theological Reflection in the Asian Context*, thesis 8. FABC Papers No. 60 (FABC: 16 Caine Road, Hong Kong, 1991).

83. *For All Peoples* (1997) 195.

84. *For All Peoples* (1992) 34.

85. *For All Peoples* (1992) 35: 'We believe that with deeper study and understanding, with prudent discernment on our part and proper catechesis of our Christian people, these many indigenous riches will at last find a natural place in the prayer of our churches in Asia and will greatly enrich the prayer-life of the Church throughout the world.' For the FABC's theology of liturgical inculturation, see Jonathan Tan Yun-ka, 'Constructing an Asian Theology of Liturgical Inculturation from the Documents of the Federation of Asian Bishops' Conferences (FABC)', *EAPR* 36/4 (1999) 383–401.

86. *For All Peoples* (1997) 163.

87. See Michael Amaladoss, *Beyond Inculturation: Can the Many Be One?* (Delhi: Society for Promotion of Christian Knowledge 1998) 20-23 and Aylward Shorter, *Toward a Theology of Inculturation* (Maryknoll, NY: Orbis 1988) 13–16.

88. For the FABC's theology of human liberation, see Peter C. Phan, 'Human Development and Evangelization: The First to the Sixth Plenary Assembly of the Federation of Asian Bishops' Conference', *Studia Missionalia* 47 (1998) 205–27.

89. *Varietates Legitimae* has reminded the bishops that 'they should not ignore or neglect a minority culture with which they are not familiar' (no. 49).

90. The *Dalits* (literally, 'broken') are considered too polluted to participate in the social life of Indian society; they are the untouchable. Between two-thirds and three-quarters of the Indian Christian community are *Dalits*. On *Dalit* theology, see Sathianathan Clarke, *Dalit and Christianity: Subaltern Religion and Liberation Theology in India* (New Delhi: Oxford University Press 1998); James Massey, *Dalits in India: Religion as a Source of Bondage or Liberation with Special Reference to Christians* (New Delhi: Mahohar 1995); and M. E. Prabhakar, *Towards a Dalit Theology* (Madras: Gurukul 1989). On Tribal theology, see Nirmal Minz, *Rise Up, My People, and Claim the Promise: The Gospel among the Tribes of India* (Delhi: ISPCK 1997). See also *Frontiers in Asian Christian Theology: Emerging Trends*, ed. R. S. Sugirtharajah (Maryknoll, NY: Orbis 1994) 11–62.

91. On *minjung* (literally, 'people') theology, see *An Emerging Theology in World Perspective: Commentary on Korean Minjung Theology* (Mystic, Conn.: Twenty-Third Publications 1988) and Peter C. Phan, 'Experience and Theology: An Asian Liberation Perspective', *Zeitschrift für Missionswissenschaft und Religionswissenschaft* 77/2 (1993) 118–20.

92. See Aloysius Pieris, *An Asian Liberation Theology* (Maryknoll, NY: Orbis 1988) 45-50.

93. See ibid., 41–2; 53; 85.

94. See Aloysius Pieris, 'An Asian Paradigm: Inter-religious Dialogue and Theology of Religions,' *The Month* 254 (1993) 131–2. Michael Amaladoss offers a comprehensive discussion of popular Catholicism in his 'Toward a New Ecumenism: Churches of the People', in *Popular Catholicism in a World Church: Seven Case Studies in Inculturation*, 272–301. He sees popular Catholicism to be characterized by the desire for a good earthly life, a concern to ward off evil, a connection with the world of spirits and ancestors, an inclination toward sacramentality and community, and a suspicion of modern ideologies. For a presentation of Catholic popular devotions with respect to Asia, see José M. de Mesa, 'Primal Religion and Popular Religiosity', *EAPR* 37/1 (2000) 73–82; Kathleen Coyle, 'Pilgrimages, Apparitions and Popular Piety', *EAPR* 38/2 (2001) 172–89 and Peter C. Phan, 'Mary in Vietnamese Piety and Theology: A Contemporary Perspective', *Ephemerides Mariologicae*, forthcoming in 2002.

Chapter 7

1. The country has changed name several times in history: the Belgian Congo during the colonial period, the Democratic Republic of Congo or Congo-Kinshasa at its independence in 1960, Zaire from 1971 to 1997, and, starting in May 1997, it became the Democratic Republic of Congo again. The Zairean Rite was approved when the country was called Zaire. Therefore, we use this name when we talk about the Zairean Rite or the Congolese Rite.

2. T. Sanon and R. Luneau, *Enraciner l'évangile*, Paris 1982; L. Boka di Mpasi, *Théologie africaine: inculturation de la théologie. Bien-fondé, enjeux, évolution, realizations*, Abidjan 2001.

3. For instance: M. Hegba, *Théologie fondamentalement africaine*, 1956; A. Vanneste, *À la théologie africaine*, 1958; G. Bissainthe, E. Verdieu, and P. Ondia, *Une théologie indigénisée, adaptée à la mentalité locale*, 1956; J. Mbiti and R. Ralibera, *Un système théologique en Afrique*, 1959; T. Tshibangu, *Une théologie de couleur africaine*, 1960; Y. Feenstra, *Réflexion théologique autochtone*, 1968: etc.

4. *Documentation Catholique*, 7 September 1969.

5. African Synod, Message 18-19; Propositions 32–8; Ecclesia in Africa 62.

6. Episcopal Conference of Zaire, *Missel Romain pour les diocèses du Zaïre*, Editions du Sécrétariat Général, Kinshasa 1988; id., *Supplément au Missel Romain pour les dioceses du Zaïre, Présentation de la liturgie de la messe*, Editions du Sécrétariat Général, Kinshasa 1989.

7. Boka di Mpasi, op.cit., 177.

8. Paul VI declares in his Message *Africae Terrarum* of 1967: 'A common and very important element of this spiritual conception is the idea of God as the first and last cause of all things. This concept, which is felt more than analysed, lived more than thought, expresses itself in extremely diverse ways

in different cultures. In reality, the presence of God penetrates traditional African life as the presence of a superior being, personal and mysterious' (n. 8). 'Man especially is never conceived purely and simply as matter, limited to life on Earth, but we recognize in him the efficient presence and action of another element, that is spiritual, thanks to which human life is always placed in intimate rapport with life beyond'(n. 8). John Paul II expresses himself in similar terms in *Ecclesia in Africa*.

9. *Supplément au Missel Romain pour les dioceses du Zaïre, Présentation de la liturgie de la messe*, Sécrétariat Général, Kinshasa 1989, 12–13.

10. Boka di Mpasi, op.cit., 117.

11. Idem.

12. Ibid.; ID., *Libération de l'expression corporelle en liturgie africaine*. *Concilium* 152 (1980) 71–80.

13. 'A meticulous study of data of the tradition has led us to discern, all things considered, those elements susceptible to being integrated into the Holy Liturgy. This study has allowed Bishops to propose to the Apostolic See a new structure of the rites to introduce, with its consent, into the Liturgy of the Mass, keeping intact the fundamental unity of the Roman Rite,' *Decret Zairensium Diocesium*, Congregatio pro culto divino (Prot. 1520/8) of 30 April 1988.

14. L. Palomera, 'Le Rite zaïrois de la Messe. Opinion d'un liturgiste d'Amérique latine', *Telema* 8 (1982) 74–5.

Chapter 8

1. Cf. *Supplément au Missel Romain pour les dioceses du Zaïre, Présentation de la liturgie de la messe*, Sécrétariat Général, Kinshasa 1989.

Chapter 9

1. Justin, *Prima Apologia*, 67, 5.

2. Talmud of Jerusalem, $B^e rak\grave{o}t$ 10a. For an exegesis of the significant Talmudic testimony, cf. Cesare Giraudo, '*In Unum Corpus.' Trattoto mistagogico sull'eucaristia* (Cinisello Balsamo 2001) 166–8; Id., *Eucaristia per la Chiesa. Prospettive teologiche sull'eucaristia a partire dalla 'lex orandi'* (Roma 1989) 203–305.

3. Justin, *Prima Apologia*, 66, 2.

4. For an analysis of the Anaphora of Apostolic Constitutions, cf. Giraudo, '*In Unum Corpus*', 269–82; Id., *Eucharistia per la Chiesa*, 385–98.

5. While the *Targùm di Onquelos* is Babylonian – the *Talmùd* of Babylonia is actually called 'our *Targùm*' (*Quddušìm* 49a) – the other two *Targùmim* are Palestinian.

6. Cf. Bernard Botte, *La Tradition Apostolique de Saint Hippolyte* (Münster Westfalen 1963) 17, n.3.

7. Botte, *La Tradition Apostolique* 26.

8. X. Funk, *Didascalia et Constitutiones Apostolorum*, 1 (Paderbornae 1905) 522–5.

9. X. Funk, *Didascalia et Constitutiones Apostolorum*, 2 (Paderbornae 1905) 188–9.

10. In the language of Madagascar, the word *fòmba* is used for what we would call 'rite'. This term, which is normally translated as 'custom, usage, or tradition', depends on the root verb *òmba*, which expresses the idea of 'to follow'. The rite is a time 'in which people follow' and consequently, 'follow others'. In adhering to their natural inclinations, they can do no less.

11. 'Selon la lecture classique des scribes malgaches, le terme devait se prononcer régulièrement *tsa-kabiry*, et fournit donc le radical qui explique toute les formes citées. Le choix du terme paraît traduire une réflexion profonde, l'eucharistie étant effectivement dans le culte chrétien l'acte central, équivalent à ce qu'est dans le culte musulman la proclamation de la grandeur de Dieu.' M. J. Gueunier, *La langue du catéchisme malgache de 1657. Les premiers essays d'une formulation de la doctrine chrétienne*, in *Le christianisme dans le Sud de Madagascar* (Fianarantsoa 1996) 46–7.

12. For a detailed analysis of the anaphora of St Basil, cf. Giraudo, *'In unum corpus'* 313–30; Id., *Eucaristia per la Chiesa* 430–43.

13. The Roman Canon is the only anaphora of the great traditions to put the epiclesis over the offerings before the institution narrative. On the structure of the Roman Canon, cf. Giraudo, *'In unum corpus'* 381–403; Id., *Eucaristia per la Chiesa* 487–506.

14. Teodoro, *Seconda omelia sulla messa 5*, in R. Tonneau and R. Devreese (eds.), *Les homélies catéchétiques de Théodore de Mopsueste, Reproduction phototypique du ms. Mingana Syr. 561* (Vaticano 1949) 540–41.

15. John Chrysostom, *Homilia XVIII in 2 Cor* (PG 61, 527).

16. On the interest that we have to apply to the words of consecration, the formula *in persona Ecclesiae*, without losing any of the sacramental realism from the parallel formula *in persona Christi*, cf. Giraudo, *'In unum corpus'* 251–9; Id., *Eucaristia per la Chiesa* 336–45.

17. In the foundational document of a women's religious community, founded in the 1930s, the foundress wrote 'the daughters of the Church will celebrate Holy Mass together with the priest, offering the gifts of the supplicant Church, because God gives to them for the salvation of all believers the food of eternal salvation.' Madre Maria Oliva Bonaldo, *'33 foglietti'*, Editrice 'Cor Unum' (Roma 1984) 38.

18. Teodoro, *Seconda omelia sulla messa 3*, in R. Tonneau and R. Devreese (eds.), *Les homélies* 538–9.

19. Justin, *Prima Apologia*, 67, 6–7.

20. Note how *Sacrosantum Concilium* 10 presents the liturgy, and especially the Eucharist, as 'source and summit' of the Christian life.

Chapter 10

1. Collegeville 2000.
2. Ibid., quoted p. 30.
3. Ibid., quoted p. 62.
4. See Seamus Heaney, *The Redress of Poetry* (New York 1995) 169.
5. Simon Tugwell, OP, *The Way of the Preacher* (London 1979) 50.
6. Simon Tugwell, OP, *Early Dominicans: Selected Writings*, 258.
7. John W. O'Malley, SJ, *The First Jesuits* (Harvard 1993) 100.
8. Op.cit., 111.
9. Kevin Rafferty, 'Mons with Mercedes', *The Tablet* (25 May 2002).
10. Cf. Barbara Brown Taylor, *When God Is Silent: The 1997 Lyman Beecher Lectures on Preaching* (Cowley 1998).
11. Augustine Thompson, OP, *Revival Preachers and Politics* (Oxford 1992).
12. Geoffrey Preston, OP, *God's Way to be Man* (London 1978) 84.
13. Op.cit., 107.
14. Mary Catherine Hilkert, OP, *Naming Grace: Preaching and the Sacramental Imagination* (New York 1997).
15. Ibid., 56.
16. Heaney, op.cit., 175.
17. *Waiting for God*, 113.
18. *Philosophical Investigations* (Oxford 1958) no 19.
19. Peter Brown, *Augustine of Hippo*, new edition (Princeton 1999) 446.
20. George Potter and Evelyn Simpson, ed. *The Sermons of John Donne*, Vol. 9 (Berkeley, 1953–62) 350.
21. *God Matters* (London 1987) 177.
22. Op. cit., 4.
23. Op.cit., 190, quoting Thomas Hardy.

Chapter 12

1. *Ut Unum Sint, Encyclical Letter of the Holy Father John Paul II on Commitment to Ecumenism* (London 1995) 45.
2. J. Wickham Legg, *English Church Life from the Restoration to the Tractarian Movement*, 1914, 21ff.
3. George Herring, *What was the Oxford Movement?*, 2002, 37.
4. Donald Gray, *Earth and Altar: The Evolution of the Parish Communion in the Church of England to 1945* (Norwich 1986) 68, *passim*.

5. Keith F. Pecklers, *The Unread Vision: The Liturgical Movement in the United States 1926–55* (Collegeville 1998) 149.

6. Ibid.

7. *Ut Unum Sint*, 23.

8. The Consultation on Common Texts, *The Revised Common Lectionary*, 1992.

9. Horace T. Allen Jr. and Joseph P. Russell, *On Common Ground: The Story of the Revised Common* Lectionary (Norwich 1998) 79.

10. 'Common Scriptural readings for liturgical use should also be explored', Pontificum Consilium ad Christianorum Unitatem Fovendam, *Directory for the Application of Principles and Norms on Ecumenism*, 1993, 187.

11. W. Richey Hogg, 'Conferences, World Missionary', in Stephen Neill, Gerald H. Anderson, John Goodwin, (eds.), *Concise Dictionary of Christian World Mission* (Nashville 1971) 133ff.

12. *Faith in the City: A Call to Action by Church and Nation*. The Report of the Archbishop of Canterbury's Commission on Urban Priority Areas, 1985, 15.8.

13. Ibid., 6. 110.

14. *The Whole Works of the Rt Revd Jeremy Taylor, DD, With a Life of the Author by Heber*, revised C. P. Eden, vol. 18, 'The Worthy Communicant', 1,2,4, 1854 (originally published 1661).

15. Bruce Kendrick, *Come Out the Wilderness*, 1963, 26.

16. Gray, op.cit., 226.

17. 'Ite Missa Est and Catholic Action', in *Orate Fratres*, March 1937, 206–8.